# exam ✓ success

## in

# BUSINESS

## for Cambridge International AS & A Level

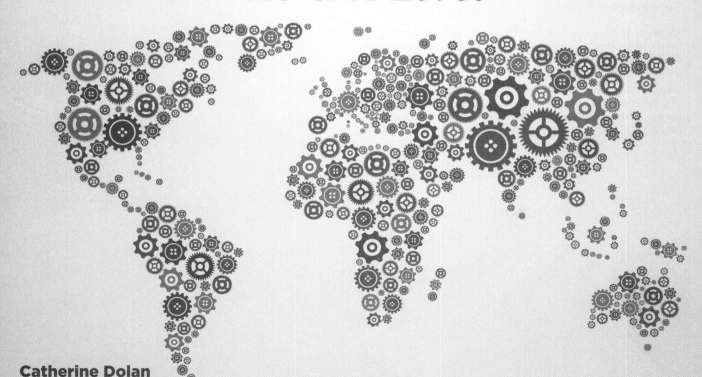

Catherine Dolan
Stefan Wytwyckyj

**OXFORD**
UNIVERSITY PRESS

**OXFORD**
UNIVERSITY PRESS

Great Clarendon Street, Oxford, OX2 6DP, United Kingdom

Oxford University Press is a department of the University of Oxford.
It furthers the University's objective of excellence in research,
scholarship, and education by publishing worldwide. Oxford is a
registered trade mark of Oxford University Press in the UK and in
certain other countries

British Library Cataloguing in Publication Data
Data available

978-0-19-841279-3

10 9 8 7 6 5 4 3 2 1

Paper used in the production of this book is a natural, recyclable
product made from wood grown in sustainable forests.
The manufacturing process conforms to the environmental
regulations of the country of origin.

Printed in India by Multivista Global Pvt. Ltd

**Acknowledgements**
The publishers would like to thank the following for permissions to
use copyright material:

Cover image: iconeer/iStock

Although we have made every effort to trace and contact all
copyright holders before publication this has not been possible in all
cases. If notified, the publisher will rectify any errors or omissions at
the earliest opportunity.

Links to third party websites are provided by Oxford in good faith
and for information only. Oxford disclaims any responsibility for
the materials contained in any third party website referenced in
this work.

# Contents

Access your support website for additional content here:
www.oxfordsecondary.com/9780198412793

# Introduction

The *Exam Success* series will help you to reach your highest potential and achieve the best possible grade. Unlike traditional revision guides, these new books show you what examiners expect of candidates.

*Exam Success in Cambridge International AS and A Level Business* covers the requirements of the AS Level and A Level Cambridge 9609 Business syllabus. Units 1–11 cover the syllabus content, while Unit 12 provides advice on making your study time more effective; and Unit 13 consists of exam-style questions. Unit 14 provides case studies that are referred to in questions and examples throughout the book.

Cross-references are given to the OUP student book *Business for Cambridge International AS & A Level*, should you wish to study the topic in more depth. Throughout the book, a grey vertical bar shows AS content, and a green bar shows A Level content.

Each *Exam Success* book has common features to help you do your best in the exam:

## Worked examples
These give examples of questions, and show you how best to answer them.

### Key terms
These give you easy-to-understand definitions of important terms.

### X Common errors
These are errors that students have made in past exams, helping you to avoid similar mistakes.

### Link
These show where in the book you can find more information on a topic, and also which case study to use for a data response question.

### ✓ What you need to know
These provide you with useful summaries of the main features of topics you would need to demonstrate an understanding of in the exam.

### Remember
These include key information that you must remember if you are to achieve a high grade.

### ★ Exam tip
These provide guidance and advice to help you understand exactly what examiners are looking for.

## ⬆ Raise your grade
Here, you can read answers by candidates and find out how to improve their answers.

### Maths skills
These remind you of the mathematical skills that you need in order to carry out business calculations.

## Revision checklist
These summarise what you need to show that you can do in the exam. Check them off one by one when you are confident.

## ? Exam-style questions
Each unit has examples of the sort of questions to expect in the exam. Answers are available on the OUP support website.

## Key topics

➤ enterprise

➤ business structure

➤ size of business

➤ business objectives

➤ stakeholders in a business.

## 1.1 Enterprise

This topic is concerned with:

➤ what is enterprise?

➤ the nature of business activity

➤ the role of the entrepreneur

➤ social enterprise.

### What is enterprise?

Whenever there is demand for a product or service, there will always be a person or a business who will take the chance of satisfying that demand.

**Enterprise** is the action taken to fulfil an identified need by either **adding value** to an existing product or filling a gap in the market by creating a product or service to fill it.

### The nature of business activity

Business responds to the needs and wants of the customer, and success or failure is determined by the ability to use available resources to their maximum potential. Entrepreneurs are vital to a country's economy as they provide employment, innovation and economic growth.

Adding value to a product could be: refining a product, repackaging a product or choosing a more suitable location to sell the product.

Economic activity is governed by the relationship between the business and the consumer; the consumer wants to buy many items but has limited capital, while the business can only produce a limited number of products as it has limited resources to allocate.

### ✗ Common error

Not all consumers who 'want' a product or service are customers, as some cannot afford to buy the product or service.

Whenever a decision is made, there is always a choice; option A, or option B. Both customer and businesses need to calculate the best option with the information available. There is always an **opportunity cost** to any decision which must be considered.

A successful business depends on its ability to provide something that its customers are willing to pay for. This depends on its ability to satisfy an identified **want** or **need**.

### ✓ What you need to know

Enterprise consists of land, labour, capital and entrepreneurship. All need to be present for enterprise to occur.

### Key terms

**Enterprise:** when a person or business creates a product or service to meet the needs and wants of an identified target customer.

**Adding value:** manipulating (changing) existing products and services to make them more valuable than the sum of the parts.

**Opportunity cost:** the next best option foregone (not chosen).

**Want:** a product or service desired but not essential for daily functions to occur.

**Need:** a basic product or service essential for normal daily functions to occur.

### 💡 Remember

Customers can be other businesses who will use your product to make a further profit or the end user, who will use the product without the intention to make further profit.

**AS Level**

1

An unsuccessful business may identify a want or need but will not have the skills or resources to meet this need.

## The role of the entrepreneur

Entrepreneurship requires a person to spot the gap in the market or an unmet need. This person is referred to as an **entrepreneur**. Entrepreneurs find inspiration in many places and may work for themselves or for a large(r) business.

Entrepreneurs are necessary for business to flourish. There are three main reasons why an economy needs entrepreneurs:

**Employment**
- entrepreneurs need help providing goods and services, so this creates employment
- cost of employment is often required to be kept low, so low skilled/young labour is recruited.

**Creating large businesses**
- most large businesses started with one person and one idea
- the new businesses that are created help to replace those in decline.

**Economic growth**
- quick response to improved economic conditions – can drive growth
- wider economic growth employs more people as a whole than large businesses.

▲ **Figure 1.1** Why an economy needs entrepreneurs

### Worked examples

1  Define an entrepreneur. [2 marks]

2  Explain entrepreneurship. [3 marks]

3  Briefly explain how an entrepreneur may add value to an existing product. [3 marks]

### Answers

1  An entrepreneur is a person who identifies ✓ and meets a gap in the market. ✓

2  Entrepreneurship is the process of an entrepreneur risking/investing their own time and money ✓ to satisfy ✓ an unmet ✓ gap in the market.

3  An entrepreneur may find a new untapped market ✓ that has no easy access to the product ✓ and will add value by providing the good to a suitable location. ✓

There is an identified process for the basic steps taken by an entrepreneur as illustrated in Figure 1.2.

**✗ Common error**

Failure of a business often focuses exclusively on cash or cash flow problems. Cash and cash flow are not sufficiently different to be classed as two examples.

**💡 Remember**

Opportunity cost is a concept – there is no actual cost incurred by not choosing an option.

Many businesses fail in their first year due to a number of reasons, often a combination of more than one.

**Key term**

**Entrepreneur:** a person who *identifies* an unmet need and takes the risk of investing their time, money and/or effort in order to meet their organisational goal, which is often to make a profit.

**💡 Remember**

There are many ways to manipulate (add value) to a product to make it more valuable to the end user.

Adding value is more than the sum of the raw materials and time taken; it can also include intangible aspects that make a product or service desirable.

**✗ Common error**

Entrepreneurs do not just 'run the/a business'; this common answer is too vague and could relate to a shareholder or a manager.

An enterprise is not just 'a business' there needs to be some specific elements such as creating a product or meeting the specific needs of customers.

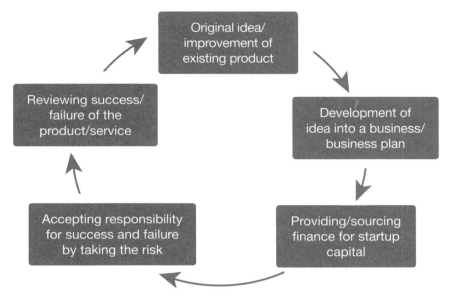

▲ **Figure 1.2** The role of the entrepreneur

**Key terms**

**Social enterprise**: an organisation that applies commercial (business) strategies to meet both organisational and social objectives such as the triple bottom line.

**Corporate social responsibility/triple bottom line**: aims to meet the needs of people, planet and profit. Each is as important as the other.

## Social enterprise

While most businesses are created to make profit for the shareholders (in small businesses usually a sole trader or partnership) some businesses are developed to meet the needs of other groups of people or even areas. These are called **social enterprises** which cater for the **triple bottom line**.

---

 **Raise your grade**

### Paper 1

**1 (a)** Define the term 'value added'. [2]

*Adding value to an existing product.* ✗

> **[0 marks]** This is mostly repeating the words in the question; this will not be awarded ANY marks. A better answer would be: The difference [1] between the selling price and the cost of raw materials. [1]

**(b)** Briefly explain two ways a business could add value to their product. [3]

*They could process a raw material or improve the packaging.* ✓

> **[1 mark]** Not sufficient information – this is a list only and the question asks for explanation – could add a simple example for the processing [1] and explain why improved packaging would increase the desirability. [1]

**2** Explain why many new businesses fail within their first year. [5]

*Businesses fail because they have insufficient capital,* ✓ *fail to understand their customers,* ✓ *over-expand* ✗ *and are unable to respond to external environmental change.* ✗

> **[2 marks]** Insufficient answer – this is a list which does not 'explain'. To get higher marks, select the two reasons you are most confident about and explain each, i.e. insufficient capital [1] as banks are reluctant to lend to start-ups [1] with no credit history [1] **and** do not have enough market research to understand their customers' needs [1] which leads to a product led business. [1]

**3 (a)** Analyse the qualities of a successful entrepreneur. [8]

A successful entrepreneur needs to be multi-skilled ✓ because there may not be many employees ✓ and must also be committed and self-motivated ✓ because there are many challenges when opening a small business. ✓

> **[4 marks]** This is a basic answer that shows some analysis [L2], but each point could be explained further by highlighting how the entrepreneur would need to learn lots of new skills in the short term [L3] and identify some challenges such as competition and long opening hours to meet customer needs.

**(b)** Discuss why senior managers leading large public companies might decide not to have corporate social responsibility (CSR) as a business objective. [12]

CSR or the triple bottom line ✓ might not be a business objective in a large public limited company (sells shares on the stock exchange) ✓ **because** if they spend money on non-essential expenditure ✓ **they are** imposing a tax on shareholders, ✓ **which means** that their dividends might be less. ✓ **if** businesses also 'do good' **they may not** focus on their core activities ✓ and the business might fail, ✓ **which would mean** that the senior managers would not risk their reputation on the triple bottom line. ✓ **This means that** most senior managers **are more likely** to focus on their core priorities such as profit seeking and shareholder satisfaction. ✓✓✓✓

> **[12 marks]** This good answer builds up in layers. It goes through knowledge, application to the question, analysis and finally evaluation. The bold text shows how each layer is built upon the other to connect points and ensure that each level is met.

**4** 'Because there is conflict between profit and corporate social responsibility (CSR), private sector businesses should not have CSR as an objective.' Do you agree? Justify your view. [20]

CSR, which considers society and the environment ✓ as well as profit when making business decisions ✓ means that there is a debate about having it as a corporate objective.

CSR might include paying higher wages and cutting waste and pollution, ✓ which while beneficial for society and the environment, ✓ affects the profit negatively as there are higher costs in the short term due to a higher wage bill and new or improved machinery, for example. ✓✓ However, if staff earn more they may be more motivated which will be a benefit to the company in the long term if employees worker more efficiently to justify their higher wages. ✓✓

If a business sets CSR as an objective, this can be set as a marketing campaign ✓ which could improve the profile of the company, getting more loyal customers in the long term ✓✓ which could increase profits which is a net benefit for shareholders in the long term. ✓✓

I do not agree with the above statement because not having CSR as an objective is only a short term benefit to the company. ✓ Even though it may be more expensive and affect shareholders negatively, ✓ if they do not have CSR as an objective then they may lose market share to competitors who do and have lower profits in the long term. ✓

> **[16 marks]** This is a good answer which follows a logical structure and answers the specific question set. However, while the analysis is sufficient for a question of this size, the evaluation is lacking in depth and the arguments are too basic.

## Worked example for Paper 2

José is walking in his local park and because it is a hot day, would like a cold drink. However, he cannot see a shop anywhere where he can buy one. He notices that there are other people walking, sitting down and playing with their friends, and wonders if they might also like to buy a cold drink.

**a)** Explain how José could become an entrepreneur and who his target customer might be. [3 marks]

**b)** Explain one reason why John might be taking a risk. [3 marks]

**c)** How would José be adding value to a product? [2 marks]

### Answer

**a)** José could bulk buy soft drinks elsewhere, ✓ then come back and sell them to the people in the park ✓ for more than he spent. ✓

**b)** José is risking his own money ✓ (capital) and time because other people might not want to buy a drink off him ✓ as they have brought their own. ✓

**c)** José would be adding value to a product by buying chilled drinks in a shop further away ✓ and then selling them in a convenient location in the park for his target customer. ✓

★ **Exam tips**

**Key features of the sample answer**

➤ José is an entrepreneur because he has spotted a potential opportunity (a gap in the market) and if he starts selling drinks, will be taking a risk to meet his objective of making a profit.

➤ José is adding value to a product that he bought because he is making it more convenient to the end user. People will often pay more money for something if it is easier and takes less effort.

## 1.2 Business structure

This topic is concerned with:

➤ economic sectors

➤ legal structures.

### Economic sectors

This topic aims to develop understanding of the different stages of the economy, the types of business ownership and the benefits and drawbacks of each and how they fit into a country's economy. A business needs to ensure it has the most appropriate method of structure and ownership depending on various factors such as size and scope.

### Primary, secondary and tertiary sector businesses

Central to the understanding of the economic sectors are the activities that each play in the broader business environment. What each business does is critical to understanding which sector a business belongs to. Businesses can be divided into three different sectors; **primary sector** which deals with **raw materials**, **secondary sector** which deals with manufacturing, manipulation and production and **tertiary sector** which deals with the **end user**, but not the **industrial market**.

---

✗ **Common error**

Candidates often choose a business which is unsuitable for the sector in question. It is very important, especially in high mark questions, that a correct example is chosen, otherwise the answer will be marked NAQ (not answered question) and marks will be lost.

**Key terms**

**Primary sector**: businesses directly related to the extraction and/ or exploitation of natural resources. Involves farming (growing crops, rearing animals), fishing and mineral extraction (drilling for oil, mining coal). These *raw materials* are usually sold unprocessed to the secondary sector via the *industrial market*.

**Raw materials**: unprocessed, basic product sold in its natural state.

**Secondary sector**: transforming (manufacturing) inputs, either directly from the primary sector or from another secondary sector business. If a secondary business sells to another secondary business it is operating in an *industrial market*. The secondary sector also sells finished good to the tertiary sector.

**Tertiary sector**: provides finished goods and services to the final user. This is the *consumer market*.

**End user/consumer market**: the final consumer (user) of a finished product (B2C).

**Industrial market**: businesses that produce products that will be used in another product (B2B).

The economic sector is often linked to the state of the country's economic progression; **ELDC** countries generally have either primary sector businesses such as farming, mining and fishing, or secondary manufacturing businesses which are both labour intensive. More developed countries are often based on the tertiary sector and have businesses in the service sector, such as banking, insurance and sales. As businesses expand, they sometimes try to **integrate vertically** to gain control and supply security.

The basic model for progression through the economic sectors is:

➤ Primary sector: Farmer plants crops (e.g. wheat), waits for it to grow and harvests. Sells to:

➤ Secondary sector: Buys raw materials (wheat) and transforms into bread. Sells to:

➤ Tertiary sector: A shop such as Carrefour who sells it to the end customer.

### Public and private sectors

Businesses are owned either by the government (**public sector**) or by private individuals (**private sector**). Each sector has different aims and priorities; the public sector exists to aid and allow the private sector to create value by creating the country's basic infrastructure.

### Legal structures

### Main features of different types of legal structure

When sitting a business exam it is essential know be able to identify and understand the different sizes and ownership structures of a business. Each legal structure has its own benefits, disadvantages and unique features. It is essential to be able to choose a suitable model and justify your choice.

▼ **Table 1.1** Business ownership structures

| Sole trader | | One owner | |
|---|---|---|---|
| ✓ | No formal, legal structure | ✗ | Unlimited liability |
| ✓ | Simple and easy to set up and manage | ✗ | Often a lack of start up and running capital |
| ✓ | Simple decision making | ✗ | Often a lack of skills necessary for the running of all aspects of the business |
| **Partnership** | | **Between two and 20 owners (UK)** | |
| ✓ | Increased level of capital | ✗ | (Usually) **unlimited liability** |
| ✓ | Additional skills – each person will have a speciality | ✗ | All partners responsible for the actions of one |
| ✓ | Decision making, workload and losses shared | ✗ | Longer decision making |
| | | ✗ | Sharing of profits |
| **Private Limited Companies (Ltd)** | | **One or more owners** | |
| ✓ | **Limited liabilities** – more risk taking | ✗ | Costs time and money to set up |
| ✓ | Separate legal identity to the owner(s) | ✗ | Profits shared between all shareholders |
| ✓ | Increased status to a sole trader | ✗ | Publicly available accounts |
| | | ✗ | Sale of shares restricted – restricts capital |

| Public limited company (plc) | | One or more owners | |
|---|---|---|---|
| ✓ | Sale of shares to general public – huge capital opportunity | ✗ | Very expensive and long process |
| ✓ | Larger public profile | ✗ | Public scrutiny of all aspects of business |
| ✓ | Board of directors manage the company | ✗ | Increased risk of takeover |
| | | ✗ | More short term v long term objectives |
| **Franchises** | | **Legal relationship (not ownership)** | |
| ✓ | Franchisee can use the established name and practice of a successful company | ✗ | Proportion of profits paid to franchisor |
| ✓ | Benefits of Economies of Scale | ✗ | Rigid model – lack of freedom |
| ✓ | Access to expertise | ✗ | Weakness of franchisee when negotiating with franchisor |
| **Co-operative** | | **Members each own a share of the business** | |
| ✓ | Working together increases Economies of Scale | ✗ | Limited amount of finance |
| ✓ | Better business decisions due to many view points | ✗ | A lack of a range of expertise |
| ✓ | Greater market power | ✗ | Complex decision making as all consulted |
| **Joint venture** | | **Two independent businesses working together** | |
| ✓ | Shared investment | ✗ | Sharing of profits |
| ✓ | Access to expertise of different companies | ✗ | Differing corporate aims |
| ✓ | Less risk | ✗ | Lack of continuity |

**Key terms**

**Unlimited liability:** no separation between the owner and the business – any debts accrued by the business can be claimed from the owner's personal possessions – sole traders and partnerships.

**Limited liability:** the owner(s) and the business are separate legal entities – any liabilities that the business holds are not guaranteed by the owner's personal possessions.

**✓ What you need to know**

The most suitable legal structure for a business and the advantages and disadvantages of that structure.

 **Raise your grade**

These are generic questions as found in Paper 1, which have no stimulus material and require retained knowledge.

**Short answer questions**

1 Distinguish between a local and national business. [2]

A local business caters to one specific area ✓ and a national business caters to more than one area. ✓

**[2 marks]** A good answer with two specific points.

2 Briefly explain one advantage of national businesses. [3]

A national business has more customers, ✓ so makes more profit. ✗

**[1 mark]** While correct, there is not enough detail; three marks means three good points are needed; candidate could add '… more customers, so can bulk buy stock [1] which reduces costs. [1]

**3** Explain why small businesses are important to a country's economy. [5]

Small businesses bring lots of jobs to the country ✓ and that means lots of people are employed ✓ which means that more people can afford to buy products raising the country's economy. ✓

> **[3 marks]** While correct, there is not enough detail; a five-mark question is asking the candidate to explain two points in some detail, so candidate could add '… and can react quickly to market changes [1] [understanding] which capitalise on new technologies and developments to become a market leader. [1] [effective explanation]

## Essay question

**4** Peter, a sole trader, wants to expand his business to deal with larger businesses. This requires an investment in expensive machinery requiring finance, so he is considering changing his legal structure. Recommend the most appropriate legal structure. [20]

A sole trader has unlimited liability, which means that he is personally responsible for any losses his business may make. This means he may lose his house. Another legal structure he could use is a partnership as a partner would bring in additional finance and new skills. The other appropriate legal structure could be a private limited company, which gives the benefit of limited liability, so his personal assets are safe if the business owes money, and more confidence to larger businesses.

> **[4 marks]** Level 1 answer – understanding of legal structures.
>
> This answer gains full marks for Level 1 – no additional knowledge is needed and expanding the answer further would only waste time.

*If* the sole trader enters into a partnership, *then* he would gain investment into his business which would reduce the amount of finance he would need to borrow from another source, such as a bank loan. *This means* that there would be *less risk* from meeting bank repayments and *greater chance* of survival. *However*, Peter would have to share the ownership of the business with someone *who may* not have the same long-term views *so* Peter could lose control of the direction of the business and not achieve his own aims.

> **[13–16 marks]** Good analysis due to connective words highlighted, thus Level 4 answer is achieved as there is also limited evaluation.

I would recommend that Peter does enter a partnership because he would get the finance and experience he would need even though he loses some of the ownership.

> **[17–20 marks]** Level 5 is not achieved as the evaluation is limited – there is no comparison made against another legal structure.

## How to improve this answer

In order to gain full marks, the candidate must also analyse a second legal structure such as a private limited company, repeating the process for the analysis of a partnership. If the candidate does this, the evaluation can be strengthened by comparing the best feature of a partnership (the source of finance has less short-term risk) to the best feature of a limited company (limited liability) and recommending which is the most suitable. Any answer would gain full marks.

## 1.3  Size of business

This topic is concerned with:

➤ measurements of business size

➤ significance of small businesses

➤ internal growth.

### Measurements of business size

#### Different methods of measuring the size of a business

This topic aims to develop the understanding and relevance of size to businesses. AS Level focuses on **small to medium** businesses and A Level questions will be based on larger, **national** or **multinational** businesses.

All measures of size must be quantifiable (measurable) so comparisons can be made against either internal business aims or external competitors. Below are four main methods explained with benefits and drawbacks.

▼ **Table 1.2** Methods of measuring the size of a business

| | Turnover | Market capitalisation | Number of employees | Market share |
|---|---|---|---|---|
| Description | Value of sales in a given time period.<br><br>Quantity sold x price. | Total value of the shares in a business.<br><br>Share price x number of shares. | Number of people employed. | Portion of a market controlled by a company or product.<br><br>Total sales or revenue of company/industry total sales. |
| Usefulness | Compare the success of the business against previous years or external competitors. | Shows the confidence of investors in a business and capacity for risk. | Can measure the growth of the business in labour intensive industries. | Calculates the relative size of the business in comparison to competition and chances of expansion. |
| Drawback | Does not take into consideration costs so a high turnover does not mean high profits. | Can only be used by incorporated businesses.<br><br>Share prices fluctuate on confidence and are unstable. | Many businesses are automated and this can be misleading. | Depends on the sector or whether the business is a niche or mainstream company. Difficult to define market. |

**Key terms**

**Small/medium business**: limited number of outlets and employees located in a limited geographical area, usually sole trader, partnership or private limited company (Ltd).

**National business**: large number of outlets and employees located in many geographical areas within one country, often a private (Ltd) or public limited company (plc).

**Multinational business**: business activities located in more than one country, often has large numbers of employees and outlets and is almost always a plc.

## Advantages and disadvantages of being a small business

To be a **small business** you have to compare it to another. It is also dependent on the relative size of businesses in the sector and the country. 'Small' in business has many meaning; a business with few employees could still be 'large' as it is a technology based company and has many employees.

Businesses often choose to remain small as there are a number of advantages over becoming larger; when small:

➤ the decision-making process is often faster, meaning more responsiveness to change

➤ there is often a closer relationship with customers, leading to a more personal service

➤ there is control of all processes and procedures, meaning the vision is clear.

However, there are some disadvantages to remaining small:

➤ you have less economics of scale, meaning unit costs may be higher

➤ customers may doubt the security and guarantees of small businesses

➤ less potential profit as revenue is often small.

## Strengths and weaknesses of family businesses

Central to the success of a **family business** is the culture of the home country. Some advantages and drawbacks of family businesses candidates could use in exams are:

### Key terms

**Small business**: can be categorised a small depending on the measurement used – this is a subjective measure.

**Family business**: usually partnerships or limited companies, all the owners are members of one family. Employ more people than incorporated businesses in most countries. Family businesses can be small, medium or large.

### Remember

It is useful to use more than one measure to define the size of a business as each has weaknesses and can be subjective. What is an appropriate measure for one business can be inappropriate for another.

### What you need to know

Definitions of small businesses vary from country and industry. According to the European Union, a small business has less than 50 employees; in Australia, it is less than 15 employees.

▼ **Table 1.3** Advantages and disadvantages of family businesses

| Advantages | Disadvantages |
|---|---|
| Joint personal stake | Family disagreements hurt the business |
| Common sense of purpose | Lack of access to capital |
| Long term view | Nepotism and promotion based on family not ability |
| Trust and a paternal leadership can keep harmony | Problems covered up by loyalty |

## Significance of small businesses

### The importance of small business and their role in the economy

The economy consists of relatively few large businesses and many smaller and family businesses. Large businesses often **subcontract non-core** activities such as transportation and IT services to specialist businesses that are often much smaller in size.

Small businesses are vital to the economy because:

➤ **Innovation** is fast due to a smaller decision making process.

➤ *Response times* are quicker due to the smaller size.

➤ Increases competition and creates jobs, *leading to a downward pressure on price and inflation.*

### The role of small business as part of the industry structure

For a large business, such as a car manufacturer to succeed, there needs to be a huge network of small businesses supplying smaller components, which are more cost effective to buy than make themselves. This allows the large business many advantages:

➤ There is less **capital investment** needed; this lowers the investment needed.

➤ Small businesses can work for many large companies offering better economies of scale.

➤ Large businesses only purchase the exact amount of products needed leading to less wastage of resources.

## Internal growth

### Why and how a business might grow internally

Some small businesses either want to grow or have to grow to remain competitive. Some of the internal main reasons for growth are:

➤ Economies of scale: leads to reduced costs.

➤ A reduction in average costs as production/sales increase; **fixed costs** per unit are decreased.

➤ **Diversification**: lowers risk.

➤ To remain competitive against larger businesses.

➤ To access additional customers and/or markets.

These can lead to:

➤ Increased profit margins.

➤ Increased profits or investment opportunities.

**Key terms**

**Subcontract**: to provide a contract for another business to provide a specific service related to the main business activity.

**Non-core**: relates to activities a business does not see as within their skills base or specialism; i.e. soft drinks manufacturers buy cans from specialist providers as their core activity is creating the drink itself.

**Innovation**: translating a new idea or invention into a product or service.

**Capital investment**: finance needed to purchase high value goods without which businesses cannot function; i.e. machinery and factories.

**Fixed costs**: costs which do not change with output such as rent and salaries.

**Diversification**: entering a new market the business does not currently compete in.

**X** | **Common error**

Candidates often write individual sentences without linking points. When working towards analysis marks, individual points have to be linked in a continuous process of cause and effect for they will be marked as simple knowledge.

**Internal growth** can be achieved in many ways. What is suitable for one business may not be suitable for another due to internal or external factors such as finance and competition.

▲ **Figure 1.3** Ways to achieve internal growth

## 1.4 Business objectives

This topic is concerned with:

➤  business objectives in the private sector and public sector

➤  objectives and business decisions.

## Business objectives in the private sector and public sector

Although every business has one or more objectives, they differ depending on the aims of the organisation. Private sector businesses usually have the ultimate aim of making a profit, while Public sector businesses usually have the ultimate aim of fulfilling a social need.

### The nature and importance of business objectives at corporate, departmental and individual levels

A business will have different **objectives** depending on which business level the objective targets. At corporate level, the objective is to allow all stakeholders to understand the overall aim of the business. This **mission statement** may or may not be realistic and is often very general. This is then broken down into a **strategy** that is an overall plan for a particular department or sector. Each strategy is then broken down into **tactics** that guides individual teams or people on how to achieve their part in the overall objective of the business.

It is important to know and separate common aims for the private and public sector. These aims are not always exclusive.

▼ **Table 1.4** Aims for the private and public sector

| Private sector aims | Public sector aims |
| --- | --- |
| • To become the largest … | • To provide social care |
| • To build brand reputation | • To provide unbiased services |
| • To build brand loyalty | • To provide affordable essential services |
| • To be a market leader | • To provide a minimum level for all |

> 💡 **Remember**
>
> Just because an objective is usually for one sector does not mean the other sector cannot use it.

### Corporate social responsibility (CSR) as a business objective

Due to increased exposure to pressure groups and media, businesses have to ensure their corporate image (see objectives above) is suitable. The list of important **stakeholders** now includes society, which requires businesses to have **corporate social responsibility**. Some common CSR policies include:

➤ Caring for the environment; planting three trees for every one used.

➤ Wages, recruitment and health and safety; employee welfare, paying a living wage and providing all recommended equipment free of charge.

➤ Energy usage; using solar or wind power and reducing the carbon footprint.

➤ Community programmes; sponsoring a school or a hospital.

➤ Selecting partners carefully; avoiding business partners who have controversial business practices.

These policies have to be balanced against other regular business objectives as seen earlier in this chapter to ensure that major stakeholders are all satisfied with the business activities. As with all business objectives, there are costs and benefits to CSR:

**Key terms**

**Objective**: a specific, often measurable target to help achieve the mission statement.

**Mission statement**: a general statement of a business' intent which all stakeholders can easily understand.

**Strategy**: an overall plan of action influencing tactics to achieve a long-term objective.

**Tactic**: a specific, short-term course of action for the day-to-day running of the business to meet part of an overall strategy.

**Stakeholder**: a person or organisation that has an interest, affects or is affected by the operation of a business.

**Corporate social responsibility**: a way in which a business can demonstrate responsibility to all stakeholders in their operations. Also known as the triple bottom line. Exceeds legal requirements.

**✗ Common error**

Candidates often write that **all** public sector organisations do not aim to make a profit. While this is true in some cases, some public sectors do make a profit, such as tax departments; all profit, however, is re-invested instead of being given to shareholders.

Not all private sector organisations aim to make a profit either, they may have different aims such as Corporate Social Responsibility, satisficing, charity or training.

▼ **Table 1.5** Costs and benefits to CSR

| Benefits | Costs |
|---|---|
| • Public awareness | • Increased financial costs |
| • Customer loyalty | • Lower profit/profit margins |
| • Goodwill | • Loss of loyalty, trust and custom if caught in controversy |
| • Marketing opportunities | • Cultural conflicts; differing values |

**The relationship between mission statements, objectives, strategy and tactics**

To make an effective tactic you must first know what the outcome of the operation should be. This is why most businesses start with a general mission statement and then gradually create **SMART** tactics through breaking down each large objective into separate components.

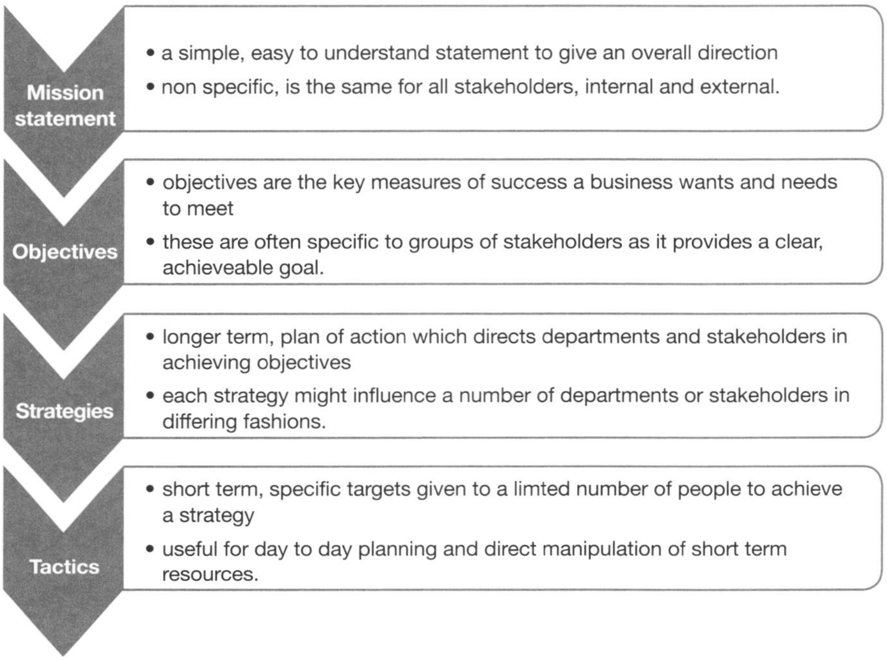
Mission statement
• a simple, easy to understand statement to give an overall direction
• non specific, is the same for all stakeholders, internal and external.
Objectives
• objectives are the key measures of success a business wants and needs to meet
• these are often specific to groups of stakeholders as it provides a clear, achieveable goal.
Strategies
• longer term, plan of action which directs departments and stakeholders in achieving objectives
• each strategy might influence a number of departments or stakeholders in differing fashions.
Tactics
• short term, specific targets given to a limted number of people to achieve a strategy
• useful for day to day planning and direct manipulation of short term resources.

▲ **Figure 1.4** Creating smart tactics

**✗ Common error**

Candidates often address CSR as meeting the legal requirements – this is incorrect. CSR is a voluntary code which exceeds legal requirements and differentiates a business.

**Key term**

**SMART**: acronym for Specific, Measurable, Achievable, Realistic and Time-based. This ensures a target has a high chance of succeeding.

**Remember**

While you can give objective Specific, Measurable and Time based objectives, the achievable and realistic elements are more subjective.

**✓ What you need to know**

Unless a question specifically asks for a definition, candidates do not need to define SMART when answering questions about objectives. Show understanding by using the framework accurately.

## Worked examples

1 Explain one benefit of a SMART objective. [3 marks]

2 Identify two benefits of CSR for a business. [2 marks]

3 Explain one benefit of CSR for a business. [3 marks]

**Answers**

1 If an objective is SMART, then it will give employees a timeframe to complete their task, ✓ which means their project will be ready for when it is needed ✓ so the overall strategy will be achieved. ✓

2 One benefit is increased customer loyalty ✓ and another is that it is a marketing opportunity. ✓

3 The benefit of increased customer goodwill ✓ is that if there is a problem or bad publicity, then because the business has a reputation for doing the right thing ✓ customers may give them the benefit of the doubt and not boycott the company straight away. ✓

## Objectives and business decisions

### The different stages of business decision making and the role of objectives in the stage of business decision making

Decision making is an iterative process – it needs to be constantly adapted and changed due to factors both internal and external. The most important reason could be that with practice comes improvement. The process of turning an idea into an outcome has many influences that can affect the objective. Each stage of decision making is influenced by stakeholder objectives which in turn influences the path the process will follow.

The process of decision making starts with an idea or objective and follows a process of identifying issues, and collecting and analysing information, through evaluating data and making a decision. Once the decision is made, the process is then reviewed and the process starts again to either improve the outcome or react to external influences.

### How objectives might change over time

Objectives do not stay constant. There are internal and external factors that influence the path of the business. As businesses develop, priorities change which influences the direction of business activities. Below are some main change factors.

▲ **Figure 1.5** Factors influencing objectives

### Translation of objectives into targets and budgets

When a business decides upon its strategic objective, this can be split into a number of departmental strategies and then targets, these are then shared with departments and individuals who use them to guide business operations.

Each individual action will have an associated financial cost: this action therefore needs a budget to maximise the success of the action.

### The communication of objectives and their likely impact on the workforce

Candidates will study management styles such as Drucker, McGregor and Taylor within Topic 2: People in Organisations. Candidates will need to understand the link between the style and the impact of management on workers.

Objectives, when used appropriately are inspirational and encourage employees. When used badly, they can be demotivating and reduce morale and output.

Top down planning often will demotivate employees. Employer involvement has proved to ensure objectives are seen as SMART and motivational as discussed in Topic 2.

---

**Key terms**

**Iterative**: repetition of a process.

**Internal**: the business has control over and can influence. This can be either a strength or a weakness.

**External**: the business has no control over this and can usually only react. This can be either an opportunity or a threat.

**Budget**: an estimate of capital, income or expenditure for a specific time period.

---

✓ **What you need to know**

Whether a change factor is internal or external and its effect on objectives.

---

💡 **Remember**

Strategic objectives are often not very detailed. To be useful for individual teams, they need to be turned into targets. These targets need to SMART. Without the finance available, no objective can be translated into an action.

---

💡 **Remember**

Whether objectives are good or bad depends on the perspective of the stakeholder and the ability to communicate an objective in a suitable fashion.

| Corporate | Departmental | Individual |
|---|---|---|
| Increase sales revenue | Marketing – special offers | Designing a new advert aimed at a new target segment by December |
| | Sales – set higher targets | Increase individual targets by 10% in one year |
| Increasing profits/ profitability | Manufacturing – reducing factory costs | Reduce the labour costs by 12% by the next accounting period |
| | Purchasing – reducing raw materials costs | Increase bulk buying economies of scale by 15% within two months |
| Growth – become market leader | Marketing – target a larger customer base | Identify two new untapped markets within one year |
| | Manufacturing – increase output to meet demand | Increase production efficiencies to ensure maximum output by 15% |
| Improve corporate image | Marketing – produce positive adverts | Highlight awareness of CSR in local areas for a two month period |
| | Production – reduce health and safety accident rate | Increase spending on health and safety by 10% annually |

## How ethics may influence business objectives and activities

**Ethics** vary from country to country and depend upon the social and moral views of not only the population as a whole, but the viewpoints of different groups.

Behaving within the laws of the land does not make a business ethical. Behaving ethically does not mean that the business is acting legally.

It may upset some of the most important stakeholders. For private sector companies, the main objective is usually making a profit to divide between the shareholders. CSR can be very expensive, so businesses have to make a choice between short term profit and long-term success.

**Key term**

**Ethics:** a moral viewpoint and set of guidelines that governs decisions and behaviour.

▲ **Figure 1.6** Balancing profit and ethical concerns

Aims give an overall target for all areas of the business. *For example, a candidate may aim is to achieve a specific grade in the exam.* Objectives break aims down into manageable and specific targets for individuals or departments. *For example, this objective might be achieved by studying a specific topic on a particular night.*

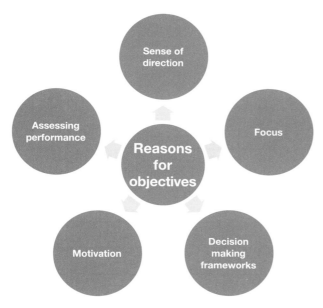

▲ **Figure 1.7** Reasons for objectives

### Objectives – corporate and departmental level

To make objectives specific, manageable and motivational, they must be SMART:

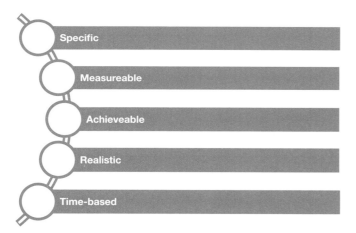

▲ **Figure 1.8** SMART objectives

Objectives differ depending on the department in question and are often specific to the responsibilities of the department. Some may have similar themes but have different outcomes.

## 1.5  Stakeholders in a business

This topic is concerned with:

➤ business stakeholders

➤ the importance and influence of stakeholders on business activities.

> **✗ Common error**
>
> Candidates often misread the term 'stakeholder' with 'shareholder' and vice versa. While a shareholder is an example of a stakeholder, that is often not what the question is asking.

## Business stakeholders

### Individuals or groups interested in the activities of business

This topic aims to develop the candidate understanding of the role, impact and influence of **stakeholders** on businesses and their decisions. A business decision or activity is neither good nor bad, however the effect it has on various stakeholder groups influences the stakeholder reaction. Stakeholder groups can be internal or external to the business, however what is good for one internal stakeholder may have a negative influence on another as shown below.

**✗ Common error**

Corporate social responsibility or behaving ethically is NOT a right; it may be expected and demanded however there is no legal requirement to do anything more than the basic legal requirements of the country.

### Roles, rights and responsibilities of stakeholders

▼ **Table 1.7** Stakeholder groups

| Stakeholder group | Role | Rights | Responsibilities |
|---|---|---|---|
| **Internal** | | | |
| Shareholders/ owners | Invest, make strategic decisions. | Expect employees to provide services. | To manage and deliver all stakeholder expectations. |
| Employees | Provide labour to complete set tasks. | To be treated within legal requirements. | |
| **External** | | | |
| Lenders/finance | Finance operations. | To receive prompt payment (interest) and correct information. | To ensure all supporting documents are accurate and correct. |
| Suppliers | Provide services as agreed. | To receive prompt payment for products and services. | To supply the correct product or service requested within an agreed time period at an agreed standard. |
| Customers | Purchase products/ services/create demand. | Products that comply with legal requirements including marketing and aftersales. | To follow seller instructions and requirements for warranty or use. |
| Local community | Provide external infrastructure (non-core needs). | To have disruption kept to a minimum and laws such as environmental respected; to be kept informed of major impacts on the community. | None. |
| Government | Provide support, regulate and tax activities. | To expect all businesses to abide by all laws and regulations. To expect all taxes to be paid. | To provide a fair and competitive environment to all stakeholders. |
| Pressure groups | Minimise negative impact of business activities and influence CSR. | None. | To act within legal boundaries. |

**★ Exam tip**

When a question asks a candidate to discuss the stakeholders, pick the most important two unless specifically asked, and then analyse these well. Weak answers have many examples of stakeholders but analysed poorly. This wastes time and effort.

## The importance and influence of stakeholders on business activities

### Impact of business decisions/actions on stakeholders, and their reactions

An important analysis point for candidates will be the reaction of stakeholders and how important their reaction will be when a business makes a decision. Candidates must be able to match a likely reaction, explain the impact and show what they likely effect will be.

**Example:** A business is considering mechanising a labour-intensive process.

**The impact on:**

➤ **Shareholders** – increased short term investment through additional capital or reduced dividend, **however**, increased long-term return on capital.

➤ **Employees** – fewer jobs available leading to redundancy, **however**, increased opportunities for skilled labour.

➤ **Government** – increased productivity leads to increased tax returns, **however**, increased unemployment which leads to dissatisfaction and increased social costs.

➤ **Customers** – decreased costs lead to reduced prices, **however**, increasing mechanisation may threaten their own jobs.

**Their reaction:**

➤ **Shareholders** – focus on their strategic aim – short term returns or long-term profit **that might depend upon** how much bad publicity the decision will bring.

➤ **Employees** – worry about job security and potentially look for other jobs, **which causes** instability for the business.

➤ **Government** – may look forward to increased tax revenues **but** will insist the business looks after all employees who lose their jobs.

➤ **Customers** – will most likely buy the most cost-efficient option.

### How and why a business needs to be accountable to its stakeholders

Accountability can be both moral and legal. The government expects a business to be accountable for both financial and legal issues. Customers and the local community expect businesses to be accountable for the products and the environment, whilst employees expect the business to be accountable for safe working practices and conditions.

The three main aspects of accountability are:

➤ Legal requirements:

  ➤ payments – tax to the government or wages to the employees within legal requirements

  ➤ treatment of staff – including health and safety and equal opportunities

  ➤ shareholders – published accounts must be made available for incorporated businesses customers – to ensure published claims are met.

➤ Ethical requirements:

  ➤ corporate social responsibility – a responsibility to provide above minimum legal requirements.

➤ Commercial requirements:

  ➤ transparency – improving relationships with supplier and customers, to ensure non are lost to competitors.

---

**★ Exam tip**

Business owners have to balance the different reactions of stakeholders of decisions made in business. Business is not just taking one stakeholder perspective as there are many different external influences.

**✗ Common error**

Candidates miss out on analysis marks as consequences related to a simple piece of analysis are not linked together; (see bold type above) they are written down as individual elements which reduces the level of complexity in an answer.

**Key term**

**Accountability**: the obligation to account for activities and accept responsibility for their actions.

**✗ Common error**

Accountability is not just a legal matter; you may act in a legal manner yet still be accountable to the moral judgement of your customer.

### How conflict might arise from stakeholders having different aims

It is important to remember that when one stakeholder gets an advantage another will be disadvantaged. A business can aim to either **satisfice** the needs of the majority/the most important stakeholders, or meet the wants of the most important. The difference in approach is directly related to the relative strength of the stakeholder.

Common stakeholder conflicts:

- customers requiring high quality and low costs *v* shareholders requiring maximum return on investment (profit)
- suppliers wanting prompt/early payment *v* businesses (customers) wanting to delay payments
- shareholders wanting short term returns *v* managers and employees wanting long term investment.

**Key term**

**Satisfice**: to meet the minimum requirements for a particular goal.

**★ Exam tip**

Basic knowledge as shown above has limited importance – most questions will require you to *explain* or *analyse* conflicts. *Always link points* using connective words such as: because; this leads to; although.

### Worked examples

1 Explain one reason why a customer may be in conflict with another stakeholder. [3 marks]

2 Define the term stakeholder. [2 marks]

3 Explain the role the local community has in the decision-making process. [5 marks]

**Answers**

1 A customer may want lower prices, ✓ which would be in conflict with shareholders ✓as they want maximum profits. ✓

2 A stakeholder is someone who has an interest ✓ or is affected by a business or enterprise. ✓

3 The local community is interested in the corporate social responsibility of the business ✓ and will want the business to ensure they take the needs of the local community into consideration ✓ such as any increase in traffic or pollution. They can lobby the local government to minimise disruption ✓ which can put restrictions on the times when traffic can be busy ✓ which will affect whether the local area is suitable for business expansion. ✓

### How changing business objectives might affect its stakeholders

Stakeholders have different requirements as businesses change and develop. To successfully analyse the effect you must first know some key business objectives and the impact at each stage on some key stakeholders.

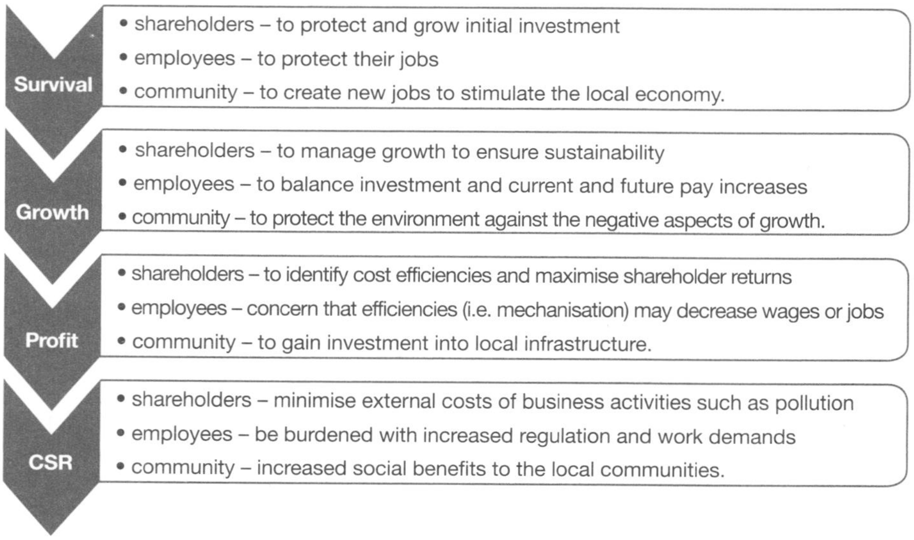

Survival
• shareholders – to protect and grow initial investment
• employees – to protect their jobs
• community – to create new jobs to stimulate the local economy.
Growth
• shareholders – to manage growth to ensure sustainability
• employees – to balance investment and current and future pay increases
• community – to protect the environment against the negative aspects of growth.
Profit
• shareholders – to identify cost efficiencies and maximise shareholder returns
• employees – concern that efficiencies (i.e. mechanisation) may decrease wages or jobs
• community – to gain investment into local infrastructure.
CSR
• shareholders – minimise external costs of business activities such as pollution
• employees – be burdened with increased regulation and work demands
• community – increased social benefits to the local communities.


▲ **Figure 1.9** The impact of objectives on key stakeholders

**★ Exam tip**

Do not try to think of intricate or complicated answers for questions: examiners expect you to be taught similar answers and these are just as valid and less likely to be wrongly interpreted. Simple, straightforward answers are less likely to be analysed incorrectly.

## Revision checklist

**I can:**

➤ define an entrepreneur and an enterprise ☐

➤ explain and give examples of added value ☐

➤ explain the concept of opportunity cost and apply it to a scenario ☐

➤ describe factors that can make a business succeed or fail ☐

➤ describe the characteristics of an entrepreneur ☐

➤ explain the impact an entrepreneur has on a country ☐

➤ explain the concept of social enterprise and the reasons people start them. ☐

## ⬆ Raise your grade

### Paper 1 questions

> ★ **Exam tip**
>
> Make sure to look at the marks allocated to a question; this will show you how much detail is needed. Do not write whole paragraphs for a question with two marks and do not jot down simple statements for a five-mark question.

1 Describe one measure of size. [3]

Sales turnover. ✓ It is the value of sales over a period of time. ✓

Market capitalisation. Value of a business total number of shares. ✗

> **[2 marks]** While sales turnover and market capitalisation are both correct answers, the question only asked for one example, so the market capitalisation is NAQ (Not answered question) or REP (repeated information). To improve the answer, you could add to sales turnover, '… and can help compare size against your competitors'. [1]

2 Explain one measure of size. [3]

Profit is a measure of size because it shows how much money a business has made this year. This shows how much money the business has to invest or share between shareholders. ✗

> **[0 marks]** It does not matter how good your explanation is if your measure is incorrect. Profit is not a measure of size because some very successful companies (Twitter, Starbucks UK) have made huge losses but are still international businesses. Ensure you choose one of the measures in the textbook.

3 Explain why a sole trader may want to expand his business. [3]

A sole trader may want to expand his business to increase his revenues. ✓ This could lead to an increase in his profits. ✓

> **[2 marks]** Remember to check the number of marks available for the question. This has three marks for a general comment which means there should be three points, one for the knowledge and two points for the extended answer. '… and help him to expand' would be needed for the third mark. [1]

4 Describe one strength of a small business. [2]

They have a quick decision-making process. ✓

> **[1 mark]** Remember to read the question carefully; this asks you to describe, not just identify. You need to describe the strength of the decision-making process, e.g. '… which means they can react quickly to changes in the market.

**5**   Analyse why it is important for small businesses to manage cash flow.   [8]

Cash flow is the balance of money coming in and going out of the business. ✗ It is important to manage because small businesses need to make sure they have enough money coming in to meet the short-term expenses of the business ✓✓ such as paying wages and buying new stock without which a business cannot operate. ✓✓ Small businesses often have limited sources of finance to cover any shortfall as banks might not give big enough overdrafts, ✓✓ so you have to monitor if customers are paying their bills on time and make sure there are procedures for collecting outstanding debts. ✓✓

**[8 marks]** This answer shows how an answer can be built up by using connecting words. Even though the first sentence does not gain the candidate any marks [NAQ], it is useful to make sure the student is focused in the right direction. A good answer does not need to be very long, it needs to meet the level requirements which you can learn by studying past exams. This answer would score the full 8 marks.

### Paper 2 questions

**6**   Describe one way in which you could measure the size of Paul's business.   [2]

🔗 **Link**

Questions 6–9 are data response questions, based on Case study 2: Paul's Paper Supplies in Unit 14.

You could use the number of customers Paul has (12) ✓ and compare that against his competitors. ✓

**[2 marks]** This answer uses data from Table 1 of the case study, so there is a direct link to the case study. This is necessary to score the second mark.

**7**   Explain why Paul's Paper Supplies may want to expand its business.   [4]

A sole trader may want to expand his business to increase his revenues. ✓ This could lead to an increase in his profits ✓ and help him to expand. ✗

**[2 marks]** Even though the answer is correct, remember this is a data response question referring to Paul's Paper Supplies. The answer has no reference to the case study, so the marks are limited (in this case to two marks).

**8**   Describe one strength of Paul's business.   [2]

Paul has a quick decision-making process as he makes all the decisions himself, ✓ so he can respond to changes quickly. ✓

**[2 marks]** It is important to describe a specific point from the case study, such as working by himself, to make sure you get the application mark. Often, candidates think that something is too obvious to write down. It isn't.

**9**   Analyse why it is important for Paul to manage his cash flow.   [8]

Cash flow is the balance of money coming in and going out of the business. ✗ It is important for Paul to manage cash flow because his business has to make sure he has enough money coming in to meet the short-term expenses of his business ✓ such as covering the 30-day credit period his customers expect. ✓ His business has limited sources of finance as he only has a small overdraft. ✓✓ So he has to monitor his customers are paying their bills on time and make sure there are procedures for collecting outstanding debts. ✓✓

**[6 marks]** Although this answer is very similar to the answer for question 5 above, there are small differences that make the difference between getting half marks and full marks. In this question, the candidate refers to Paul rather than a generic business, as in the Paper 1 question. While the candidate uses specific examples from the case study and explains them for analysis (a small overdraft), his extended analysis is too generic; replacing 'paying their bills on time' to 'paying within 30 days' would have increased this answer to full marks.

## ? **Exam-style questions**

This section will allow you to practise writing answers for exam-style questions. Remember, it is useful to be aware of the mark schemes for the questions which can be found on relevant websites or from your teacher.

**Paper 1**

**Short answer questions**

1 (a) Define market capitalisation. [2]

 (b) Briefly explain one reason why a sole trader would not use market capitalisation as a measure of size. [3]

2 Explain the importance of small businesses to a country's economy. [5]

3 (a) Briefly explain a small business. [2]

 (b) Explain why a small business might be more responsive to change than a larger business. [3]

4 Explain two reasons why a small business would aim for internal growth. [5]

5 Explain two disadvantages of remaining a small business. [5]

6 (a) Identify two methods of measuring businesses. [2]

 (b) Explain a benefit of each measure. [3]

7 (a) Define internal growth. [2]

 (b) Explain two methods of internal growth. [3]

8 (a) Identify and briefly describe one potential small business objective. [2]

 (b) Explain one reason why a small business objective might change. [3]

9 (a) Identify two stakeholders in a business. [2]

 (b) Briefly explain why a shareholder would not be happy with CSR policies. [3]

**Long answer questions**

10 (a) Analyse the importance of businesses effectively knowing their size in the market. [8]

 (b) Discuss how knowing the size of a business may influence stakeholders in a business. [12]

11 Discuss why governments would want to encourage the development of small businesses in a country. [20]

12 (a) Analyse how a business might use market share for pricing decisions. [8]

 (b) Discuss the best ways a small retailer could use its knowledge of its market share to achieve internal growth. [12]

13 Discuss the most important factors that could influence a business when changing its objectives. [20]

14 'Shareholders are the most important stakeholders in a business.' Discuss this statement. [20]

**Paper 2**

🔗 Link

Refer to Case study 1: Dingle's Dairy in Unit 14.

1 (a) Define the term 'stakeholder'. [2]

 (b) Briefly explain the term 'joint venture'. [3]

 (c) Refer to Table 1 and calculate the profit margin for 2016. [3]

 (d) Explain one way DD could use this information for decision making. [3]

 (e) Analyse two factors influencing the changing business objectives for DD. [8]

 (f) Recommend whether DD should choose expansion as a new business objective. Justify your choice. [11]

---

## Key topics

➤ management and leadership

➤ motivation

➤ human resource management.

## 2.1 Management and leadership

This topic is concerned with:

➤ management and managers

➤ leadership

➤ choice of leadership style

➤ emotional intelligence.

### Management and managers

This topic will aim to develop the candidates understanding of the difference between management and leadership. While managers identify ways in which to implement short term tactics and achieve specific goals, leaders create a vision and inspire stakeholders to believe in the long-term direction and success of the business.

### The functions of management, their roles and styles

**Management** focuses on utilising the resources available to meet the organisations goals and objectives. **Managers** are reactionary (react to) not visionary (big picture); managers will try to make efficient use of resources to minimise costs or maximise efficiency. This does not necessarily make them popular and/or inspiring.

The two theorists that candidates will need to identify, explain and link to management theory are:

#### Henri Fayol – the functions of management

Henri Fayol saw the role of management as controlling and **hierarchical**, based on a scientific principle. Instructions come from senior managers and are clear to ensure all employees focus on the same overall objective. This is associated with a very traditional form of management.

1. Plan

2. Organise

3. Command

4. Co-ordinate

5. Control and monitor

By their nature, these functions maximise efficiency and may not inspire employees. These focus on meeting business objectives and are based on **rational** thought, and business decisions are made based on the most important influencing factors – communication is likely to be one directional and top down.

---

**✗ Common error**

While a manager may be able to direct a team, this is not the same as being a leader – not all managers can be effective leaders, and not all leaders can manage effectively.

**Key terms**

**Management:** the process of dealing with or controlling people and resources.

**Manager:** a person who controls, directs and implements the short-term tactical decisions to achieve overall objectives.

**Hierarchical:** based on rank, with many layers of management and a clear level of seniority.

**Rational:** based on reason or logic – there is a planned reason for every action or decision.

**🔗 Link**

There is more about business objectives in Unit 1, topic 1.4.

This style of management is useful for task-based businesses where creativity is not necessary and there are clear, defined objectives.

### Henry Mintzberg – the functions of management

Where Fayol saw management as an orderly process for the efficient use of resources, Mintzberg's theory sees management as having three specific roles. This theory assumes there are 10 different functions a manager can fulfil, in three different categories.

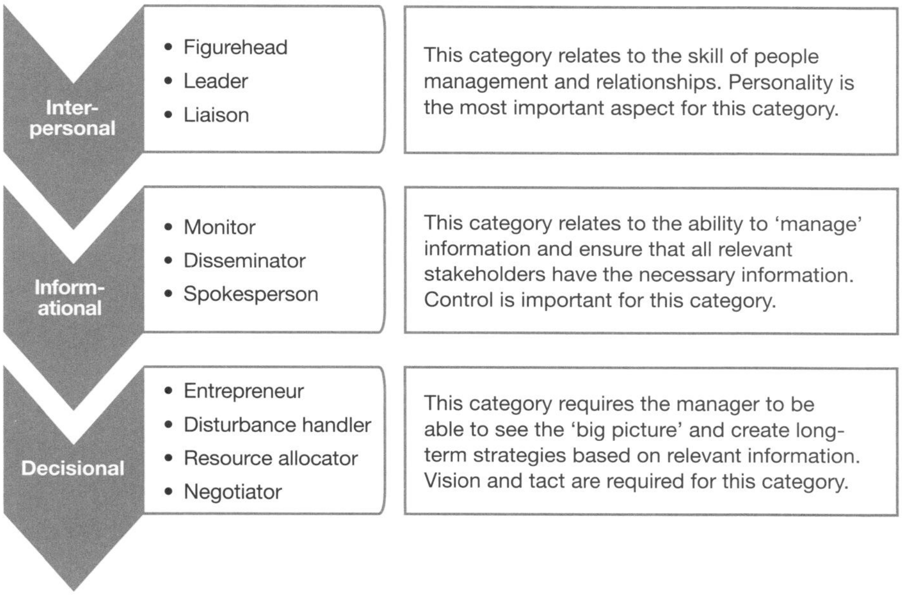

**Inter-personal**
- Figurehead
- Leader
- Liaison

This category relates to the skill of people management and relationships. Personality is the most important aspect for this category.

**Inform-ational**
- Monitor
- Disseminator
- Spokesperson

This category relates to the ability to 'manage' information and ensure that all relevant stakeholders have the necessary information. Control is important for this category.

**Decisional**
- Entrepreneur
- Disturbance handler
- Resource allocator
- Negotiator

This category requires the manager to be able to see the 'big picture' and create long-term strategies based on relevant information. Vision and tact are required for this category.

▲ **Figure 2.1** Mintzberg's functions of management

This idea of management has three different styles depending on the function identified. Mintzberg suggested that while a manager may be able to fulfil each of the three categories, the manager will have one particular strength.

---

**Worked examples**

1   Briefly explain why managers might require control.  [3 marks]

2   Briefly explain one of Mintzberg's areas of management.  [3 marks]

**Answers**

1   According to Fayol, ✓ managers need control as they need to ensure that resources are used efficiently ✓ to meet organisational objectives. ✓

2   One area of management is the interpersonal role. ✓ This area relates to the skill of people management ✓ and personality is important for this role. ✓

---

## Leadership

### The purpose of leadership

Candidates must be able to understand that the role of leadership relates to the ability of not only creating a clear vision, but also being able to share this with others, making sure that they will follow willingly.

A **leader** may have a number of different purposes:

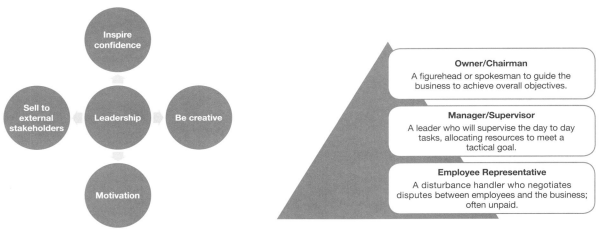

▲ **Figure 2.2** Purpose of a leader      ▲ **Figure 2.3** Leaders and their roles

---

## Worked examples

**1** Identify two purposes of a leader.      [2 marks]

**2** Briefly explain the purpose of leadership.      [3 marks]

### Answers

**1** To motivate stakeholders to follow the vision ✓ and to be creative to set organisational goals. ✓

**2** The purpose of leadership is to create a vision ✓ that can be shared with stakeholders ✓ that stakeholders will want to follow. ✓

---

### Leadership roles in business

Leadership does not necessarily mean the person has a position of power within the business; a leader may have a small or large role, and may or may not be paid for the leadership role. The table below gives some examples of leaders and their roles.

### Qualities of a good leader

A leader has different qualities to a manager. A manager has to meet organisational targets while a leader has to create organisational goals. Some main differences are:

| Manager | Leader |
|---|---|
| • Organised <br> • Practical <br> • Realistic <br> • Commanding <br> • Planner | • Self-confident/self-belief <br> • Intelligent, thoughtful and reflective <br> • Creative <br> • Charismatic <br> • Multi-skilled <br> • Inspirational |

★ **Exam tip**

You may want to include an example of a well-known leader; this may help to show your understanding of the subject by relating the person and identifying a leadership skill and purpose to gain a developmental mark.

Just because a quality is mainly associated with a manager or a leader does not mean that this cannot be associated with the other. Marks are lost when definite claims are made which show a basic and undeveloped understanding of the subject.

---

## Worked examples

**1** Briefly explain the difference between a manager and a leader.      [5 marks]

**2** Briefly explain one quality of a leader.      [3 marks]

### Answers

**1** A manager is responsible for efficiently allocating resources ✓ to achieve a tactical goal related to an organisational objective ✓ while a leader may create the organisational objective ✓ and inspire employees, including managers, ✓ to work towards the overall goal. ✓

**2** One quality a leader may have is charisma, ✓ as this is necessary to make people want to follow a leader ✓ which is one of the main aims of leadership. ✓

## Choice of leadership style

Different businesses need different leadership styles depending on the objectives of the business. There are three main generic styles and one management theory which you will be required to know.

### Leadership styles

▼ **Table 2.1** Leadership styles

| | Autocratic | Democratic | Laissez-faire |
|---|---|---|---|
| Characteristics | • One-way communication.<br>• Close supervision and limited freedom. Little trust in employees.<br>• Work methods and processes are dictated and followed exactly. | • Two-way communication.<br>• Trust is a key feature employee participation is encouraged.<br>• Work methods are discussed and employees have ownership. | • Two-way communication.<br>• Trust is key and employees make their own decisions.<br>• Work methods are left to the employee to do as he/she feels best. |
| Advantages | • Quick decision making.<br>• Smaller chance of mistakes.<br>• Useful for emergency situations. | • Employee involvement and motivation.<br>• Employee insights may create more efficient processes. | • Employee self-discipline.<br>• Trust can be motivating.<br>• Flexibility and freedom to make decisions to suit the employee. |
| Drawbacks | • Lack of trust can be demotivating.<br>• Lack of employee innovation. | • Slower decision making.<br>• Can create dissatisfaction if employees do not agree. | • Can create lazy managers and employees.<br>• Loss of management control. |
| Likely used in | • Armed forces.<br>• Manufacturing.<br>• Low skilled businesses. | • Progressive businesses.<br>• Medium skilled business. | • Creative businesses.<br>• Highly skilled businesses.<br>• Research and development. |

### McGregor's leadership styles

The above management styles are *descriptive* and focus on the three main types of management. Douglas McGregor created the theory of X and Y to outline *how* managers might view their employees:

| Theory X | Theory Y |
|---|---|
| • Employees are lazy and will avoid work where possible.<br>• Clear instructions and targets are needed to ensure tasks completed.<br>• Employees do not want responsibility and may avoid opportunities. | • Employees get job satisfaction and enjoy work.<br>• Employees are creative and contribute ideas.<br>• May seek responsibility if recognised and rewarded. |

**Key terms**

**Autocratic**: hierarchical management structure with decisions made by senior team. Lack of trust in employees.

**Democratic**: business leaders take into account the views of all levels of the organisation. Majority view is often accepted although senior managers make the final decision.

**Laissez-faire**: reduced management control and a flat managerial structure.

**Theory X manager**: distrusts staff and is likely to be an autocratic manager. Controlling and supervisory.

**Theory Y manager**: trusts employees and is likely to be either democratic or laissez-faire. Values workers' opinions and input.

## Emotional intelligence

### Goleman's four competencies of emotional intelligence

Management and leadership is **evolving**. Daniel Goleman suggested that as employees and management are not machines, it is important to be aware of and understand emotions. This theory is called **emotional intelligence**.

This theory can help managers to identify what **motivates** employees and how this knowledge can help improve performance. There are four main strands to this theory.

▼ **Table 2.2** Goleman's four competencies of emotional intelligence

|  | Self awareness | Self management | Social awareness | Social skills |
|---|---|---|---|---|
| **Description** | Knowing and understanding own emotions. | Applying own emotions to a situation. | Ability to recognise the emotions of others. | To manage relationships and emotions of other people. |
| **Importance** | To recognise and understand the influence of own emotion on others. | Self-regulation and self-motivation; managing own emotions to minimise their influence on others. | To be sensitive to the emotions of others and recognise others' individual needs and motivation. | To appreciate the cause of emotion and manage a situation to restore calm. |

## 2.2 Motivation

This topic is concerned with:

➤ motivation as a tool of management and leadership

➤ human needs

➤ motivation theories

➤ motivation methods in practice.

### Motivation as a tool of management and leadership

This topic will aim to develop the candidates understanding of the different methods managers and businesses use to motivate their employees to meet

**X Common error**

Candidates can often focus on the methods of motivation but fail to apply them to the business or, apply incorrect methods to the case study. This will lose application marks for knowledge and analysis.

business objectives. Different objectives and businesses require different approaches to meet the needs of not only the business but also the employees themselves.

### The need to motivate employees to achieve the objectives of the business

Business needs motivated employees to meet the specific business objectives. **Motivation** can lead to specific outcomes for the businesses, which have to be analysed to gain higher marks.

**Link**

There is more about business objectives in Unit 1, topic 1.4.

**Key term**

**Motivation**: a reason for acting in a particular fashion; the drive to achieve a specific goal.

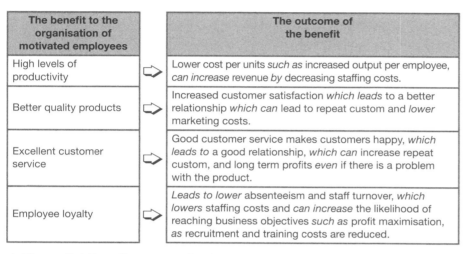

| The benefit to the organisation of motivated employees | | The outcome of the benefit |
|---|---|---|
| High levels of productivity | ⇨ | Lower cost per units *such as* increased output per employee, *can increase* revenue *by* decreasing staffing costs. |
| Better quality products | ⇨ | Increased customer satisfaction *which leads* to a better relationship *which can* lead to repeat custom and *lower* marketing costs. |
| Excellent customer service | ⇨ | Good customer service makes customers happy, *which leads to* a good relationship, *which can* increase repeat custom, and long term profits *even if* there is a problem with the product. |
| Employee loyalty | ⇨ | *Leads to lower* absenteeism and staff turnover, *which lowers* staffing costs and *can increase* the likelihood of reaching business objectives *such as* profit maximisation, *as* recruitment and training costs are reduced. |

▲ **Figure 2.4** Benefits to organisations of motivated employees

**Remember**

To gain good analysis marks, you must link your separate points using transition phrases that create a complex sentence. Transition phrases are highlighted in Figure 2.4 in *italic*.

---

### Worked examples

1 Identify and briefly explain one advantage of motivated employees. [3 marks]

2 Explain two possible consequences for a business of poor employee motivation. [5 marks]

### Answers

1 One advantage is high levels of productivity ✓ as fixed costs will be shared over more units ✓ which will lead to the objective of profit maximisation being achieved. ✓

2 One possible consequence is that there might be poor customer service ✓ which will lead to customers feeling their needs aren't being adequately met ✓ which may reduce repeat customer in the future. ✓ Another consequence is that employees may decide to leave the business and find a better job ✓ which will decrease productivity levels as new staff will have to be trained. ✓

---

### Human needs

It is important for candidates to realise the difficulty of motivating employees if managers do not understand their employees' **human needs**. Incorrect methods of motivation can be expensive and even reduce motivation.

### A simple explanation of human need

Humans are complex and have differing needs. While some needs are generic and needed by most, every person will have independent needs that have to be met in order for employees to meet organisational needs.

Humans usually have two levels of needs; the basic requirements such as food, shelter and society, which are the basic functions that have to be satisfied.

Satisfaction however, is a basic need; most people want more that what they currently have; this could be **tangible** goods or **intangible** rewards.

**Key terms**

**Human needs**: a set of requirements that can include wants (desires) that have to be met to satisfy the basic requirements of people.

**Tangible**: items that physically exist and can be touched, such as a material product.

**Intangible**: something which cannot be touched – for example, an idea or a service.

### How human needs may or may not be satisfied at work

It is important for managers to realise whether their staff work to exist or exist to work.

If employees work mainly for the material rewards such as pay, then they will have a different set of motivators than employees who love their job and are defined by their role in the workplace.

Those who work for material rewards are *less likely* to be motivated by intangible rewards such as praise and additional responsibility. A business will therefore motivate them with financial rewards, however, the social needs will be neglected within the workplace to maximise the earning potential.

Those who work for intangible rewards are *more likely* to require attention, however, when working in a team, individual contributions may be harder to spot and may lead to decreased satisfaction levels.

## Motivation theories

### Ideas of the main content theorists and process theorists

> **✓ What you need to know**
>
> Candidates will be required to explain and apply the following theorists:
>
> **Maslow – Hierarchy of needs:** the lowest level needs to be satisfied before the next can be met.
>
> **Taylor – Economic man:** people are motivated by money only and cannot be trusted.
>
> **Mayo – Hawthorne experiment:** teamwork and observation increases productivity.
>
> **Herzberg – Two factor theory:** people cannot be motivated until their basic needs are met.
>
> **McClelland – Motivational needs theory:** motivation is achieved through achievement, authority and affiliation.
>
> **Vroom – Expectancy theory:** employees expect to be rewarded according to their effort.

> **💡 Remember**
>
> A number of theories borrow heavily from Maslow's theory – therefore, it is often the most well-known and must be fully understood before most motivation exam questions can be attempted.

**Maslow's hierarchy of needs**

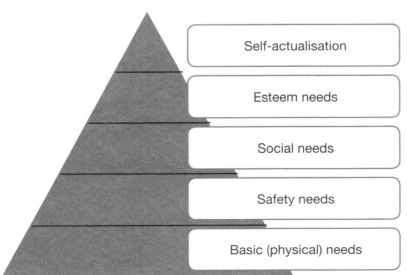

▲ **Figure 2.5** Maslow's hierarchy of needs

Most people require basic needs, such as income from a wage, as a minimum. Once this set of needs is **satisfied**, it is no longer a need.

The focus then changes to safety needs such as a contract, which allows the focus to change from short-term to longer term issues.

Once this need is met, most people require social contact, and will try to make social bonds and contacts.

Many people are satisfied at this stage, and require no further motivators. This does not mean that further motivators are unwelcome.

Some people require the approval or admiration of others, which may be as little as appreciation of work completed to rewards for targets met, to meet the self-esteem needs of a person.

The workplace is also a place that can allow a person to fulfil their potential through progression of skill and/or seniority. Less people aspire to and achieve this stage.

> **Remember**
>
> It is possible to go down the pyramid as well as up the pyramid. People can lose their jobs, be passed over for promotion or change jobs and have to create a new social circle to meet this need once more.

> **X Common error**
>
> Some candidates state that **all** people require safety and social needs. This is untrue, as some positions which rely on commission only payment have no safety needs but provide the social and financial needs required by an individual in this workplace.

### Worked examples

**1** Define the term 'social needs'.  [2 marks]

**2** Discuss the importance of Maslow's hierarchy of needs for employees in the secondary sector.  [12 marks]

### Answers

**1** Social needs refers to the third level of Maslow's hierarchy of needs ✓ which states that an interpersonal relationship is a human need. ✓

**2** Maslow's hierarchy of needs has 5 levels, from basic needs to self-actualisation. ✓✓ Safety, security and social needs may be more important for employees in the secondary sector because jobs can often be repetitive and offer little chance of meeting esteem or self-actualisation needs. Many workers in the secondary sector are also happy when they achieve a well-paying job which meets their social needs, so may not want to progress to higher levels. ✓✓✓✓✓ However, it is important to have an opportunity for those who want to be promoted and reach their self-esteem needs as without progression opportunities to team leader or management, employees may become dissatisfied and seek new jobs which may negatively affect the business objectives of staff retention and turnover. ✓✓✓✓

### Taylor's economic man

Taylor's theory of motivation focuses around control and reward. Taylor believed employees required **financial motivators** in order to meet organisational objectives.

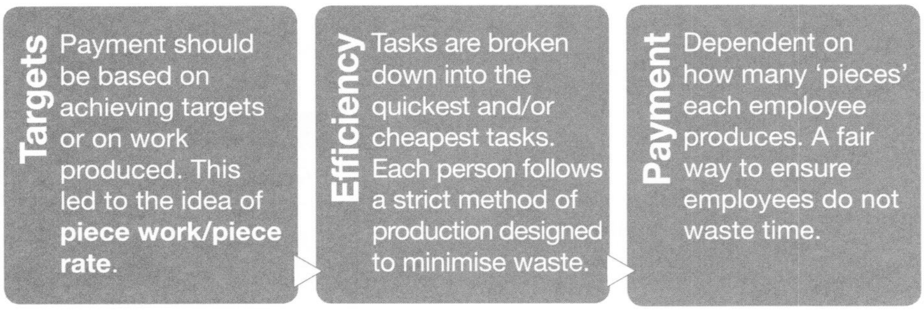

**Targets** Payment should be based on achieving targets or on work produced. This led to the idea of **piece work/piece rate**.

**Efficiency** Tasks are broken down into the quickest and/or cheapest tasks. Each person follows a strict method of production designed to minimise waste.

**Payment** Dependent on how many 'pieces' each employee produces. A fair way to ensure employees do not waste time.

▲ **Figure 2.6** Taylor's economic man

> **Key terms**
>
> **Satisfy**: to meet the basic needs. This does not make a person happy, it removes the need to worry.
>
> **Financial motivators**: monetary reward or incentive given to employees.
>
> **Piece work/piece rate**: payment relates to the amount produced. This assumes money is the main motivator for employment.

### Mayo's Hawthorne experiment

Mayo based his theory on one group of employees in one factory. He started with Taylor's theory and swiftly developed it to take into account **non-financial** motivators, namely team work and esteem needs.

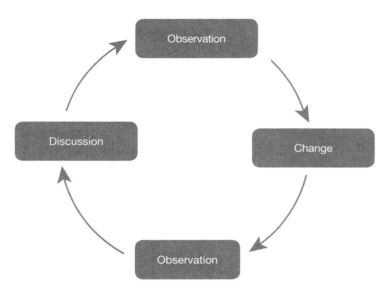

▲ **Figure 2.7** Mayo's Hawthorne experiment

**X | Common error**

Candidates often recite a theory from memory, however will not link it to business objectives or the case study. A generic or unsupported answer will cost valuable additional marks.

### Herzberg's two factor theory

Herzberg believed that there are two elements necessary to cause motivation: causes of dissatisfaction need to be removed or minimised by meeting employee basic needs, only then will employees be able to feel the benefits of motivation.

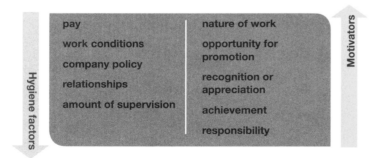

▲ **Figure 2.8** Herzberg's two factor theory

### McClelland's motivational needs theory

This **process theory** separates the key motivation forces that drive managers and employees. A person will need elements of all three of these to be motivated. Whichever force is dominant will influence the character of the employee or manager.

**Key term**

**Non-financial**: a method of motivation which takes into account non-monetary methods, such as the social and esteem needs of Maslow's pyramid.

**Key term**

**Process theory**: motivation theory that emphasises psychological drivers used to encourage employee involvement.

32

**Worked examples**

1   Define the term 'non-financial' motivation.                                    [2 marks]

2   Briefly explain the benefit of one method of non-financial motivation.          [3 marks]

**Answers**

1   Non-financial benefit means a method of motivation which motivates by means other than money ✓ such as promotion or training. ✓

2   Training allows for employees to learn new skills ✓ which a business can utilise to meet organisational objectives ✓ such as increased productivity. ✓

| Achievement | Authority | Affiliation |
|---|---|---|
| • Achievement of realistic yet challenging goals.<br>• A need for feedback and accomplishment.<br>• Can lead to high pressure and demotivation in others. | • Need to make an impact and influence others.<br>• Desire for leadership and dominance of their ideas.<br>• Can be for individual or organisational outcomes. | • The need to have friendly relationships.<br>• Requires interaction and often teamwork.<br>• Can hinder effective decision-making when difficult decisions have to be made. |

▲ **Figure 2.9** Motivational needs theory

**Vroom's expectancy theory**

A very simple theory that has four main stages that need to be present for the theory to succeed, which is based upon the theory that employees will work if their efforts are rewarded. Similar in principle to Taylor's economic man theory.

| Skills and equipment | Appropriate appraisal | Attractive rewards | Rewards received |
|---|---|---|---|
| The necessary training and equipment is provided for successful completion. | There is appropriate appraisal to ensure targets are met and feedback is given. | Rewards have to meet employee expectations and be suitable for the type of employee. | Rewards promised have to be delivered to ensure staff motivation levels are kept high. |

▲ **Figure 2.10** Vroom's expectancy theory

**Remember**

Theories are not real life. They are simplistic by nature and do not take into account any external factors which may affect the outcome.

## Motivation methods in practice

It is important to realise a number of key points; theory is not real life and there are external factors which can affect the basic theories. Another key influence into the practical implementation of these theories is that the case studies used by theorists were very narrow in scope, and were expanded with many assumptions.

### The theories in practical situations

If a theory is applied to a practical situation, it will often have limitations due to external factors. Some factors are identified and explained below.

▼ Table 2.3 Motivational methods in practice

| | | |
|---|---|---|
| Achievement | ⇨ | A common theme for many theories; may cause pressure on others not motivated by achievement and can act as a demoralising agent. |
| Achievement (2) | ⇨ | With the growth of teamwork, the opportunity for personal recognition of achievement is minimised, which can act as a demoralising agent especially when team members are rewarded equally for limited contributions. |
| Financial limitations (1) | ⇨ | Theory assumes financial rewards will be appropriate for the task, or that the finance is available for the training and development necessary which may not be the case in small organisations with limited budgets. |
| Financial limitations (2) | ⇨ | Theory assumes quality will be constant regardless of the speed of production. Quantity and quality are not always positively linked. |
| Human social needs | ⇨ | An important factor for many theories, however, fails to take into account that social needs often have time and financial costs which may differ from the stated objectives of profit maximisation or efficiency. |
| Scope of investigations | ⇨ | Theorists such as Hawthorn and Mayo used specific and limited samples which related only to a specific sector. These results may not be representative of a wider cross section. |

## Different payment methods

A payment method is the compensation acceptable to both the supplier and the receiver.

> **X Common error**
>
> Wages and salaries are different. A wage is time based and may vary monthly, while a salary is an agreed amount that remains constant throughout the period of employment.

▼ Table 2.4 Different types of pay

| | Time based | Salary | Piece rate | Commission | Bonus | Profit sharing | Performance related pay |
|---|---|---|---|---|---|---|---|
| Description | Related to the number of hours worked. | An agreed amount (usually) paid monthly. | An agreed amount for every item produced. | Payment made according to the number of sales. | An addition to normal pay for success. | Employees are shareholders and benefit from higher profits. | (PRP) Payment based on meeting or exceeding specified targets. |
| Used for | Roles where demand is changeable, and this is a benefit for the business. | Skilled positions where employee retention is required. | Skilled job production where individual items are created. | Sales positions as an incentive for high sales. | An incentive to meet organisational targets. | Cooperative businesses. | Positions where performance can be measured, i.e. sales or customer service. |
| Disadvantages | Employees do not have a guaranteed or regular amount of income. | Can be expensive for the business in time of economic downturn. | It is often difficult to identify the individual contribution of an employee due to teamwork and mass production. | The pursuit of sales means suitability can come second to profitability and ease of sales, leading to reduced repeat custom. | Can become expected if regular and can demotivate when bonuses are not received. | When there are losses, employees may suffer financially. | Unrealistic targets can demotivate and reduce productivity. Can be irrelevant for those who are not motivated by money. |

## Different types of non-financial motivators

Non-financial rewards are needed as a motivator *in addition to* financial compensation. Each meets a specific need when related particularly to Maslow's theory.

▼ **Table 2.5** Rewards related to Maslow's theory of needs

| | Basic | Safety | Social | Esteem | Self-actualisation |
|---|---|---|---|---|---|
| Training/Development/Job redesign | ✓ | | | ✓ | |
| Induction | ✓ | ✓ | ✓ | | |
| Promotion/Status | | | | ✓ | ✓ |
| Team working | | | ✓ | | |
| Empowerment | | | | ✓ | ✓ |
| Participation | | ✓ | ✓ | ✓ | |
| Fringe benefits/perks | | | | ✓ | |

## Ways in which employees can participate in the management and control of business activity

Participation allows a sense of belonging and ownership of the business, as views and opinions are listened to and considered. Participation does not need to be direct.

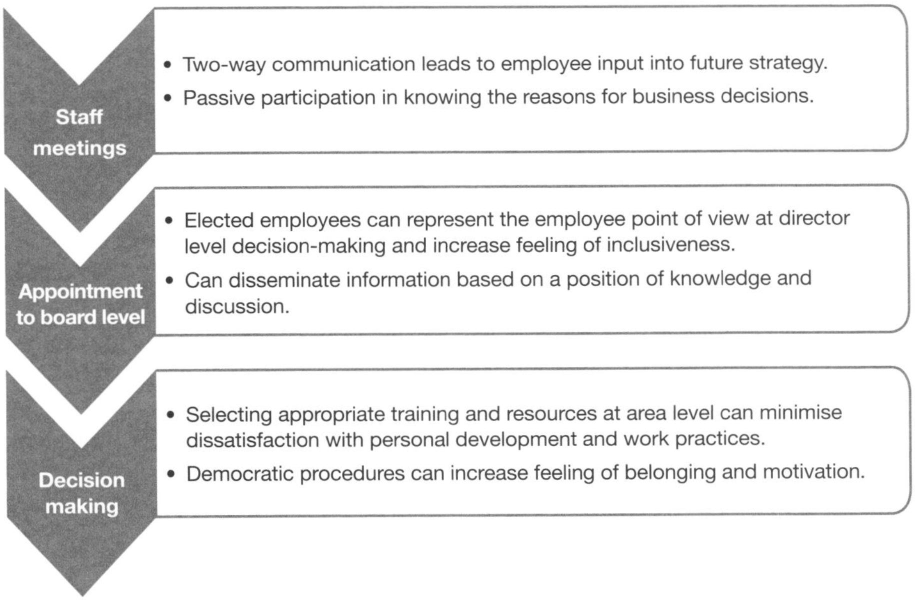

**Staff meetings**
- Two-way communication leads to employee input into future strategy.
- Passive participation in knowing the reasons for business decisions.

**Appointment to board level**
- Elected employees can represent the employee point of view at director level decision-making and increase feeling of inclusiveness.
- Can disseminate information based on a position of knowledge and discussion.

**Decision making**
- Selecting appropriate training and resources at area level can minimise dissatisfaction with personal development and work practices.
- Democratic procedures can increase feeling of belonging and motivation.

▲ **Figure 2.11** Participation of employees in management

**Remember**

To score high marks for analysis, unless specifically asked for only benefits or drawbacks, you must highlight and analyse an opposing view of the stance identified.

---

**✗ Common error**

Many candidates confuse piece rate, commission and PRP. Piece rate is for manufacturing, commission is for sales and PRP is for target based, quantifiable positions.

**Remember**

Just because some people are not motivated by money does not mean that money is irrelevant. Employees *require* financial payment, but not all are *motivated* by financial rewards, and therefore need non-financial motivators.

**Key terms**

**Empowerment:** the responsibility given to employees to make decisions relating to their area of business activity.

**Participation:** employee involvement in business decisions.

**Fringe benefits/perks:** benefits given to an employee which have little or no monetary value and are not essential but can be nice to have.

**✓ What you need to know**

Induction is training in areas unrelated to the position or area of work, such as fire safety and office layout and hierarchy.

## Worked examples

**1** Define worker participation. [2 marks]

**2** Analyse why it is important for a business to have employee participation. [8 marks]

### Answers

**1** Worker participation is the involvement of employees ✓ in business decision making ✓ such as deciding training needs or appointment to the board of directors.

**2** It is important to have employee participation because this is a source of non-financial motivation which helps employees meet esteem needs and can also ensure businesses reach their organisational goals such as productivity or profitability. ✓✓✓✓ If employees participate in board meetings, they may be able to suggest solutions to problems identified by employees such as inefficient work processes, which may increase efficiency and ultimately increase the productivity. ✓✓ This employee involvement will also allow dissemination of strategic decisions made which will empower employees and give them a sense of belonging and understanding of the direction of the business. ✓✓

## 2.3 Human resource management

This topic is concerned with:

➤ purpose and roles of HRM

➤ recruitment and selection

➤ job descriptions, person specifications, job advertisements

➤ employment contracts

➤ redundancy and dismissal

➤ staff morale and welfare

➤ staff training.

### Purpose and roles of HRM

This topic will aim to develop the candidates understanding of the different methods businesses use to ensure that its stated objectives are met. **HRM** aims to supply the organisation with the skilled and unskilled employees with the required level of skills and training to complete specific tasks.

### The role of HRM in meeting organisation objectives

Although HRM looks after the needs of employees, the reason for this care is to ensure employees are mentally and physically able to meet the needs of the organisation. A dissatisfied employee will not work efficiently which means an organisational goal may not be achieved.

Organisational goals such as 'exceeding customer expectations' or 'increasing profit margins by 10%' may not seem to be compatible, but these goals will be reached by the same methods employed by **HR**:

> **X Common error**
>
> Candidates often refer to HRM as looking after employee needs – this is not true. HRM looks after the organisation's needs by ensuring the most effective use of human resources.

> **Key terms**
>
> **HRM**: the function of ensuring the employees of a business are available and used in the most efficient and effective method possible.
>
> **HR**: human resources is the department that looks after human resource management.

> **Remember**
>
> The words in *italic* link each point and create a developed chain of analysis. Using conjunctions such as these are likely to increase your mark.

▲ **Figure 2.12** HR methods to achieve organisational goals

## Recruitment and selection

As shown above, recruitment and selection is one of the main functions of HRM. An organisation is only as good as the people it employs.

> **Worked examples**
>
> 1 Identify and briefly explain one advantage of a method of selection. [3 marks]
>
> 2 Explain the possible consequences for a business of poor recruitment and selection. [5 marks]
>
> **Answers**
>
> 1 One method of selection is face to face interviews. ✓ One advantage is that it allows the interviewer to assess the quality of the response ✓ and employ the right candidate. ✓
>
> 2 One consequence is that an unqualified person may gain the job ✓ which means the business will have to spend time and money on training ✓ which may reduce output and revenue. ✓ Another consequence is that if interpersonal skills are needed and the candidate does not have any, it may cause customer service problems ✓ which could annoy customers and they won't have repeat orders. ✓

### Labour turnover, methods of recruitment and selection

This **turnover of labour** has to be managed and any gaps in the organisation have to be filled with effective **recruitment** and **selection**.

> **Maths skills**
>
> $$\text{Labour turnover} = \frac{\text{Number of employees leaving in a period of time}}{\text{Total number of employees}} \times 100$$

While businesses may try to retain its skilled employees, some leave for reasons such as retirement, dismissal, relocation, promotion or new jobs. It is important to understand the consequences of labour turnover.

▼ **Table 2.6** Advantages and disadvantages of labour turnover

| Advantages | Disadvantages |
|---|---|
| New skills and experience are brought into the organisation. | Valuable skills may be lost. |
| A different viewpoint may be given. | May demotivate remaining employees. |
| May disrupt existing bonds within departments. | Replacing leads to business expense. |

**Key terms**

**Labour turnover**: the number of employees leaving a business over a period of time expressed as a percentage.

**Recruitment**: defining a vacant role and finding a candidate with the skills necessary to fulfil the job requirements.

**Selection**: the process of identifying the best candidate to fulfil the requirements of the vacant position.

**Workforce planning**: assessing the number of employees available and the skills required to meet business aims and objectives.

Once a business has identified that there is a gap that needs to be filled, the recruitment process begins. Recruitment involves **workforce planning** which compares the future needs of the organisation with the existing workforce and creates a plan of outcomes to allow the organisational aims to be met.

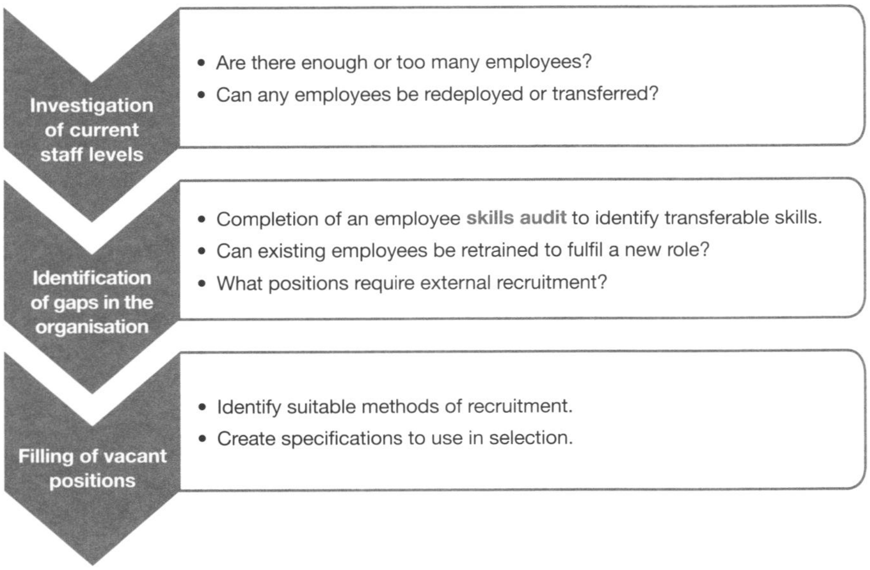

**Investigation of current staff levels**
- Are there enough or too many employees?
- Can any employees be redeployed or transferred?

**Identification of gaps in the organisation**
- Completion of an employee **skills audit** to identify transferable skills.
- Can existing employees be retrained to fulfil a new role?
- What positions require external recruitment?

**Filling of vacant positions**
- Identify suitable methods of recruitment.
- Create specifications to use in selection.

▲ **Figure 2.13** Workforce planning

Once candidates have been identified via the recruitment process, the candidate with the most suitable skills and abilities has to be selected for the organisation. Candidates can be both internal and external. There are a number of methods, each with their own advantages and disadvantages.

▼ **Table 2.7** Selection of suitable candidates

| Method | Advantage | Disadvantage |
|---|---|---|
| Interview | • Can be done face to face or via distance communications.<br>• Same questions asked to ensure fairness.<br>• Questions selected to identify required skills/experience. | • Easy to prepare/provide untruthful answers.<br>• Responses can be viewed subjectively.<br>• Some candidates may be nervous and it may not be a fair reflection of ability. |
| Aptitude test | • Practical tests can allow candidates to demonstrate skills.<br>• Harder for candidates to claim proficiency.<br>• May reduce training costs. | • Difference in ability due to experience may influence results.<br>• Nervousness may result in poor performance. |
| Psychometric tests | • Written questions unrelated to the task may show candidate aptitude and decision-making abilities.<br>• May show natural strengths and weaknesses of candidates. | • May not be understood by candidates and may provide false representation.<br>• Some may not fill in the answers and put in random answers. |
| Presentations | • Useful for positions where candidates are required to have visible roles and need confidence.<br>• Can judge the ability of a candidate for the role. | • Candidates are usually briefed in advance, so have lots of time to prepare – may show unrealistic or heightened skills. |

### Worked examples

**1** Define a psychometric test. [2 marks]

**2** Discuss the importance of a skills audit. [8 marks]

### Answers

**1** A psychometric test is usually a written list of questions with different answers which tests the aptitude of candidates ✓ to help select those with the most relevant thought processes. ✓

**2** A skills audit identifies the existing skills and attributes of a businesses' employees. ✓✓ If a business does this, then they may find suitable candidates for redeployment or promotion ✓✓ which can potentially save them the time and cost of recruitment and selection which may also improve the motivation and job satisfaction of an employee, ✓✓ however, some employees may lie as they think that they may be made to do more work for less pay if a business exploits unknown skills. ✓✓

> 💡 **Remember**
>
> Exam questions need to be built up through the different levels according to the mark schemes.

## Job descriptions, person specifications, job advertisements

### Purpose of job descriptions, person specifications and job advertisements

Following an analysis of the position that needs to be filled, a detailed list of functions that will need to be carried out is compiled. This is called a **job description**. Once this is completed, the HR department then creates a list which specifies the type of person required to fill the role. This is called the **person specification**.

To attract suitable candidates, the job must then be advertised in a legal manner. In the EU for example, you cannot ask for only male or only female workers, or workers aged between 18–35. This is **discrimination**.

Job advertisements are designed to attract suitable candidates. They can be internal or external and must be suitable for the type of position advertised. Some main methods are outlined below.

> ✗ **Common error**
>
> Many candidates confuse job descriptions and person specifications, but these have different roles.

> **Key terms**
>
> **Job description**: outline of the details of the position which allows a candidate to understand the requirements of the role.
>
> **Person specification**: outlines the essential and desirable skills, qualifications and personal qualities required of the applicant to be able to complete the job.
>
> **Discrimination**: the prejudicial treatment of different categories of people, including race, age and sex.

▼ **Table 2.8** Different types of job advertisements

| Recruitment method | Benefit | Drawback |
|---|---|---|
| **Business website** | Ensures only interested and motivated candidates apply. | Many candidates will not check all business websites as there may be too many. |
| **Recruitment agency** | A guaranteed supply of candidates available at short notice. Much of the initial selection work is completed by the agency. | Expensive to use and initial selection may be done by the agency which may not know your requirements. |
| **Headhunting** | Useful for attracting highly skilled employees with valuable skills who may not be actively looking for new opportunities. | Very expensive and the candidate may not be loyal if he agrees to leave his existing business for increased benefits. |
| **Job centres** | Ideal for lower skilled positions where applicants may receive government training. | Many applicants may apply which makes selection much more difficult. |
| **Personal contacts** | Existing employees are unlikely to recommend an unsuitable person as it reflects badly on them. | Limited pool of candidates and the best candidate may not be chosen. |

## Employment contracts

An **employment contract** gives security and peace of mind to both the employer and the employee. It allows the employee to know what is expected, what he will receive in return for his labour and it allows the employer to set minimum requirements of the employee.

Key term

**Employment contract**: a legal agreement between the employer and employee stating terms and conditions of employment.

### Main features of a contract of employment

Benefits of a contract:

- Agreed expectations of employee and employer.
- Allows peace of mind.
- Can resolve disputes as all main points should be stipulated.
- Breaches of contract can be identified and used for dismissal or industrial action.
- States clear conditions of termination.

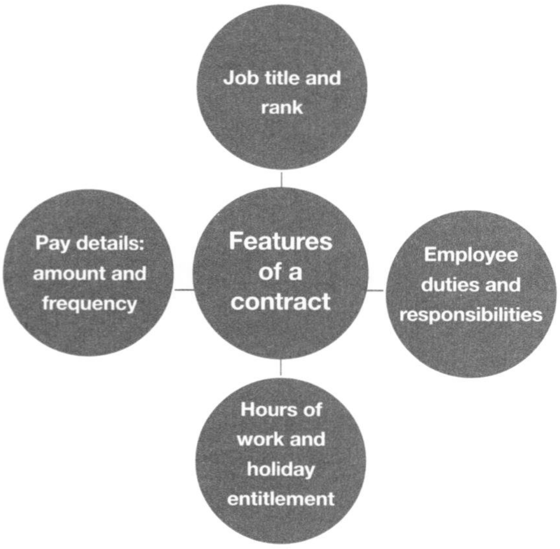


▲ **Figure 2.14** Features of a contract

## Redundancy and dismissal

### Difference between redundancy and dismissal

To ensure that business objectives are met, HR may have to make an employee **redundant** due to a change in work practices or demand, or **dismiss** an employee if their actions may cause harm to the business.

Causes of redundancy may be:

- mechanisation/obsolescence of roles
- decline in demand/economy.

Cause of dismissal may be:

- repeated lateness/absence
- not completing tasks to a required standard.

## Staff morale and welfare

It is important for businesses to ensure that staff **morale** and **welfare** are high; motivated employees work hard and help achieve organisational objectives. HRM may investigate internal and external causes of dissatisfaction in order to ensure staff are working at maximum efficiency.

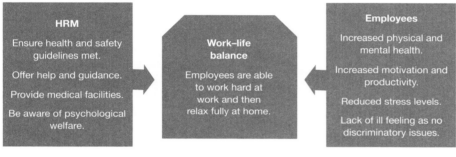

▲ **Figure 2.15** Relationship between HRM, staff morale and welfare including **work–life balance**

### Policies for diversity and equality

Each country has its own laws and regulations relating to **equality** and **diversity**, with minimum levels that must be met to ensure a business is acting legally. These policies may be exceeded if a business objective is to be seen as an equal opportunities business for marketing purposes.

Examples of areas where equality is required:

- sex
- race
- age
- religion.

Reasons why equality is required:

- to attract the best candidates
- to avoid charges of discrimination
- to be used for marketing and promotion purposes.

**Key terms**

**Redundancy**: when a position is no longer required and there is no work available for the employee.

**Dismissal**: termination of a contract due to a condition of contract being unfulfilled.

**Morale**: the confidence and enthusiasm of a person at a particular place or time.

**Welfare**: the health and/or happiness of a person or group.

**Work–life balance**: employees cannot work efficiently 100 per cent of the time and need to relax and enjoy their life outside of the workplace. This aims to balance work and career and family and friendship commitments.

**Equality**: treating each employee fairly in relation to rights, responsibilities or opportunities regardless of differences such as sex, race or colour.

**Diversity**: a reflection within an organisation of the differences between people found within a country such as race or religion.

> **Remember**
>
> If a 2-, 3- or 5-mark question does not ask you to 'define', then you do not have to define as you will gain no extra marks – your answer will show your understanding of the concept.

## Staff training

HRM provides training in order to allow employees to have the required knowledge and expertise required to fulfil the job role. The level of training provided depends on the organisational aims and level of skill required.

- **Induction training**: General training to help employees familiarise themselves with the business and rules and regulations – unrelated to the actual job or position.

- **On-the-job training**: Training directly related to a specific role and occurs at the workplace.

- **Off-the-job training**: Training which may not be directly related to the role, however, develops understanding. Occurs away from the workplace.

> **Remember**
>
> Each type of training has its own unique characteristics and benefits. 'Training' may not be a detailed enough answer for an extended question.

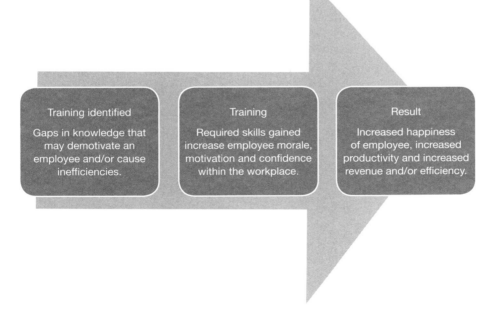

▲ **Figure 2.16** The purpose of staff development/training as a means of securing required skills and motivating the workforce

## Revision checklist

**I can:**

➤ explain the difference between managers and leaders ☐

➤ identify and apply two theories of management ☐

➤ identify and explain the qualities of a leader and explain how this affects leadership styles ☐

➤ explain and apply the term emotional intelligence ☐

➤ explain and apply the main motivational theories of a case study ☐

➤ explain the need for human resource management and recruitment and selection. ☐

## ⬆ Raise your grade

**Short answer questions**

1 **(a)** Define the term leadership. [2]

Directing and persuading others ✓ to work towards the organisation's goals. ✓ This can be achieved by using Mintzberg's functions of management. ✓

> **[2 marks]** While there are three points and three ticks here, there are only two marks available. However, in a short answer question like this, it is always useful to give an example as this could help the examiner decide whether a vague point you have made is relevant.

**(b)** Briefly explain two qualities of a leader. [3]

One quality of a leader is self-confidence ✓ – this is because it encourages others to believe in your vision ✓ which allows organisational aims to be met. ✗

Another quality is intelligence. ✓

> **[2 marks]** Because the question asks you to 'briefly explain two qualities', you cannot get the third mark without an explanation of the second point, even though the second quality identified is correct and the first point is very well explained.

2 Explain the possible consequences of a leader choosing an autocratic leadership style. [5]

There are four leadership styles: laissez-faire, autocratic, paternalistic and democratic. ✓ Laissez-faire is when a manager trusts their staff and allows them to manage themselves, ✓ autocratic is when a manager makes all of the decisions, paternalistic is when a manager treats their staff like children and listens but makes the final decision regardless of what staff say, and democratic is when staff are allowed a meaningful say. ✗

An autocratic leadership style is used when there are tight deadlines and you need to make sure employees are producing work to a high standard, because you can measure their performance and use financial motivators and punishments effectively. ✓

> **[3 marks]** Even though the candidate clearly has excellent knowledge of leadership styles, the majority of the answer is wasted as the student has not read or answered the question.
>
> 'Possible consequences' is asking for a minimum of two consequences, and here, even though the (positive) consequence is effective, there is only one, which means the student may not achieve higher than 3 marks.

**3** Explain two methods of financial reward. [5]

Salary is one method of a financial reward, ✓ which pays an employee a regular income, usually every month ✓ which allows the employee to feel financially secure. ✓

Commission is another method of a financial reward, where employees are rewarded based on the level of their sales or profits, ✓ which motivates employees to work hard to increase the amount of money earned. ✓ This is usually used in sales positions. ✓

> **[5 marks]** This is a full answer because it exactly answers the question. Each point is 'soundly explained', which means that there are two or more connected effects to each point. Note that there are 6 ticks for a 5-mark question. The extra effort here may well be rewarded if two of the points are similar or within the same marking criteria.

**4** Explain the possible benefits for a business of internal recruitment. [5]

One benefit of internal recruitment is that promotion is an employee motivator, ✓ which encourages employees to work hard to gain promotion ✓ which can improve the morale within the organisation. ✓

Another benefit of internal recruitment is that the member of staff will know all of the internal processes and procedures, ✓ however, this may mean that the promoted person will know all of the short cuts and may weaken the organisation's structure. ✗

> **[4 marks]** This answer only receives four marks as only one benefit is explained – the second benefit, even though correct, is answered with a disadvantage which is not answering the question asked. The second point needs an advantage such as 'this would reduce training time and cost for the business'. [1]

**5** Distinguish between a person specification and a job description. [5]

A person specification outlines the personal qualities, skills and qualifications ✓ needed by the applicant ✓ to successfully carry out the job. ✓

The job description is a list of information such as the job title and tasks and responsibilities which the business needs the candidate to be able to complete. ✓ The person specification is usually written based on the job description. ✓

> **[5 marks]** This receives full marks as each element is 'soundly explained'. Each point is also written as a separate paragraph which helps the examiner distinguish each separate point, it also ensures that the candidate can check they have answered each element fully.

## Long answer questions

**1 (a)** Analyse the qualities of a successful leader. [8]

A leader will have a number of qualities that make him successful, but it depends on the type of organisation he/she works in. According to Mintzberg, a successful leader would have good interpersonal ✓ skills, as these are required to give guidance and inspiration. ✓ If the leader is working in a team of sales people for example, the leader would have to motivate and encourage their staff to meet organisational targets such as a specific number of sales per day. ✓

> At this point, the candidate is showing some understanding of a leader and is also applying the quality needed to a business context, however the analysis is still quite weak and not yet strong enough for a Level 3 answer.

Another quality is self-confidence. ✓ Without self-confidence, a leader would not be able to inspire those around him/her as people are usually inspired by those that believe strongly in themselves and the direction that they are leading their team in. ✓ In a sales environment, there is a lot of pressure and sometimes when the team is not meeting its targets, it is very easy to become dispirited and this is when a strong, self-confident leader will be able to make others believe that 'the next person' will be the best customer and allow the team to work their way towards a target. ✓

> At this point, Level 3 has been achieved as there is 'some analysis of the qualities needed by a leader to be successful' however it has not yet reached the level of 'good analysis' which could be achieved with a critical stance.

However, it is very important that a leader is aware of the impact of his/her qualities. As even if a leader was self-confident, this might put too much pressure on his/her team to achieve unrealistic targets. ✓ If a leader is too self-confident and sets demanding targets, which if not reached, can be demotivating and lead to members of staff feeling inadequate and leaving the organisation – causing high level of staff turnover or poor sales techniques that may harm the long-term prospects of the company by using high pressure tactics that may put customers off using the business again. ✓

> At this point, Level 4 has been achieved as there is now 'good analysis of the qualities needed by a leader to be successful'. It is very important that you look at the number of marks available and try to make sure that you follow a limited number of points through to a good depth, rather than trying to give many examples to show the breadth of your knowledge of the qualities of leadership.

**(b)** Discuss why senior managers leading large public limited companies might decide to use democratic styles of leadership to reach organisational goals. [12]

A large public limited company may operate in more than one country or business sector, which means that there are many different elements of the business which need to be considered.

Senior managers in plc's usually deal with strategic rather than tactical issues, ✓ and the supervision of individual national or regional teams is left to more junior managers. This means that a senior manager would rather use a democratic style of leadership as ✓ it allows a two-way method of communication and if junior managers are allowed to participate in the decision making, ✓ their local knowledge might help to ensure tactical decisions are appropriate for their particular area, leading to a business being able to make the right decisions to increase sales revenue and meet their organisational goal of revenue maximisation. ✓ In addition to this, it is very easy to check on the progress and direction of your junior managers as information technology has increased the speed of communications which means that it is much easier than 20 years ago to monitor what your teams are doing and intervene at an early stage if an incorrect decision has been made. ✓✓

> At this point, the candidate has shown 'understanding' of senior managers/democratic leadership and public limited companies, [L1] as well as some limited analysis and application of arguments for using a democratic style of leadership. [L2]

However, this often leads to a flatter organisational structure which places more power into the hands of junior managers, who may not always see the 'bigger picture' and advise their managers to make decisions which may be good for that department or country, but not for the business as a whole. This increase in a junior member's power means that there is more risk for the senior manager who has to trust each of his regional managers to make the correct decisions, as ultimately it is the reputation of the senior manager which is at risk if there is a mistake to be made. ✓

> At this point, the level of analysis is sufficient for a good Level 2 answer. Remember, as this is a 12-mark question, the amount of marks awarded for analysis is usually only up to half of the marks; 6 marks are allocated for the evaluation.

Therefore, even though the level of risk is increased for senior managers by using democratic styles of management, ICT has made it possible to monitor many teams in a short amount of time, which decreases the risk to a senior manager and a plc in general of junior managers acting in a way that would harm a business's overall strategic direction as a senior manager could intervene very quickly to correct a course of action to protect the businesses reputation or bottom line. ✓

> At this point, Level 3 has been achieved as 'Limited evaluation of why senior managers might use a democratic style of management' however it is not yet effective evaluation as this would need some contrasting comments.

Senior managers may decide to use the democratic style as traditional methods such as the authoritarian style of leadership are only useful for specific situations, such as when there is no need to take into account influences such as religion or culture and there is a need for specific rules and regulations which need to be followed, for example in a factory setting where there are strict regulations and no tolerance given.

To get the best out of your employees, you must be able to trust them and give them a chance to use their initiative and regional or cultural knowledge to maximise sales and/or meet customer expectations. This then means that the democratic style of leadership is the most useful style for modern plc's. ✓

> At this point the candidate has neatly wrapped up his/her evaluation by showing how the democratic style is better than another style, such as the authoritarian style of leadership. There is 'effective evaluation' and this answer would be scoring maximum marks in this setting.

2   'Because the democratic leadership style encourages participation in decision making, this helps achieve organisational goals'. Do you agree? Justify your answer.   [20]

I agree with this statement because democratic leadership styles allow for two-way communication and are often seen in flatter business organisations with fewer levels of hierarchy. ✓ This allows for employees from all levels of the organisation to contribute their ideas ✓ and observations which may improve the efficiency of some operations. ✓

Because there is two-way communication, this means that employees are usually given more information about the direction of the business which motivates ✓ employees and improves efficiency. ✓ Employees may also have suggestions on how to improve the efficiency of operations as they do the job every day, which managers may not be aware of as they are removed from the job. ✓ This may help to achieve the organisational goal at departmental levels of increasing profits by reducing expenditure through suggesting money saving ideas. ✓

> At this point, the candidate is within the Level 2 boundary as there is some limited analysis which means that the points are not developed well and/or this is only a one sided view. This answer would receive a score of between 5 and 10 marks.

However, democratic leadership may not help achieve organisational objectives as it may take a long time to take the views of all of the employees of business. ✓ This long period of decision making may mean that a business misses an opportunity to exploit a gap in the market, ✓ as time has to be taken for voting, opinions, debate and the communication of the results to the employees. ✓ This means that competitors may beat you to the market and gain first mover advantage, gaining customer loyalty which may mean that your organisational goal of increasing market share may not be met. ✓

> At this point, there are two developed paragraphs which are showing 'analysis of the statement in relation to achieving business goals'. This would now be achieving a grade of 11–12 marks, as there is no evaluation of the statement.

I agree with the statement that democratic leadership styles help achieve organisational goals such as reducing costs to increase profits, ✓ as employees who actually do the work are often the ones who find short cuts which managers may not be aware of. ✓

> At this point, there is now a limited evaluation with some justification which answers the question. This is, however, a very low level answer as it is not developed and there is no effective evaluation which takes into consideration any negative issues. This would now be achieving a grade of 13–14 marks. A better evaluation is below.

I agree that democratic leadership may be useful in achieving organisational goals if managers use the style effectively. ✓ When there are decisions that are made which are not time critical and may affect a particular department, then democratic leadership style would help in achieving some organisational goals ✓ such as reducing costs or improving quality, due to the knowledge and input of employees, however may be less useful in aims such as gaining market share as employees ✓ may not have relevant knowledge of the market and may provide biased opinions not based on data. ✓ However, businesses need to be careful of allowing a full democratic operation as this may reduce ✓ the speed of decision making which would reduce the chances of achieving corporate objectives such as increasing market share. ✓

> At this point, the candidate is now achieving a Level 5 answer as there is effective evaluation of the statement as there is a reasoned judgement referring to agreeing/ disagreeing with the statement.

# ❓ Exam-style questions

This section will allow you to practise writing answers for exam-style questions. Remember, it is useful to be aware of the mark schemes for the questions which can be found on relevant websites or from your teacher.

## Paper 1

### Short answer questions

1   (a) Distinguish between 'management' and 'leadership'. [2]

    (b) Briefly explain **two** styles of leadership. [3]

2   (a) Define 'motivation'. [2]

    (b) Briefly explain **two** types of financial reward. [3]

3   Explain the possible consequences for a business of poor workforce planning. [5]

4   (a) Define the term 'job description'. [2]

    (b) Briefly explain why a business might decide to use more than one selection method. [3]

### Long answer questions

5   (a) Analyse why it is important for a business to have policies on redundancy and dismissal. [8]

    (b) Discuss the importance of staff training and development for employee welfare in a tertiary sector business. [12]

6   Discuss how a large national retailer could develop an effective sales force. [20]

7   (a) Analyse how a business might use non-financial rewards as a way of improving staff morale. [8]

    (b) Discuss the qualities that are likely to be essential for a manager in a car manufacturing business to be effective. [12]

## Paper 2

 **Link**

Refer to Case study 2: Paul's Paper Supplies in Unit 14.

1   Analyse methods of staff training Paul could use for new employees when expanding his business. [8]

2   Recommend whether Paul should create a formal training and development plan when expanding his business. [11]

## Key topics

➤ what is marketing?

➤ market research

➤ the marketing mix.

## 3.1 What is marketing?

This topic is concerned with:

➤ the roles of marketing and its relationship with other business activities

➤ supply and demand

➤ features of markets: location, size, share, competitors, growth

➤ industrial and consumer markets

➤ niche versus mass marketing

➤ market segmentation.

### The roles of marketing and its relationship with other business activities

This topic will aim to develop the candidates' understanding of the role of marketing. While there are many different methods of marketing a product, each has its own unique characteristics and will work best in specific situations.

The main role of marketing is to ensure a business can sell its product for the maximum price to maximise the profitability of a product. It is important to realise however that marketing is not a standalone function and needs to cooperate closely with all the other main departments of a business in order to be successful, therefore a **marketing strategy** is essential to meet the corporate objectives.

### The link between marketing objectives and corporate objectives

**Marketing** is the process of identifying and satisfying customer needs by getting the right product sold in the right place and attracting customers by using the right methods of promotion. These are commonly known as the 4 Ps, which will be investigated further in a later topic.

It is important to understand that marketing has many different aims and each of these aims is dependent on the corporate objective it is meant to achieve.

The success of a business is determined by its ability to meet its corporate objectives. In order to meet these corporate objectives, a business must attract potential customers to buy the product or service offered. In order to do this, a **marketing objective** is created.

> **✗ Common error**
>
> This topic can be poorly answered as candidates do not read the question properly and use generic marketing techniques such as 'television and newspapers' without reading the context.

> **Key terms**
>
> **Marketing strategy:** a plan of action designed to promote and sell a product in order to meet the marketing and corporate objectives.
>
> **Marketing:** promoting and selling products or services; making potential customers aware of a product or service.
>
> **Marketing objective:** a goal/goals set by a business when promoting products or services that should be achieved within a specific time frame.

> **🔗 Link**
>
> There is more about the 4 Ps in Unit 3, topic 3.3.

AS Level

## Marketing objectives

A marketing objective is necessary to promote and sell the product effectively. You need to be aware of the current strength of your brand and how to maximise the brand exposure for the minimum cost.

▲ **Figure 3.1** The link between corporate objectives and marketing objectives

## Supply and demand

The marketing objective of a business will often be determined by the quality and/or quantity **supplied** of the product and the amount of **demand** in the market place.

**Key terms**

**Supply:** the quantity of products or services available for purchase at a particular time.

**Demand:** the quantity of customers who are willing and able to buy the product at that time.

## Factors influencing the supply and demand for the products/services

The two main factors which influence supply are the *selling price* and the *cost of production*.

▼ **Table 3.1** Factors influencing supply

| Selling price | If the selling price of a product or service is increasing and the **barriers to entry** are low, this will increase the level of supply as more businesses try to capitalise on the product or service. |
|---|---|
| Cost of production | However, if the cost of raw materials increases profit margins will decrease. If the amount of profit is likely to decrease, this will make some businesses change focus to a more profitable product or service which will reduce the supply of a product. |

**Costs of production**
- labour, materials, fuel and rent
- an increase in these leads to an increase in manufacturing costs that can affect supply.

**Advances in technology**
- high costs of purchasing and updating hardware
- however, new technologies reduce unit costs enabling a rise in supply.

**Taxes and subsidies**
- taxes on **demerit goods** increase costs which reduce the supply
- **subsidies** on **merit goods** increase the supply as costs are reduced.

**Government and regulation**
- laws such as health and safety add costs and time which can reduce supply
- these can act as barriers which make the production of a product unviable for production.

▲ **Figure 3.2** Factors which influence costs

**Key terms**

**Barrier to entry**: an obstacle that prevents a new business from easily entering an industry or area of business, i.e. high start-up costs or limited licenses.

**Demerit goods**: a product or service that is 'bad' and has an external cost, such as cigarettes and alcohol, so is heavily taxed to reduce demand.

**Subsidies**: money provided by the state to help reduce the price of a product or service.

**Merit goods**: a product or service considered to have a positive effect may be under-consumed due to cost; therefore, it is likely to be subsidised.

There are four main factors which influence costs.

The demand of a product is influenced by many different factors; some of the main factors are identified and explained in Table 3.2.

**▼ Table 3.2** Factors of demand for products

| Factor | Explanation | Example |
|---|---|---|
| Price of similar products | A competitor may have aggressive pricing strategies to undercut your product. | Sales and predatory pricing strategies may lower the price of competing products. |
| Income | A rise or fall in income levels in your target market will also affect the ability of potential customers to access the product. | A fall in income levels means customers may switch to lower priced products.<br><br>A rise may influence customers to buy 'premium products' instead. |
| Customer attitudes and fashion | Brand loyalties, ethical concerns and fashion crazes can increase demand or decrease if deemed unpopular. | While real fur used to be a luxury it is now seen as cruel and unpopular, while electronic brands rise and fall with fashion and technology levels. |
| Seasonal factors | Demand changes according to the external natural environment. | Ice-cream is popular in summer while warm clothing is popular in winter. |
| Demographic factors | As distribution of age, gender and even religion can affect the demand for products. | A younger population is more likely to demand fashionable items while an older generation is likely to be more cost conscious. |

> 💡 **Remember**
>
> Supply and demand are very closely linked, and one factor may influence both supply AND demand. Make sure to explore each factor thoroughly.

---

**Worked examples**

1  Explain two different factors which can influence demand.                    [5 marks]

2  Define the term 'barriers to entry'.                    [3 marks]

**Answers**

1  One factor which can influence demand is income. ✓ If a person's level of income rises then they may have more disposable income, ✓ which can increase demand for luxury goods. ✓ Another is seasonal factors. ✓ Businesses must make sure that they sell suitable products for the season to minimise waste ✓ and ensure accurate levels of stock. ✓

2  A barrier to entry is an obstacle that limits entry to an industry ✓ such as government regulation or licenses ✓ which may reduce the amount of demerit goods. ✓

---

**Interactions between price, supply and demand**

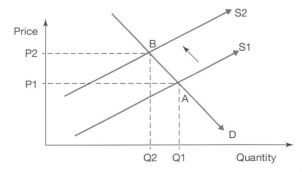

> ⭐ **Exam tip**
>
> You will never have to draw a supply and demand graph, although you may have to be able to interpret one and being able to draw a simple diagram may help you to explain a particular point.

▲ **Figure 3.3** Interactions between price, supply and demand

This simple diagram shows the relationship between supply, demand and price.

- Supply has **shifted** to the left (S1 moves to S2). This is due to less products being supplied in the market.

- This means that the quantity demanded has decreased (Q1 moves to Q2). This is because the price has increased as the **equilibrium point** has moved from A to B.

### Features of markets: location, size, share, competitors, growth

Markets have many different characteristics and it is important for the candidate to be able to accurately define, assess or apply a specific market to the question asked.

### How markets may differ

There are many different types of markets:

▼ **Table 3.3** Types of premises

| | |
|---|---|
| Physical location | Shops and premises that you can visit and enter. |
| Electronic market | Online or virtual shops which you access via technological means and have no physical contact. |
| Sub markets | One area can be vast and is usually broken up into more specific markets which cater for a specific need. |
| Competition | A market can be competitive if there are many competitors selling identical or **substitute goods**. |
| Consumer market | Selling products and services to individual buyers who will consume or use the product without the intention of reselling for further profit. |
| Producer market | A location where producers buy goods and services with the intention of transforming them into a sellable product with the purpose of making a profit. |

> **Key terms**
>
> **Shift**: when a supply or demand curve (which is a straight line) shifts to the left or right, due to an external change in supply or demand.
>
> **Equilibrium point**: where the supply equals the demand for a product – there is no waste.
>
> **Substitute goods**: a product or service which is different but has the same purpose, i.e. water is a substitute for fizzy drinks.

---

**Worked examples**

1  Briefly explain a shift in demand.　　　　　　　[2 marks]

2  Briefly explain one feature of an electronic (e-) market.　[3 marks]

**Answers**

1  A shift in demand is when there is an external influence on the level of demand ✓ such as an increase or decrease in competitors or customers. ✓

2  One feature is a lack of a physical selling location such as a shop, ✓ which means there is little or no personal contact between seller and buyer, ✓ but a buyer can purchase at any time of the day or night. ✓

Markets can also be categorized into national, regional and international settings.

▼ **Table 3.4** National, regional and international markets

| National | Companies that sell their products and services in more than one geographical location within one country's borders. Often have multiple sales outlets and advertising on national television channels, national newspapers and advertise heavily online. |
|---|---|
| Regional | Companies which sell their product or service in a region which has its own identifiable characteristics and needs. This could be a small market or a larger market such as Europe, North America or Asia. Products and services will often be similar but have minor variations to cater for individual customer needs. |
| International | Often larger companies that sell their product or service globally. Products and services must have a common, identifiable message across cultures and regions, although products and services may be altered as with regional businesses. |

## The differences between product and customer (market) orientation

A business may have a **product orientation** or a **customer orientation**.

▼ **Table 3.5** The differences between product and customer (market) orientation

| Product orientation | Customer orientation |
|---|---|
| The design of the product attracts customers. | Products are designed to meet the needs of customers. |
| Homogenous product sold with little or no adaptation to suit local needs. | Lots of adaptation with regional, cultural or financial influences catered for. |
| Saves on market research costs. | High expenditure on market research. |
| Businesses produce according to organisational strengths and abilities. | Businesses produce what markets desire and ask for which widens customer base. |
| Can be risky if there are few customers attracted to the design. | Can stretch the resources of a business as many different options need to be included. |

## Problems associated with measuring market share and market growth

In order to be able to assess the success of a business's marketing strategy, there must be methods of measuring progress. The two main measures are **market share** and **market growth**; however, these have many problems associated with them:

- It can be difficult to define the market – Who are your direct and indirect competitors? Should substitutes be included?

- Markets can change rapidly – a competitor today may not be a competitor tomorrow.

- Data on competitor sales and profits can be difficult to obtain.

- A high market share does not mean high profits – low prices and margins may make your business seem very successful.

## Implications of changes in market share and growth

Businesses can use changes in market share and growth to identify strengths, weaknesses and areas for exploitation, expansion or contraction:

▼ **Table 3.6** Identifying what changes in market share and growth mean for a business

| | |
|---|---|
| Increasing market share | Means the business may become market leader and can control prices and features. |
| | However, may increase competition as other businesses try to reduce your dominant position by reducing prices or offering new features. |
| Low market share | This identifies that a business's product is losing popularity and either needs to be replaced, updated or removed from sale. |
| | However, it may also mean that a competitor has captured the market with a new product, meaning that you have to increase investment into promotion and marketing to ensure the business objective of survival is reached. |
| Sharp increase in market growth | Identifies a potential trend, which can mean an increase in production is viable. |
| | However, this will attract competitors into the market which may increase competition and reduce prices, customers and profit margins. |
| Slow decrease in market growth | Identifies a slowing market and the need to reduce investment in that particular area. |
| | However, increased advertising and/or a change in pricing strategy may be needed to combat other businesses trying to maximise sales in a shrinking market. |

## Industrial and consumer markets

▼ **Table 3.7** Classification of products and differing marketing styles

| | **Characteristics** | **Communications/marketing** |
|---|---|---|
| Industrial | • Buy raw materials.<br>• Buy in bulk.<br>• Intention is to add value and resell. | • Direct communications to individual businesses.<br>• Focus on technical specifications and price. |
| Consumer | • Buy finished products.<br>• Buy individual/few items.<br>• Intention is to use, not make a profit. | • Often mass media/above the line.<br>• Promotion may be from retailers.<br>• Promotions focus on desirability or practicality. |

⭐ **Exam tip**

In the exam you may be asked for consequences or implications of a change in a variable. It is important to develop a few points fully to gain analysis marks, rather than listing many points that will only gain limited knowledge marks.

✓ **What you need to know**

The two types of customer that businesses may target are **industrial** and **consumer markets**. A candidate must be aware that each type of market has its own characteristics and marketing will be developed accordingly.

**Key terms**

**Industrial market**: customers who buy a product with the intention of adding value and to make a profit.

**Consumer market**: final customers who buy a product to consume.

## Niche versus mass marketing

A business must understand its objectives and their customers before creating marketing objectives and a marketing plan. The marketing plan must consider whether the customers are **niche** or **mass market**.

### Reasons for and benefits/limitations of mass marketing and niche marketing

**Niche market:**

A small segment of a large market aimed at particular customers who must be identified, their specific requests met and a product or service tailored to this need.

Markets are often unprofitable for large scale producers due to a limited number of customers.

Products are often more unique and also more expensive. Often high quality and there are less economies of scale due to the limited quantities produced.

However, due to the unique nature, profits are often higher and there are few competitors.

**Mass market:**

A large market where a generic product appeals to the majority of the market.

Products are often standardised, produced in high volume and often widely available at a comparatively low price.

Brands are often synonymous with mass markets and quality is often associated with particular brands.

Products are made and then customers are located, usually through mass marketing techniques which are often expensive, however, gain a brand identity and large volumes of sales meaning **unit costs** are low.

**Key terms**

**Niche market**: a small, specialised market for specific products and services.

**Mass market**: a wide market for generic goods produced on a large scale.

**Unit costs**: total expenditure needed to produce a single unit – all costs divided by the number of products produced.

**✓ What you need to know**

Marketing is related to objectives and finance as well as the intended customer – you must be able to start bringing together different strands to create a rounded argument.

### Worked examples

1 Explain two different benefits of niche marketing. [5 marks]

2 Define the term 'industrial market'. [3 marks]

**Answers**

1 One benefit of niche marketing is that the target audience is smaller ✓ which means you can focus your advertising to a specific market segment, ✓ which should reduce your marketing costs. ✓ Another benefit is that you can make the advertising personal, ✓ which may increase the amount of customer loyalty, which helps to develop a long-term relationship. ✓

2 An industrial market is one that sells to other manufacturers and not the end customer. ✓ These manufacturers will then add value to the product ✓ with the intention of reselling and making a profit. ✓

## Market segmentation

Promoting a product is expensive and can require a huge investment of capital. To minimise costs, businesses segment their markets to ensure that capital invested into marketing strategies is not wasted.

Market segments must have identifiable characteristics and have be large enough to provide the required number of sales for a business to be profitable.

▼ **Table 3.8** Benefits and limitations of market segmentation

| Benefits | Limitations |
|----------|-------------|
| Reduces the number of potential customers, which increases the ability to create targeted advertising. | Excludes potential customers who you may not have thought about which reduces the potential market size and therefore opportunity for sales. |
| Can produce a specialised product which can increase the profit per unit. | Specialised products can be harder to sell if trends or market conditions change. |
| Communications to the customer are more personal and may reduce marketing costs. | Personal communications can create a brand image that may be hard to change if fashions change, which can limit the size of the market. |

## Methods of market segmentation

Markets can be segmented in many ways depending on the product, the business objectives and the amount of potential customers. While there are many different methods of segmentation, it is better to identify the main methods and analyse them fully.

▼ **Table 3.9** Methods of market segmentation

| Method | Reason | Explanation |
|--------|--------|-------------|
| Gender | Advertising can be directed towards gender specific areas such as magazines/ television channels. | A product for a male is not always sold in a male market – sometimes the opposite gender buy products as presents. |
| Household type | If you are selling to families, single people or couples, the approach will need to be accessible. | Marketing a product to a family with children will not gain the attention of different lifestyles. |
| Age | The interests and requirements of teenagers will differ to those of retirees or middle-aged people. | Marketing a high fashion item to retirees is unlikely to gain the attention of potential customers. |
| Socio-economic | Income, education and occupation can influence the buying habits of potential customers. | Low income groups are more likely to be potential customers for lower price goods, while higher income groups are likely to require better quality and branded goods. |
| Psychographic | Attitudes, lifestyle and location influence the products that may be required. | Early adopters may require the newest trends while working people may require convenience food to fit in with busy lifestyles. |

**Key terms**

**Promotion:** the publicising of a product or service to increase sales or awareness.

**Market segmentation:** dividing a large market into smaller, more manageable groups based on different characteristics.

**Remember**

What may be a benefit for one company may be a limitation for another depending on the objectives, the product and the amount of capital available for a business.

**Remember**

Market segmentation requires the marketer to make assumptions based on lifestyles which may be based on either research or pre-conceived ideas. The important element of market segmentation is the reasoning for the segmenting of the market.

## 3.2 Market research

This topic is concerned with:

- primary and secondary research
- methods of information gathering
- sampling methods
- market research results
- cost effectiveness.

### Primary and secondary research

**Market research** can be separated into two different types – **primary research** and **secondary research**. Each has its own characteristics and uses and candidates must be able to choose the *most appropriate method* for the situation identified in the exam. The data gathered can be **quantitative** or **qualitative**.

| | |
|---|---|
| **Customer/ market profiling** | • identify customer/market characteristics and preferences<br>• segment the customers and the market into appropriate measures<br>• identify trends and competitor decisions. |
| **Quantitative information** | • allows the relationship between sets of data to make marketing decisions<br>• can be used to identify cause and effect. |
| **Qualitative information** | • allows the analysis of information based on expressive opinion<br>• can be used to explain reasons for customer and market motivation and behaviour. |

▲ **Figure 3.4** Purpose of market research

### Methods of information gathering

**Common error**

Many candidates either list many methods or explain a secondary method when a primary method is required. Read the question and the command words carefully.

| **Primary** | **Secondary** |
|---|---|
| Original data – direct from source. | Second-hand data already gathered for alternative use. |
| Often takes time to gather. | Relatively quick to find information. |
| Can be expensive in comparison to desk research. | Is much less expensive than primary research. |
| Information is ALL relevant to the business. | Information is not always relevant and can be difficult to discover. |

▲ **Figure 3.5** Distinction between primary (field) and secondary (desk) research

**Key terms**

**Market research**: the process of gathering information about markets, customers and competitors to assist in the creation of marketing objectives and strategies.

**Primary research**: gathering new information specific to your needs direct from original sources – often known as field research.

**Secondary research**: using data which has already been collected and for a different purpose – often known as desk research.

**Quantitative**: data concerning quantity, amount or range, usually measurable and able to be analysed mathematically.

**Qualitative**: data that describes attitudes, views and opinions and is difficult to be measured mathematically. Provides reasons not figures.

**Remember**

Even though primary and secondary research have their own advantages and disadvantages, both are still useful and usually used together.

**Common error**

Candidates may think that primary research is expensive but it does not always have to be – it depends on the size and scale of the primary research completed.

▼ **Table 3.10** Methods of primary research and their advantages and disadvantages

| Method | Advantages | Disadvantages |
|---|---|---|
| Observation | o Can observe true behaviour.<br>o Can identify common patterns. | o Does not explain reasons for behaviour.<br>o Depends on observer bias. |
| Surveys | o Generic word to describe any type of questioning activity.<br>o Can use open and closed questions depending on requirements.<br>o Can be structured or unstructured. | |
| Interview | o Can gather detailed qualitative data.<br>o Can ask deeper questions to understand reasons. | o Some respondents may lie or give 'expected' answers.<br>o Can be expensive and time consuming. |
| Questionnaire | o Easy method to gather large quantities of quantitative data.<br>o Can also collect some qualitative data to expand quantitative data.<br>o Cost effective when used on websites. | o Some respondents may rush and give incorrect answers.<br>o Construction of questionnaires may be subject to bias.<br>o No control of quality of respondents or method of judging responses. |
| Focus group | o Selected people from an identified segment representative of target market.<br>o Discussion leads to freedom of respondent answers. | o Individuals may be influenced by others.<br>o Individuals may not give true views on sensitive or controversial issues. |
| Test marketing/ trials | o Sales data provides a clear reflection of popularity.<br>o Can be used in conjunction with observation. | o May give false views as customers are inquisitive of a new product.<br>o Often used with promotions which may influence buying habits. |
| Loyalty cards and databases | o Provides a range of qualitative data on purchasing habits.<br>o Easy to build customer profiles and identify trends. | o Very expensive to administer.<br>o Can provide too much information. |

**Key term**

Bias: prejudice for or against one person or group which can be considered unfair.

Customer profile: a portrait of a customer by identifying similar goals and characteristics that can be used in the implementation of a marketing plan.

▼ **Table 3.11** Sources of secondary information

| Method | Definition | Example |
|---|---|---|
| Internal | o Information which is not publicly available but is generated for a different reason within the business. | o Sales reports.<br>o Turnover figures.<br>o Management reports. |
| External | o Information which has been compiled from an external source and is not directly related to the business. | o Competitor company reports.<br>o Journals.<br>o Books.<br>o Newspapers. |
| Printed | o Hard copy information. | o Newspapers.<br>o Articles books. |
| Web-based | o Located in an electronic format in the virtual world (internet). | o Newspaper web pages.<br>o E-libraries. |
| Paid for | o Information which has been collected and sorted by a third party. | o Trade journals.<br>o Government sources.<br>o Data companies. |

## Worked examples

**1** Identify and briefly explain one source of secondary data. [3 marks]

**2** Explain a possible consequence for a business of only using quantitative data. [5 marks]

### Answers

**1** One source of secondary data is company reports. ✓ These may be internal or external, ✓ and will give historical data about success and achievements. ✓

**2** One consequence is you may get too much information, ✓ which tells you the results but does not explain why they are important. ✓ Without any quantitative data, a business may make the wrong decision ✓ as any external influences are unknown, ✓ which could have a negative effect on business objectives. ✓

> 💡 **Remember**
>
> While secondary information may be relatively cheap and easy to access, it may be out of date, or incomplete or hidden within a larger document. It is often used as a starting point for primary research.

## Sampling methods

A business cannot ask all of its customers when doing research. Therefore, a business must select a representative sample of its customers to make sure that answers are spread evenly between ALL customers, not just one segment.

▼ **Table 3.12** Sampling: the appropriateness and limitations to given situations

| | Definition | Appropriateness | Limitations |
|---|---|---|---|
| Random | Every person has an equal chance of being chosen. There is no method. No samples are entirely random. There needs to be a specific method of random sampling. | Relevant random sample can save time and cost. | Bias in the determining of sample – may be too scary or too old. May be a disproportionate number of one segment. May not sample target segment. |
| Stratified | Population is divided into groups with defined characteristics. | It is possible to target specific segments relevant to the investigation. | It may exclude those who do not fit the criteria and valuable information is not gathered. |
| Quota | Set numbers of people with different characteristics are chosen within the sample. | Can get a representative sample of the population or customer base. | May limit the information as once the quota is reached no more people are asked. This can lead to incomplete data sets. Also depends on bias and assumptions. |

> 💡 **Remember**
>
> No sample is ever random, and bias is inbuilt to the collection of data. There is no one perfect method of sampling and often methods will be mixed, such as a random stratified sample.

## Market research results

It is important to understand the data that is collected. It is important to understand how reliable the data is and the best methods of analysing results.

### The reliability of data collection

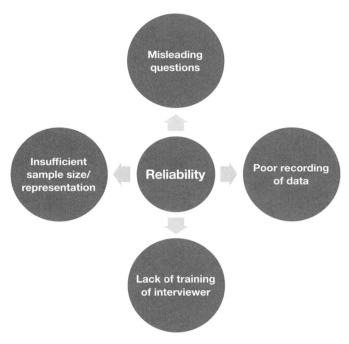

▲ **Figure 3.6** The reliability of data collection

Effective analysis can only be completed when the analysis takes into consideration the reliability of the data collection. Some factors which need to be considered in this respect are as follows.

### Analysis and interpretation of results obtained from market research

Analysis of information must relate to business and marketing objectives. Candidates must be able to read information and justify their analysis of relevant data. Information will usually be provided in the form of graphs or tables.

---

### Worked examples

1   Identify and briefly explain one sampling method.                                [2 marks]

2   Explain why online surveys may not be reliable.                                   [5 marks]

### Answers

1   One sampling method is the stratified sample. ✓ This is when the population is divided into groups with defined characteristics. ✓

2   They may not be reliable as there is little control over who answers the survey ✓ and there is no way of checking whether the information is correct or made up. ✓ It is also difficult to ensure you have a representative sample, ✓ which may mean there is a negative bias in the results, ✓ which could provide results which are not representative of the whole market. ✓

---

The main way of interpreting quantitative data is using the following calculations:

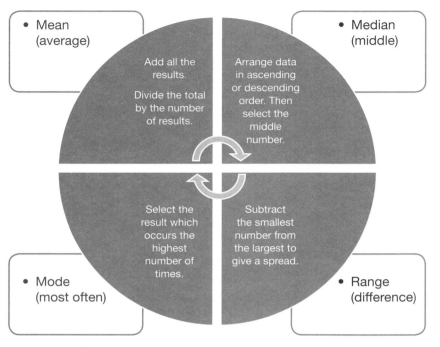

▲ **Figure 3.7** Interpreting quantitative data

## Cost effectiveness

### Cost effectiveness of market research in given situations

Businesses invest in market research to meet their organisational goals. If a business spends too much money on market research then they will not be able to satisfy their objectives. Therefore, effective planning and budgetary control are necessary for the success of a marketing project.

## 3.3 The marketing mix

This topic is concerned with:

➤ the elements of the marketing mix (the 4 Ps)

➤ the role of the customer (the 4 Cs)

➤ product

➤ product life cycle

➤ types of pricing strategies

➤ price elasticity of demand

➤ promotion methods

➤ channels of distribution

➤ using the internet for the 4 Ps/4 Cs

➤ consistency in the marketing mix.

## The elements of the marketing mix (the 4 Ps)

This topic will aim to develop the candidates understanding of the different elements of the marketing mix and their role in achieving the marketing objectives. The **marketing mix** aims to create a set of guidelines which make sure that customer requirements are met in an effective and coherent way.

## Product, price, promotion, place

The **4 Ps** is an internal, business focussed model which aims to identify the ways in which the product should be marketed.

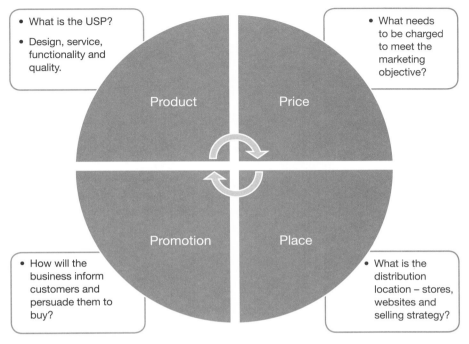

▲ **Figure 3.8** The 4 Ps

## The role of the customer (the 4 Cs)

The **4 Cs** is an external, customer focused model which aims to understand the requirements of the customer and the target market.

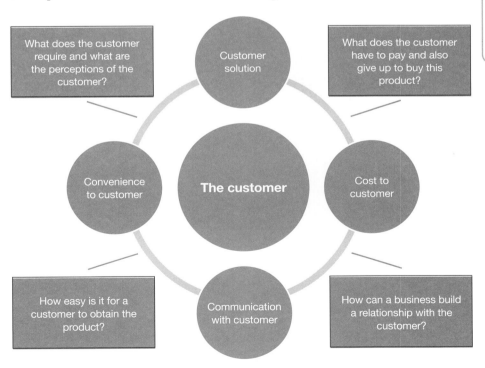

▲ **Figure 3.9** The relationship between the customer and the business (the 4 Cs)

**Key term**

**4 Ps**: an internally focused model commonly known as the marketing mix.

**Remember**

The elements of the marketing mix are not separate, they need to be integrated and support each other in a coherent way. A high quality product cannot be sold in a discount store.

**X Common error**

Candidates often try to use some of the seven Ps or even any other words that begin with 'P' as they cannot remember the original 4 Ps! It is essential to remember the correct Ps.

**Key term**

**4 Cs**: an externally focused model that aims to think like a customer and anticipate their requirements.

## Ways in which customer relations can be improved

Due to the increase in competition from multiple selling channels, it is crucial to interact effectively with customers and potential customers to be a successful business. There are three main ways in which customer relations can be improved:

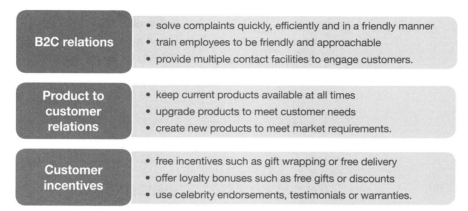

**B2C relations**
- solve complaints quickly, efficiently and in a friendly manner
- train employees to be friendly and approachable
- provide multiple contact facilities to engage customers.

**Product to customer relations**
- keep current products available at all times
- upgrade products to meet customer needs
- create new products to meet market requirements.

**Customer incentives**
- free incentives such as gift wrapping or free delivery
- offer loyalty bonuses such as free gifts or discounts
- use celebrity endorsements, testimonials or warranties.

▲ **Figure 3.10** Improving customer relations

## How the 4 Cs relate to the 4 Ps

There is a close relationship between the 4 Ps and 4 Cs. You must be able to identify the similarities and differences between the two models.

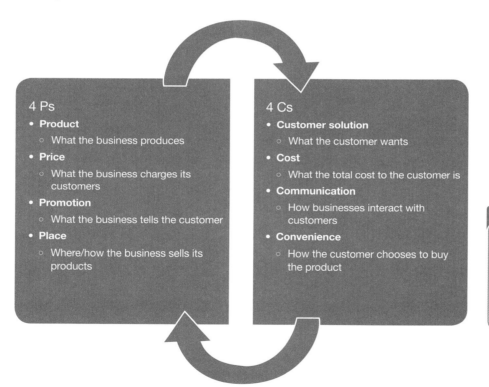

**4 Ps**
- **Product**
  - What the business produces
- **Price**
  - What the business charges its customers
- **Promotion**
  - What the business tells the customer
- **Place**
  - Where/how the business sells its products

**4 Cs**
- **Customer solution**
  - What the customer wants
- **Cost**
  - What the total cost to the customer is
- **Communication**
  - How businesses interact with customers
- **Convenience**
  - How the customer chooses to buy the product

▲ **Figure 3.11** Relationship between the 4 Ps and 4 Cs

**Worked examples**

1  Briefly explain the term 'USP'.                                                [2 marks]

2  Explain two reasons why it is important to consider the 4 Cs.                  [5 marks]

**Answers**

1  USP is the unique selling point of a business or a product, ✓ which might be quality or design, ✓ such as an ergonomic cup.

2  One reason it is important to consider is because there is more choice from e-commerce, ✓ which means businesses must consider cost to the consumer ✓ to ensure they are getting the best value possible. ✓ It is also important to the convenience to the customer such as home delivery, ✓ as e-commerce also allows the customer to choose the most convenient option which may reduce the appeal of your product. ✓

## Product

### Goods, services

The final **product (good)** or **service** received by the customer may be considered the most important element of the 4 Ps. It does not matter if the product is well promoted or sold at a competitive price if the product does not meet requirements.

### Recognising that products have a combination of tangible and intangible attributes

When a product is purchased, it is not always because of the **tangible** assets; often, products are purchased over substitute or competitor goods due to an **intangible** asset:

| Tangible features | Intangible features |
|---|---|
| ☐ Shape and size – is the shape attractive or fit for purpose? | ☐ Brand – is the image suitable for the customer/market? |
| ☐ Colour – does the product look aesthetically appealing? | ☐ Perception – does the product make the owner feel powerful/attractive/wealthy? |
| ☐ Quality – are the materials suitable for the product and price? | ☐ Fashion – is the product a fashionable item and currently in trend? |
| ☐ Packaging – is it suitable for the product and the intended customer? | |

▲ **Figure 3.12** Reasons for purchasing a product

### The importance of product development

Why do you upgrade your products? People no longer upgrade or replace their products solely due to a product not working, products are upgraded to keep up with fashion trends and new developments in the market.

Methods of product development include:

➤ modification

➤ presentation

➤ new formulation of an existing product.

---

**Key terms**

**Product** a tangible article that has physical properties and can be touched.

**Service**: a system, method or other intangible form that fulfils a need.

**Tangible**: an object that has physical properties and can be touched.

**Intangible**: does not have a physical presence and cannot be touched or held.

💡 **Remember**

Customers buy products for many reasons, and what might be an attractive feature for one stakeholder may well be irrelevant for another.

💡 **Remember**

Product development does not mean fundamentally changing a product, it might just be a simple update to use modern materials and methods.

Reasons for developing products include:

➤ gaining and keeping market dominance

➤ maintaining a competitive edge

➤ entering new markets.

Due to:

➤ Asset led development – using research and development to improve an existing product – including:

  ▪ technological influences

  ▪ employee skills and abilities.

➤ Market led development – using market research to identify customer wants and needs – including:

  ▪ technological influences

  ▪ competitor based influences.

## Product differentiation and USP (Unique Selling Point)

Products are differentiated by the use of Unique Selling Points (USP), which are aimed to convince the customer that the product or service has an advantage over competitor products with similar features.

Methods of **differentiation** and **USP**s include:

➤ Promotion – advertising and marketing campaigns to increase desirability.

➤ Product design – making the product visually appealing.

➤ Improved/superior performance – faster or stronger than competitors.

➤ Aftersales and guarantees – customer assurance.

➤ Branding and packaging – creating brand loyalty.

## Product life cycle

A product has a life similar to a human being – this **product life cycle** influences the marketing and sales activities of a product.

> **Key terms**
>
> **Product differentiation**: the marketing of similar products with minor variations to attract customers.
>
> **USP**: the key factor that differentiates a product from its competitors.
>
> **Product life cycle**: the stages a product goes through from introduction to withdrawal from the market.

---

### Worked examples

1   Identify and briefly explain one intangible feature of a product.   [3 marks]

2   Analyse the importance of product development for a business or brand.   [8 marks]

### Answers

1   One intangible feature might be the brand associated with the product. ✓ A well-known brand can add value to the basic features of the product ✓ and increase the desirability leading to an increase in sales. ✓

2   Product development is important for a business as it allows a product to remain competitive. ✓ A modification ✓ of a mature product, such as improving the processor on the Samsung mobile phone range, may be used to extend the product's life and stop it from entering the decline phase as quickly, ✓ which may increase the return on investment of the original product. ✓ Another important factor is that product development will enable your product to access new markets ✓ such as the Samsung Galaxy mobile phones which have been developed for individual target segments based on price or performance according to the needs of the individual target segments. ✓ This could also extend the life of a product ✓ and increase the customer base by building on an existing product and reputation. ✓

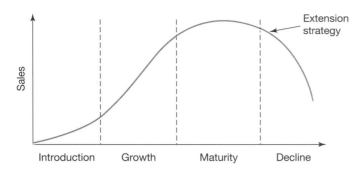

▲ **Figure 3.13** How the product life cycle stage influences marketing activities and extension strategies

▼ **Table 3.13** How the product life cycle stage influences marketing activities and extension strategies

| | Characteristics | Outcome |
|---|---|---|
| **Introduction** | New product.<br><br>Low sales.<br><br>Customers unsure of the product.<br><br>Customers likely to be early adopters. | Large spend on marketing and advertising.<br><br>Focus on raising awareness of the product and/or brand.<br><br>Price will either be very high or subsidised to attract customers. |
| **Growth** | Sales increase quickly.<br><br>Brand awareness is higher.<br><br>Retailers see the potential for profit and are likely to stock.<br><br>Customers likely to be early majority. | Continuation of spending on marketing and advertising.<br><br>Focus alters to protecting the reputation and challenging competitors. |
| **Maturity** | Sales will plateau and remain constant.<br><br>High sales, high profits and possibly a large market share. | Reduction in spend on advertising.<br><br>Focus changes on keeping brand awareness and existing customers. |
| **Decline** | A fall in sales, revenue and profits.<br><br>Increased competition from competitors and more modern products.<br><br>**Extension strategies** are used to extend the life of the product. | Marketing activity likely to:<br><br>increase if focusing on extension strategies<br><br>OR<br><br>decrease as the product is allowed to decline and be replaced by more up-to-date products. |

### Product portfolio analysis as a way of achieving marketing objectives

**Portfolio analysis** is used by businesses to:

➤ assess the range of products that are currently being sold

➤ remove any products which no longer fit into the marketing and business objectives

➤ identify any gaps in the product range which may be a missed opportunity.

**Key terms**

**Extension strategy**: a method of retaining market share by adding features or promotions to keep a product in the maturity phase.

**Portfolio analysis**: examination of the assets of a business used to determine the best possible allocation of resources.

## Types of pricing strategies

The **pricing strategy** chosen will depend on the cost of production, the competition and the customer perception of the product. The wrong pricing strategy may influence the marketing strategy negatively and cause a product to fail to live up to expectations.

▼ **Table 3.14** Influencing factors on pricing strategy

|  | **Reason** | **Effect** |
|---|---|---|
| Cost of production | The selling price must meet the objective of breaking even or making a profit. | Determines lowest possible selling price. |
| Competition | The selling price must take into account competitor and substitute pricing. | Determines maximum possible selling price. |
| Customer perception | The selling price must take into account the customer perception of the brand and the product. | Determines the range of prices a customer is likely to accept. |

▼ **Table 3.15** Use and value of alternative pricing strategies

|  | **Definition** | **Use** | **Value** |
|---|---|---|---|
| Competitive | Researching competitor pricing levels and basing your price at a similar, lower or higher level. | Low price can create a USP. | Gains market share. Creates reputation for affordability. Low profit margins but high sales figures. |
|  |  | High price can create a reputation for quality. | Brand reputation can be created which can lead to premium pricing levels and high profit margins. |
| Penetration | An initial low price set for a new product to attract a wide percentage of the market. | Increases the number of new price conscious customers. Used as a form of advertising. | Increases the number of new customers very quickly in a short amount of time. Reduced profit margins an opportunity cost of the marketing benefit. |
| Skimming | A relatively high price point set for a desirable product which usually reduces over time. | Creates an image of exclusivity and prestige. | Covers high R&D costs. Creates large profits to compensate for reduced profit when prices fall. Can increase brand loyalty. |
| Price discrimination | Setting a different price in different markets for the same product. | When it is not possible for the product to be resold at a higher price in a different market. Ensures affordability of a product in different markets. | Allows for high profit margins to be made where there is high demand. Also builds the brand image in new markets where disposable income may be lower. |
| Cost-based pricing | Setting a fixed sum or percentage onto the total production cost of the product. | Simple to calculate and guarantees a certain level of profit. Must take into consideration competitors and customer perception. | Can maintain the profit levels when raw material costs change. |

**Worked examples**

1 Define price discrimination. [2 marks]

2 Distinguish between 'tangible features' and 'intangible features'. [5 marks]

**Answers**

1 Setting the same price in different markets. ✓ For a similar or same product. ✓

2 A tangible feature is something that you can touch or feel and is real, ✓ such as the screen on a mobile phone. ✓ This can improve the actual viewing experience of the user. ✓ While the brand of the mobile phone, such as the Samsung name, is an intangible feature, ✓ as it creates an image rather than adding a real feature to the product. ✓

## Price elasticity of demand (PED)

### Define, calculate and interpret price elasticity of demand and suitable prices

This calculation allows a business to predict the likely effect on sales of a change in price. It is an essential element when making pricing decisions.

> **Maths skills**
>
> PED calculation:
>
> $$\frac{\text{Percentage change in quantity demanded}}{\text{Percentage change in price}}$$
>
> PED outcomes:
>
> <1 = Price inelastic – demand is not very sensitive to price so revenue will rise or fall with the change in price.
>
> >1 = Price elastic – demand is sensitive to price so revenue is inversely proportional to the change in price.

### Usefulness of price elasticity of demand when making pricing decisions

While it is important to know how changing the price will affect the likely demand for the product, PED should not be used as the only determinant for a price change. Important variables to consider are:

➤ Do you have the raw materials, capacity and capital necessary to increase your production levels?

➤ How will competitors react to the change in your price?

➤ Will a lower price make potential customers think the quality is low?

➤ Is your brand image strong enough to keep your customers?

➤ How many substitute goods are available?

### Promotion methods

Although there are many ways for a business to attract customers, not all methods of **promotion** are suitable for all businesses, due to a variety of factors. Two methods of promotion are identified and explained in Table 3.16: **above the line promotion** and **below the line promotion**.

> **✗ Common error**
>
> When a question asks the candidate to recommend a pricing strategy, there must be more than one strategy discussed, as it is often difficult to justify your choice if it is not compared against another method.

> **✗ Common error**
>
> Candidates often take the PED figure to be an absolute or guaranteed outcome. This is incorrect as any prediction cannot be guaranteed, and there are many external variables that can influence the PED.

> **💡 Remember**
>
> You must be able to define, calculate and interpret **price elasticity of demand**. You must also take into account any variable factors which could influence the outcome of the PED.

> **Key terms**
>
> **Price elasticity of demand**: a method of measuring the relationship between a change in the quantity demanded of a particular good due to a change in price.
>
> **Promotion**: the publicising of a product, service or organisation to increase sales or public awareness.

|  | Examples | Benefits | Drawbacks |
|---|---|---|---|
| Above the line | Television<br>Radio<br>Billboards<br>Internet adverts | Reaches a large audience.<br>Creates brand awareness. | Expensive.<br>Needs to be updated constantly. |
| Below the line | Direct selling<br>Direct mail<br>Point-of-sale<br>Sales promotions<br>Sponsorship<br>Public relations | Reaches the target audience.<br>Builds customer relationships.<br>Relatively inexpensive.<br>Product placement. | Needs a lot of organisation and control.<br>Targeting diverse cultures needs careful planning. |

## The role of packaging in promotion

The packaging of a product can be one of the main methods of promotion for a product. It is the first impression the customer will have of the product and will help to make a value judgement on the quality of the product itself.

**Protecion:** is the packaging suitable and environmentally friendly?

**Information:** is technical information clear and visible?

**Legal requirements:** are these clearly shown and following the laws of the land?

▲ **Figure 3.14** The role of packaging

## Branding as part of product/promotion

Many businesses are able to promote their brand for little or no cost as customers themselves act as promotion for the **brand**.

Brand names, logos and colours automatically conjure an instinctive reaction, either positive or negative.

It is difficult to build a positive brand; it can be very easy, however, to ruin an existing brand name with poor marketing and planning.

**Brands**

Can offer a competitve edge via a USP which can increase sales volume in short amounts of time.

Brands must be true to the product; a low value brand must not be marketed as a luxury, as this will deter all customers.

▲ **Figure 3.15** Branding as promotion

## Channels of distribution

Distribution can be either **direct** or **indirect**. Each channel has its own advantages and drawbacks which depends on the objectives of each business.

▼ **Table 3.17** Choosing between alternative types of channel of distribution

| Factor | Direct distribution | Indirect distribution |
|---|---|---|
| **Type of product:** perishable or specialist | No concerns over perishable goods rotting or specialist items going out of fashion. | Long lasting mass market goods are better suited to an indirect system that can reach more customers. |
| **Type of market:** specialist | Specialist market with detailed requirements needs close contact with both parties. | Mass market needs a channel that has access to many retailers and outlets. |
| **Customer preference** | For when customer service and direct contact is essential. | For when convenience and speed is important. |
| **Producers preference** | A producer will be able to control the marketing, pricing and all other aspects of the brand. | Useful for when the producer has little experience of selling or does not have the resources to reach a larger audience. |

> **Remember**
>
> The channel of distribution depends on the marketing and business objectives. In an exam setting, candidates must justify their decision or recommendation.

## Using the internet for the 4 Ps/4 Cs

Since the advent of the internet, there has been a huge change in the methods small and large businesses have been able to market and attract customers. This rise in **e-commerce** has changed many of the 'rules' around who can market in what way and must be a factor in the decision-making process.

### Online advertising

There are many factors which need to be considered for online advertising:

**Dynamic pricing**
- Can react swiftly to a change in demand: leads to less wastage and maximised profit potential.
- Can react swiftly to changes in external factors such as exchange rates to ensure that profit margins are always maintained.

**Social media**
- Allow businesses to connect directly to the consumer and correspond over huge distances.
- Viral advertising can reach huge numbers of potential customers using real time communications, videos and unplanned marketing events.

**Targeted advertising**
- Can reduce the capital expenditure by clearly defining a market segment which may have been too expensive using traditional methods.
- Creates huge marketing databases which can be used to produce targeted advertising based on a segmented market.

▲ **Figure 3.16** Factors to consider for online advertising

> **Key terms**
>
> **Direct distribution channel:** the producer supplies the product directly to the final consumer.
>
> **Indirect distribution channel:** the producer relies on intermediaries to distribute the product to the final customer.
>
> **E-commerce:** commercial transactions which are conducted electronically over the internet and are not reliant on personal contact.

> **Remember**
>
> Online advertising has many benefits over traditional methods however it has much bigger disadvantages as the internet is harder to control and once something is online it is difficult or impossible to delete fully, meaning the internet or e-commerce isn't always the best option.

## Consistency in the marketing mix

As mentioned earlier, the marketing mix is a combination of many factors and there must be consistency between all of the factors in order to provide an integrated message to the customers.

▲ **Figure 3.17** The need for the marketing mix to be consistent with the business, the product type and the market

### Worked example

Analyse the importance of packaging for the achievement of business objectives.     [8 marks]

**Answer**

Packaging is one of the 4 Ps and is used as a means of promoting ✓ the business by showing the customer the perceived quality of the contents. ✓ For example, if you use a simple plastic unbranded bag as the packaging for a high quality mobile phone, the packaging will not be appropriate ✓ for the target market segment who will associate a simple plastic bag with low value inferior goods ✓ so sales will be low and the business objective of sales maximisation won't be reached. ✓ If packaging is appropriate for the target market segment and the perceived quality of the product, this can create the correct image for the product ✓ and the brand which will increase the brand power and potentially attract more customers, increasing sales revenue ✓ as well as differentiating the brand from competitors who use a cheaper or less premium type of packaging so there is more visual shelf appeal. ✓

## Revision checklist

### I can:

- ➤ identify and explain different pricing strategies ☐
- ➤ understand price elasticity of demand ☐
- ➤ explain and evaluate above and below the line promotion methods ☐
- ➤ understand the role of packaging and branding ☐
- ➤ explain the different channels of distribution ☐
- ➤ understand and explain the 4 Ps/4 Cs ☐
- ➤ relate marketing strategies to a number of different situations. ☐

## ⬆ Raise your grade

### Short answer questions

**1 (a)** Define the term primary research. [2]

Primary research is gathering new data from original sources ✓✗

> **[1 mark]** While you may think that 'new data' and 'original sources' are two separate points, they are very similar as you cannot get new data from old sources, so they may be seen as the same point. It is always useful to add an extension such as 'known as field research', or an example, 'e.g. a questionnaire'.

**(b)** Briefly explain the use of qualitative information. [3]

Qualitative information is using open questions ✗ to gather expressive opinions ✓ which can be used to explain why a customer buys a particular product, ✓ which can be used to ensure marketing activities match the expectations of the customer. ✓

> **[3 marks]** It is important to read the question carefully. The question is not asking for a definition of qualitative information therefore there would be no marks awarded for the simple definition as indicated above.

**2** Explain two possible barriers to entry for a business. [5]

One possible barrier to entry is the cost of production ✓ because there might be high setup costs. ✓

Another barrier is taxes and subsidies ✗ which can make the price of a product too expensive for customers. ✓

> **[3 marks]** Even though there are two examples only one gets a mark as in the mark scheme there is only one mark for knowledge or understanding. The second and third marks are for limited understanding which is the basic explanation. To improve this mark, each explanation would have to have an extended answer, for example '...too expensive for customers who would find a cheaper substitute good'. ✓

**3** Distinguish between merit and demerit goods. [2]

A merit good is a good which the government thinks has a positive influence on society ✓ such as education which will make the population more knowledgeable and lead to a better workforce which will increase the skill level of the economy. ✗

A demerit good is considered to have a negative external cost such as cigarettes ✓ which cause cancer and mean that people are sick and need to use hospitals which puts a strain on the finances of the country and may lead to a smaller workforce than is needed. ✗

> **[2 marks]** While this is a full answer and well explained, there are only two marks available, so the candidate who writes this is wasting valuable time which often leads to the high mark questions at the end being answered poorly due to a lack of available time.

4   Briefly explain the product life cycle.                                                                    [3]

The product life cycle is the stages a product goes through from introduction to decline, ✓ which allows a business to identify and apply the most cost-efficient marketing strategies. ✓

> **[2 marks]** As this is a three-mark question, there have to be three separate points and there are only two here. The additional mark could come from 'this also shows when extension strategies could be used'. ✓

5   Explain why many new products use the penetration pricing strategy.                                          [5]

Penetration pricing is when an initial low price is set ✓ to attract a wide percentage of the market ✓ and create brand awareness. ✓ This can cause price conscious customers to choose the new product ✓ over a known competitor brand and increase market share. ✓

> **[5 marks]** A five-mark question does not need to have lots of writing – some of the best questions are clearly structured and meet the mark scheme requirements as candidates understand the difference between 'understanding, limited and effective explanation'.

**Long answer questions**

1   (a)   Analyse the importance of an effective marketing strategy.                                            [8]

A marketing strategy is the plan of action a business uses to promote and sell a product or service. ✓

> At this point, the candidate shows understanding of marketing strategies and has achieved the maximum marks available for Level 1. Therefore, no more knowledge marks are available.

A business may use a marketing strategy such as the 4 Ps or the 4 Cs to maximise customer awareness of a new or existing product to ensure the correct market segment is targeted by ensuring an appropriate price is set which matches the customers cost expectations. ✓

> At this point, Level 2 has been achieved as there is 'some explanation/application of marketing strategies in a business'.

If there is an effective marketing strategy, then the business will be able to make sure there is a co-ordinated marketing message, allowing the business to set a price which is appropriate for both the quality of the product and the customer expectations. This will allow a business to meet its corporate objective of brand awareness and acceptance. ✓

> At this point, Level 3 has been achieved as there is now 'some analysis of the importance of an effective marketing strategy'. It is important to realise that it is not the quantity of evidence, it is the quality of the evidence. If the answer was to stop here, this would achieve 6 marks out of a possible 8.

It is also important to take into account the actions of competitors and substitute brands, as a marketing strategy which doesn't take into account external factors may not succeed if the product or the price is not as suitable as its nearest competitor meaning an effective marketing strategy is very important to meet organisational goals. ✓

> At this point, Level 4 has been achieved as there is now 'effective analysis of the importance of an effective marketing strategy'. As this also incorporates the negative aspects of creating a marketing strategy which isn't effective.

**(b)** Discuss the importance of mixing above the line and below the line promotion for a tertiary sector business. [12]

Above the line promotion is a paid method of promotion which uses mass media to promote a business to a wide range of customers, while below the line promotion is a targeted method of promotion which focuses on a specific target market using direct communications instead of mass media.

> At this point, the candidate has shown 'understanding of ATL and BTL promotion', [L1] there are no more knowledge or understanding marks available, so there is no point in adding extra definitions.

If a business uses ATL promotion, then they will reach a wide number of potential customers and spread awareness of their brand to many different market segments, such as advertising the 'Samsung' brand on television. However, if they use BTL promotion, then they will spend less money on advertising as they will select the appropriate target market and focus their advertising on them, such as for the 'Samsung Galaxy S8' which will focus on the more fashion or trend conscious customers. ✓

> At this point, the level of analysis is sufficient for a good Level 2 answer. Remember, as this is a 12-mark question, the amount of marks awarded for analysis is usually only up to half of the marks; 6 marks are allocated for the evaluation.

Therefore it is important to mix ATL and BTL promotion because if you only focus on ATL, while brand awareness might be achieved, potential customers might not know about the actual products and would need to investigate themselves, which many might not do, causing a lack of customers, while only using BTL would mean that the target market would know about the product, but might not buy it because the brand itself is unknown, and fashion conscious people want other people to know that they are wearing a particular brand so they can be associated with the brand values of innovation and advanced technology in the case of Samsung. ✓

> At this point, Level 3 has been achieved as 'Limited evaluation of the importance of mixing above the line and below the line promotion for a tertiary sector business'. However, it is not yet effective evaluation as this would need some contrasting comments. This would score a maximum of 8 marks.

Therefore it is important to mix ATL and BTL promotion because if you only focus on ATL, while brand awareness might be achieved, potential customers might not know about the actual products and would need to investigate themselves, which many might not do, causing a lack of customers, **even though this is an expensive method of advertising and to get the best**

**advertising slots on prime time would be hugely expensive due to competition from other leading brands, which would make this method unsuitable for small businesses**, while only using BTL would mean that the target market would know about the product, but might not buy it because the brand itself is unknown, and fashion-conscious people want other people to know that they are wearing a particular brand so they can be associated with the brand values of innovation and advanced technology in the case of Samsung. **Although this is a cheaper method as you do not waste advertising budgets on customers who you may not want to purchase your brand such as Luis Vuitton, who only want high net worth customers to purchase their products.** ✓

> At this point, with the addition of the contrasting points, the candidate has neatly wrapped up his evaluation by showing the importance of mixing the two types of promotion to help a tertiary sector business succeed.

2   Discuss how a regional fast food retailer could develop effective marketing during a period of economic growth.   [20]

A regional fast food retailer could develop effective marketing during a period of economic growth by commissioning some primary marketing research to identify the current needs of the target market within a specific regional area, such as a city like London or Paris. As there is a period of economic growth, customers are likely to have jobs and more disposable income which might mean they would be more prepared to spend their income on luxury foods and the environment of the restaurant, so advertising should focus on customer wants rather than the financial needs of potential customers as customers are more likely to buy premium fast food in a nice location rather than focusing on the price of the product. ✓

> At this point, the candidate is within the Level 2 boundary as there is understanding of marketing, regional retailers and economic growth. Some limited analysis which means that the points are not developed well and/or this is only a one sided view. This answer would receive a score of between 5 and 10 marks.

Effective marketing needs to be based on current market research so that the fast food retailer is aware of the target customer, the target customer's needs, and the income and aspirations of the potential customer. Therefore, effective primary research such as surveys or test marketing will be necessary to determine the needs of customers to re-evaluate the products being sold and the brand values of the fast food retailer. Effective marketing will need to emphasise the aspirational aspect of the restaurant to compete against lower value options and national chains who have bigger marketing budgets. This marketing could focus on the premium product portfolio which would attract customers with more disposable income who would want a nicer fast food experience and establishing a premium feel to the fast food restaurant such as Nando's. ✓

> ✓✗ At this point, this is a good paragraph with 'Analysis of effective marketing for a fast food retailer in times of economic recession'. This would now be achieving a grade of 11-12 marks, as there is good analysis or evaluation of the statement.

However, the marketing must consider the effect of national retailers who may have a larger marketing budget and may be able to build a bigger brand awareness so the marketing may want to focus on below the line methods of promotion to attract the target audience within the specific regional area of the business by using the types of foods identified within the market research. This could be used in conjunction with the 4 Cs to identify customer expectations rather than using the internal 4 Ps marketing strategy. ✓

> At this point, there is now good analysis and some limited evaluation of effective marketing for a fast food retailer in times of economic growth. However, there needs to be more effective evaluation to achieve Level 5 and achieve the 17-20 marks.

Therefore the retailer must take care to develop his marketing based on effective primary research, as even though it may be expensive and time consuming, it will allow the retailer to gauge the current demand for products in a time of economic boom and means there will not be wasted product development and the retailer will be able to adapt to the buying habits of customers with more disposable income, who may be tempted by the above the line promotion of national retailers who have more disposable income and are able to buy their products at lower prices due to the volume of food required. This means that the marketing strategy must focus on the strengths of the business, which may be the quality of the ingredients, the menu which reflects local tastes and needs and the improved customer in store experience. ✓

> At this point, the candidate is now achieving a Level 5 answer as there is effective evaluation of the statement and a reasoned judgement referring to discussing how effective marketing could be developed.

# ? Exam-style questions

This section will allow you to practise writing answers for exam-style questions. Remember, it is useful to be aware of the mark schemes for the questions which can be found on relevant websites or from your teacher.

## Paper 1

### Short answer questions

1  (a) Distinguish between 'above the line' and 'below the line' promotion. [2]

   (b) Briefly explain **two** of the 4 Ps. [3]

2  (a) Define the term 'brand'. [2]

   (b) Briefly explain **two** distribution channels. [3]

3  Explain the possible consequences for a business of a poor marketing strategy. [5]

4  (a) Define the term 'dynamic pricing'. [2]

   (b) Briefly explain why a business must keep consistency in the marketing mix. [3]

### Long answer questions

5  (a) Analyse the importance to a business of product differentiation. [8]

   (b) Discuss the importance of identifying and meeting the needs of regional markets. [12]

6  Discuss how a large national supermarket could develop an effective marketing strategy. [20]

7  (a) Analyse how a business might use market research as a means of increasing brand loyalty. [8]

   (b) Discuss the uses of different sampling methods for a marketing department. [12]

## Paper 2

🔗 Link

Refer to Case study 1: Dingle's Dairy in Unit 14.

1  (a) Define the term 'market growth'. [2]

   (b) Briefly explain the difference between a 'product' and a 'customer'. [3]

2  (a) The total UK market size, measured in revenue, in 2015 was $800 000 and in 2016 was $1 200 000. Calculate DD's 2016 market share. [3]

   (b) Explain one way in which this data could help DD in their decision to expand. [3]

3  Analyse two potential market segments for DD. [8]

4  Recommend, using evidence, whether Fred's decision to expand his business is correct. [11]

## Key topics

➤ the nature of operations

➤ operations planning

➤ inventory management.

## 4.1 The nature of operations

This topic is concerned with:

➤ resources and the production process

➤ effectiveness, efficiency and productivity

➤ how value is added

➤ capital- versus labour-intensive production.

### Resources and the production process

Operations management refers to the systems that take an idea or need, for a good or service, to the end process of production. These systems should be designed and controlled so that the **product** meets customer expectations.

> **X  Common error**
>
> Candidates might think that the operation process only applies to physical goods. The operation process also applies to service sector businesses. The terms 'product' and 'production' can refer to physical goods and services.

Operations management ensures that products are produced efficiently and effectively – it is the process by which **inputs** are transformed into outputs. Inputs include **land**, **labour** and **capital** (including **intellectual capital**).

These resources can be combined in many different ways in order to transform inputs into outputs. There are many stages involved to get from an idea/need to a final product. There are different processes at each stage.

> **Worked example**
>
> Anwar is a writer who has had two non-fiction books published. His third book is fiction but he cannot find anybody interested in publishing this book. He has decided to produce the book himself. Explain to Anwar three important inputs he will require to be successful.
>
> [5 marks]
>
> **Answer**
>
> Anwar will need capital ✓ and labour. ✓ Capital would include a printing machine ✓ and premises. ✓ He would also need people to operate the machine. ✓

> **Key terms**
>
> **Products**: the provision of goods and services.
>
> **Inputs**: the resources used in the production process – land, labour and capital.
>
> **Land**: natural resources, which includes the physical land and the natural resources obtained from physical land.
>
> **Labour**: people who work in a business – the employees.
>
> **Capital**: machinery, equipment and buildings – physical assets.
>
> **Intellectual capital**: the intangible assets of a business, including people (human capital), relationships (e.g. with suppliers and customers), and processes.

🔗 Link

There is more about pricing decisions in Unit 3, topic 3.3.

**Worked example**

A bottle manufacturer employs 20 people. They each work an 8-hour day, 5 days per week. 12 000 bottles are produced per week. The workers are paid $12 per hour.

a) Calculate the productivity of labour per hour. [5 marks]

b) Calculate the cost of labour per bottle. [3 marks]

**Answers**

a) Productivity = output per hour ÷ number of employees ✓

Output per day = 12 000 ÷ 5 = 2400 ✓

Output per hour = 2400 ÷ 8 = 300 ✓

Productivity of labour per hour = 300 ÷ 20 ✓

= 15 bottles per unit of labour per hour ✓

b) Cost of labour per bottle = pay per worker per hour ÷ bottles produced per hour ✓

$12 ÷ 15 ✓

= **$0.80** ✓

💡 Remember

Productivity and efficiency are not the same thing. Efficiency is about getting more output from a given amount of inputs. This could be done by reducing the waste of inputs, such as materials and time. Increased efficiency should reduce unit costs and increase profits. Increasing productivity may increase efficiency but not necessarily. For example, a baker producing 20 perfect loaves an hour is **less** productive but **more** efficient than a baker producing 40 loaves an hour but burning half of the loaves.

📐 Maths skills

Labour productivity = output per time period ÷ number of employees.

**Key terms**

**Effectiveness**: is how well the product meets customer needs.

**Efficiency**: measures the resources needed for production.

**Productivity**: measures the efficiency of inputs such as the output per unit of labour over a specified period of time.

## Effectiveness, efficiency and productivity

Productivity is an important concept for business. The higher the productivity then the higher the output from the same number of inputs. As productivity increases, then average costs fall. In the worked example above, if productivity is increased so that each worker produces 16 bottles per hour then the labour cost of each bottle would fall to $0.75. A fall in average costs would allow the business to reduce the price of the bottles and keep its profit margin the same, or keep price the same which would increase the profit margin and lead to higher profits.

▼ **Table 4.1** Methods to increase productivity

| Method | Comment |
| --- | --- |
| Capital investment | Spending on new machinery and equipment can increase the speed of production and reduce unit costs over time. However, it is expensive and there might be less costly ways to achieve higher productivity by careful use and maintenance of existing equipment. |
| Training | This can increase labour productivity so that fewer mistakes (and waste) occur. Skilled labour can work more quickly and efficiently. Once again this can be an expensive option. Production may stop or slow down during training. The training has to be for the right people, for the right tasks and at the right time. |
| Improve worker motivation | Motivated workers produce more, are less likely to be absent and remain loyal to the business. However, care must be taken to employ appropriate motivation methods that recognises the individual worker's needs. |
| Change the business culture | Businesses with a strong and deep-rooted culture are often more effective than those with a weak culture. This can be a low-cost way to improve productivity but not always. It can take a long time to change culture and employees may be resistant to changes in procedures and working practices. This could be disruptive in the short term and lead to decreased productivity during the period of change. |

🔗 **Link**

See Unit 2, topic 2.3 for more on training employees.

🔗 **Link**

See Unit 2, topic 2.2 for more detail on motivation methods.

★ **Exam tip**

Productivity and production are not the same thing. If a question asks for methods to increase productivity this is very different from increasing production. Production can be increased by employing more inputs, such as labour. Increasing productivity means increasing the output per unit of input, over a specific period of time e.g. the baker, producing 20 perfect loaves per hour would show an increase in productivity by producing 22 loaves per hour.

### Worked example

Safi and Lila opened a small café a year ago. They employ five members of staff, three work in the kitchens and two serve customers. At weekends they also employ two part-time workers who help out where needed. Lila is concerned that service is slow and some customers, tired of waiting to be served, walk out without ordering. This problem seems to worsen at weekends even though they have extra staff. Lila and Safi are discussing ways to increase the number of customers served and decrease waiting times.

Analyse **two** methods that Safi and Lila can use to increase the number of customers served.                                    [8 marks]

### Answer

Safi and Lila could employ more staff ✓ [knowledge mark for identifying a method] or increase the productivity of the existing staff. ✓ [knowledge mark for identifying a method] Employing more staff may not be suitable as the problem is worse when there are two extra staff members at weekends ✓ [1 application mark for identifying context]. However, it could be the case that the café has many more customers at the weekend ✓

[application mark for using the context] so increasing the employees may help increase the number of customers served. ✓ [analysis mark for simple analysis] The productivity of existing staff could be increased by changing the numbers between the kitchen and the service sections. ✓ [analysis mark for simple explanation of increasing productivity] Three members of staff work in the kitchen and only two are serving, during the week. A change in the way things are done would be less costly than employing more staff, and could mean that the labour hours available are managed more effectively, reducing time wasted by overstaffing the kitchen. ✓ [good analysis mark for a chain of reasoning in context] However, the employees may be resistant to change which may disrupt the service of customers, demotivate staff and decrease productivity so that more customers are waiting longer to be served. ✓ [good analysis mark for a chain of reasoning in context]

## How value is added

Added value is an important operational objective for all businesses. **Value added** is the increase in value a business adds from one stage of production to another.

The success of a business is determined by its ability to meet its objectives. Design, planning, quality and workforce issues all interrelate to achieve operations objectives. Added value is linked to marketing, the operations process and operations decisions.

**Key terms**

**Value added**: value added = price − cost of bought-in goods and services.

**USP**: unique selling point – the one particular factor that makes a product different from competitor products.

**Link**

There is more about business objectives in Unit 1, topic 1.4.

**Link**

See Unit 3, topic 3.3, for methods of adding value through marketing.

**✗ Common error**

In exam questions, candidates might think that value added is **only** the value added at each stage of production. However, it can also refer to the perception, by the customer, of added value. For the customer added value may come from branding, promotion or additional services such as guarantees on electrical products. All these may mean that a business can charge higher prices than competitors.

▼ **Table 4.2** Where is value added?

| Value added and ... | Explanation |
| --- | --- |
| The operations process | At each stage of the production process value is added to the starting inputs – land, labour, capital, as these inputs are transformed into semi-finished or finished products. |
| Operations decisions | Operations decisions should lead to efficiency and effectiveness so that customer needs are met by the value added during the production process. |
| Marketing | This is giving something to customers they perceive as high value but is low cost to the producer. Marketing can add value by, for example, branding, adding accessories or by quality assurance. The added value can provide a **USP** to a product. To be successful, a business really needs to understand what its customers want. |

## Worked example

Analyse how a watch retailer could apply the 4 Cs in order to add value to its watches. [8 marks]

### Answer

Customer solution. ✓ [1 knowledge mark for identification] If the customer sees the watch as being exclusive and high status, they will be prepared to pay a higher price, cost to the customer, ✓ [knowledge mark for identification] to gain that exclusiveness and high status. Added value can be achieved by increasing the selling price as long as customers have the money to pay. ✓ [analysis mark] Another way of adding value would be to discuss, with the customer, ways of customising the watch such as an engraving, different size or different wristband. ✓ [application mark for context] This is communication with the customer. By engaging the customer the retailer is building up a relationship with that customer ✓ [analysis mark] so that the customer perceives the watch to be of high value. ✓ [analysis mark] Finally, for convenience to customers, the shop could stay open late for customers ✓ [application mark for context] who want to shop after working hours. Customers are busy and have lots of choices when buying a watch, so the shop that will stay open late is offering an additional service which is another way of adding value to the watches. ✓ [analysis mark]

## Capital- versus labour-intensive production

Businesses should optimise resources (land, labour and capital) in order to meet business objectives. Capital and labour can often be substitutes for each other. For example, a wool scarf can be knitted by hand (labour) or by a machine (capital).

Businesses have to make complex decisions in order to get the right balance between capital and labour at each stage of the production process. A significant influence on that decision will be the relative cost of each input. Other influences on the decision will be factors such as:

- the design of the product – a product with many parts, such as an airplane, is complicated to produce and it is harder to get the capital/labour mix right

- finance – a business, particularly if it is small, could have a limited source of finance and be unable to invest in the latest technology

- product type – service industries generally tend to be more labour-intensive and manufacturing more capital-intensive

- availability of inputs – some areas may have a shortage of labour which may make labour expensive or unavailable.

> **Key terms**
>
> **Capital-intensive**: a business uses more machinery and fewer workers.
>
> **Labour-intensive**: a business uses more workers and less machinery.

 **Link**

See Unit 5, topic 5.2, for more detail on sources of finance.

▼ **Table 4.3** Some benefits and limitations of capital- and labour-intensive production

| Type of production | Benefits | Limitations |
|---|---|---|
| Capital-intensive | 1. Can be cheaper than labour in the long run.<br>2. Greater precision and consistency in output.<br>3. Easier to manage.<br>4. Can work 24 hours a day. | 1. Expensive to set up.<br>2. Inflexible as only suited to one task.<br>3. Long production delays if the machine breaks down.<br>4. Not suitable for all types of products, e.g. personal service industries. |

| Type of production | Benefits | Limitations |
|---|---|---|
| Labour-intensive | 1. Flexible – can be trained for more than one task.<br>2. Cheaper where low-cost labour is available, e.g. China.<br>3. Workers can communicate ideas and help to solve production problems.<br>4. Suited to personal service industries. | 1. Cost of labour can rise over time as wages increase.<br>2. More difficult to manage than machinery.<br>3. Cannot work constantly – need rest periods, holidays etc.<br>4. Can be unreliable – absences, lateness or leaving the business at short notice. |

 **Exam tip**

In case study questions there is a lot of context. A common question is to evaluate a production decision to change processes such as a change from labour-intensive to capital-intensive production. The temptation is to just list the benefits and limitations of such a decision without reference to the context such as the design of product, the size of the business or the scale of production. For higher mark questions the expectation is that the answer will consider all these factors and apply analysis and evaluation to the context in order to access the higher marks.

## Worked example

Regular Stays Ltd (RS) is a company operating 50 hotels. Each hotel employs nine receptionists. They want to reduce costs and are considering automated check-ins at all their hotels. This would mean that a customer would check-in using a machine rather than being checked-in by a receptionist. This would reduce the number of receptionists employed to three per hotel.

Discuss the factors that would influence this decision.   [11 marks]

### Answer

Investing in 50 automated check-in machines would require a high investment, ✓ [knowledge mark] and RS should consider if it can finance the investment. ✓ [knowledge mark] The finance required would not just be for buying the machines but also for staff training and redundancy costs. ✓ [1 analysis mark] If RS decide to purchase the machines it will make about 300 staff redundant, ✓✓ [marks for contextual analysis] which will be very expensive and could lead to demotivated staff, disrupting service to hotel customers, leading to dissatisfied hotel guests and increased costs of service. ✓✓✓ [marks for good contextual analysis based on a chain of reasoning and with some evaluation]

RS should also consider the possible effect on demand for its hotel rooms. RS is in a personal service industry where customers may like to interact with employees rather than machines. Introducing automatic check-in could reduce the demand for rooms so that RS has to decrease the price of rooms, leading to lower revenue and reduced profit margins. RS should research whether the reduction in labour costs would allow a fall in prices and a higher profit margin. ✓✓✓ [marks for good contextual analysis based on a chain of reasoning with evaluation]

**Exam tip**

In higher mark questions quantity does not compensate for quality. The quality of your answers will determine the mark awarded. In the worked example, 11 marks are available. The answer does not list 11 factors. In fact, if you analyse the answer, you will see that only three influencing factors are discussed – financing the investment, effect on staff and on customer perceptions. The answer focuses on hotels as a personal service industry which allows the candidate to make some judgements when discussing the effect on staff and customers.

## 4.2 Operations planning

This topic is concerned with:

➤ operations decisions

➤ change as process innovation

➤ methods of operation

➤ factors influencing location and scale of a business.

### Operations decisions

Decisions on the organisation of resources are influenced by many factors. In this section we look at three major influences.

### 1. Marketing

Marketing is the process of identifying the needs and wants of customers through effective market research, applying an appropriate marketing mix and ensuring a strong customer focus. Marketing will influence ideas for products; design of products; price customers are willing and able to pay; location suitable for the product and how to persuade customers to buy the product.

### 2. Available resources

Many businesses would like to increase output but are limited by the cost and availability of resources. A hairdresser might be able to cut the hair of 34 customers a day. To increase the number of haircuts a day would involve employing somebody, increasing the equipment required and maybe larger premises. All this is very costly – requires finding a trained person and may require an increase in prices to cover the cost; customers might not be willing to pay the higher price. Available resources will influence the extent to which ideas for products can be carried out; decisions whether changes can be made to production and location are influenced by the availability of labour and suitable premises.

### 3. Technology

Most businesses use technology such as automated production and computer systems. Investing in technology can help reduce business costs; improve design; increase production; improve communications and enable businesses to operate globally. Computer-aided design (**CAD**) and computer-aided manufacturing (**CAM**) have contributed to major advances in areas such as the design and production processes. CAD can be used to design new products, alter existing products or provide a 3D display to customers e.g. the interior design of a house. CAM uses computers in production. This could involve robots or computer controlled machines. CAM is often combined with CAD – referred to as CAD/CAM. CAD is used to design the products and feed the design data directly into the CAM machine.

**Key terms**

**CAD**: combining computer software and hardware to design products.

**CAM**: computer software controls and manages equipment, robots and machine tools in production.

▼ **Table 4.4** Advantages and disadvantages of CAD/CAM

| Benefits of CAD/CAM | Problems caused by CAD/CAM |
|---|---|
| • Increased productivity.<br>• Reduced waste.<br>• Higher quality.<br>• Greater accuracy.<br>• More flexible design process. | • Requires high amounts of investment.<br>• Rapid technological advances can mean technology is quickly outdated.<br>• Increases staff training costs.<br>• Requires organisational change.<br>• Breakdowns in equipment can halt all production. |

## Worked examples

1   Briefly explain how marketing can influence production decisions.   [5 marks]

2   Briefly explain how the internet might influence business location.   [3 marks]

**Answers**

1   Market research can inform the pricing of a product ✓ and the quality of a product, ✓ which would influence production methods, ✓ e.g. is the customer willing to pay a high price for high quality, handmade products, ✓ or is the product better suited to a low-price mass market? ✓

2   The internet has allowed major advances in communication, ✓ allowing businesses to choose the best location world-wide, ✓ e.g. European businesses with call centres in India. ✓

## Change as process innovation

Businesses need to be able to adapt quickly to changing market environments, in order to survive. This requires **operational flexibility** in the quantity produced (volume), the timing of deliveries and the **specification** of a product.

Volume flexibility means being able to vary the amount produced so that output does not exceed demand. Demand can change over the **product life cycle** or at different times of the year. If there is no volume flexibility, businesses may not be able to meet increased demand, resulting in lost sales and profit, or have too much stock leftover as demand falls. This flexibility includes being able to supply at a quality and price that meets customer demand.

Flexible delivery times mean that the product is delivered at a time and place to suit the customer. The ability to offer flexible delivery times can give a business a competitive advantage in the market. Sometimes a business can charge a higher price for delivering at a time to suit the customer. The increasing use of just-in-time manufacturing systems means that flexible delivery times are essential for getting an order.

Flexible specifications mean that businesses offer customers products which are 'tailor made' to the customer's specification. This means that producers need systems that will enable them to respond to a wide range of specification demanded by customers. This requires considerable planning and preparation by businesses.

> **Key terms**
>
> **Operational flexibility:** how quickly and easily a productive system can adapt to a changing market environment.
>
> **Specification:** an exact description of a product in terms of size, materials, performance and aftercare.
>
> **Product life cycle:** the stages a product passes through: development, introduction, growth, maturity and decline.

>  **Link**
>
> Just-in-time production is dealt with in topic 4.3.

## Worked example

Flexible Solutions plc (FS) offers services and solutions to manufacturers at any point in the product life cycle. They offer to manufacture or assemble products to customer specifications, and to deliver direct to customers where, when and how the customer demands. They use IT systems to produce, track and monitor orders; plan and complete delivery arrangements.

Discuss the advantages to manufacturers of using the services offered by FS.   [10 marks]

**Answer**

Manufacturers will have the operational flexibility ✓ [knowledge mark] to adapt to changing market conditions. ✓ [analysis mark] Manufacturers will have volume flexibility ✓ [knowledge mark] as FS offer to make products ✓ [application mark] output can be changed quickly and easily to meet market demand ✓ [analysis mark] and enable the manufacturer to reduce the costs of holding inventory ✓ [analysis mark]. FS also offer to produce products to customer requirements ✓ [application mark] giving the manufacturer specification flexibility to provide 'tailor made' products to customers. ✓ [analysis mark] More importantly, FS offer flexible delivery times which is often essential to a manufacturer getting the order. ✓ [evaluation mark] Flexibility is very important in a rapidly changing business environment as it allows manufacturers to exploit new opportunities. ✓ [evaluation mark]

**Process innovation**

Process innovation involves changing current processes or adopting new ways of producing products, such as automation and robotics, or delivering services e.g. by improving workflow.

Process innovation can take place at all stages of the production process and can be a major change, such as investing in new technology, or a small change such as reorganising team work. Firms will consider ways to innovate processes in order to reduce costs, improve a product or to incentivise employees.

**Key terms**

**Automation**: using electronics and machinery to control a production system.

**Robotics**: using robots, machinery that resembles a human being in the operations it can perform, in a production system.

**Workflow**: managing production systems so that items are available exactly when they are needed.

**✗ Common error**

Candidates might be tempted to answer a question on process innovation by listing the benefits to a firm. However, the question might ask candidates to focus on how workers or customers or managers might be affected. It is useful to always think of process innovation as internal change so that your answer refers to change and the effects of change on stakeholders.

**★ Exam tip**

Always consider the focus of the question. If asked about the effect on employees of a change from job to batch production, you should not discuss the benefits to the firm. Such an approach would not attract marks.

**Methods of operation**

▼ **Table 4.5** Methods of operation

| Method | Definition | Advantages | Disadvantages |
|---|---|---|---|
| Job production | Producing as single items, one at a time. | • Can produce high-quality products.<br>• Can customise.<br>• Can motivate skilled workers.<br>• Good for small scale operations. | • High unit costs.<br>• Slow.<br>• Needs specialist, skilled, workers.<br>• High training costs. |

| Method | Definition | Advantages | Disadvantages |
|---|---|---|---|
| Batch production | Production is broken down into separate operations that are each completed in turn on a group or batch of products at the same time. | • Can vary batch size.<br>• Capital intensive so lower unit cost.<br>• Can change one stage if necessary.<br>• Can be used to produce several products. | • Less skilled work.<br>• Less motivating for workers.<br>• The need to reset machines between batches means production stops.<br>• Cost of inventory can be high as need to have stock ready for production. |
| Flow production | Continuous production where one operation is completed on a product that then moves on to the next operation. | • Low unit cost.<br>• Low labour cost as less-skilled workers required.<br>• Can standardise products.<br>• Fast high-volume production. | • Requires high and stable demand.<br>• Inflexible as products standardised.<br>• High set-up costs.<br>• Employees can find the work boring. |
| **Possible variations of the above methods** | | | |
| Mass production | Producing large quantities, usually through flow production but sometimes batch can be used. | • Low unit cost.<br>• Low labour costs – often uses an assembly line.<br>• Can produce high quantities quickly.<br>• Good if the firm produces for a mass market. | • Requires standardised parts.<br>• Requires high capital investment in machinery.<br>• Needs a system for organising large quantities of materials.<br>• Can demotivate employees who find the work boring. |
| Mass customisation | A flexible production system enabling customers to specify what features of a product/service they want. | • Can produce to customer specification.<br>• Easy when using job production.<br>• Benefits the marketing of the product.<br>• Can be a USP for the firm. | • Difficult/expensive if using batch, flow or mass production.<br>• If using batch and flow may require additional investment in technology.<br>• Firms may have to compromise by offering options rather than a fully customised product.<br>• May result in slower, smaller and more costly units produced. |

## Problems of changing methods of production

Planning and preparation in regard to production methods is very important. Mistakes can be costly and take a long time to put right. Growing businesses may change production methods over time but would have to plan carefully and consider the effect on stakeholders.

 **Exam tip**

If you see a question on production changes consider the impact of change, don't just concentrate on the change. See the following worked example where the focus of the question is on the factors influencing a decision rather than on a business or its stakeholders.

✓ **What you need to know**

Change is a constant for businesses and one of the key concepts around which the business syllabus is built. New enterprises are created in response to economic, cultural and social changes. Businesses have to constantly evolve and adapt to change in order to survive and grow. 'Analyse' and 'evaluate' questions, the high mark questions, will expect you to show understanding of change when considering the issues faced by business.

## Worked example

Alistair is the managing director of a glass manufacturing company, producing glass consumer products such as smartphones and computers. Through research, he has found that glass food and drink containers are in short supply. He would like to set up a new division of the company to mass produce these glass containers. As this would represent a major investment, Alistair wants to be sure that he chooses the right production method. If the company can produce low cost containers, Alistair is confident that demand will be very high from processed food and drink manufacturers. Glass production can be by batch or continuous flow processes. The best glass production process for the containers depends on many factors.

Evaluate the factors that Alistair should consider before deciding on a production process.     [16 marks]

## Answer

Batch production is where production is broken down into separate operations that are each completed in turn on a group or batch of products at the same time. ✓ [knowledge mark] Flow production is continuous production where one operation is completed on a product that then moves on to the next operation. ✓ [knowledge mark] One factor to consider is the quantity of glass containers to be produced. Flow production allows high volume and constant production, whereas batch production is for small to medium quantities. ✓ [analysis mark] Alistair seems confident of high order quantities and flow production would have a low unit cost. ✓✓ [marks for contextual analysis] Another factor would be how standardised the glass would be. Flow production is less flexible than batch if different containers required different sorts of glass. With batch production, machinery can be used to produce several different products but flow can be expensive for other than standardised production. ✓✓ [marks for contextual analysis] Set-up cost is another major factor. Continuous flow production requires quite a large space and labour to keep the process going, as well as the capital costs for the large-scale machinery required. ✓✓ [marks for contextual analysis] Another consideration is the availability of labour – flow production processes can more easily be automated, thus keeping labour costs low. ✓✓ [marks for contextual analysis]. As the processed food and drinks market is highly competitive, Alistair should aim to produce at a low unit cost so flow production would result in a lower unit cost. ✓ [mark for contextual evaluation] However, Alistair also needs to be sure that he can sell a high volume otherwise the company will have to store large amounts of inventory which will require storage space and tie up some of the company's capital. ✓✓ [marks for good contextual analysis based on a chain of reasoning] The market for food and drink containers is very large, and many containers come in standardised shapes and sizes. In order to compete in this market, Alistair should probably choose flow produce as it is more suited to mass production of items. ✓✓ [marks for an evaluative judgement]

## Factors influencing location and scale of a business

### Location

The two main influences on where a business locates are costs and ease of access to markets. Changes in the business environment may also lead to firms relocating. Some of the factors affecting location/relocation are:

- physical geography and climate
- cost and availability of labour
- laws regulating business
- political situation
- government policies – particularly taxes and subsidies
- infrastructure
- transport costs.

> **Key term**
>
> Infrastructure: the network of utilities in a location, including transport links, communications, education and health facilities, and support services.

Change is a constant for businesses and reasons for choosing a particular location often change e.g. change can be caused by changing costs, objectives, government policies etc. Changes may require relocation and can be expensive. **Industrial inertia** can occur if the costs of moving appear greater than the costs of staying. In theory, businesses can locate/relocate anywhere but most businesses face some restrictions such as the size of the business and whether it is a local, regional, national or international business. Most businesses look for a location which minimises costs – for labour-intensive businesses the main costs are those related to workers. Some businesses require workers with specific skills and will locate in areas where those skills can be found. Businesses using unskilled or low-skilled labour will locate to where wages are low.

### Economies/diseconomies of scale

**Economies of scale** occur when the **scale of operation** increases leading to a fall in costs per unit (**average cost**). **Diseconomies of scale** happen when the scale of operation increases leading to an increase in average cost.

> **X | Common error**
>
> Candidates should note that an increase in scale refers to an increase in the size of production and should **not** be confused with just an increase in output. Businesses can increase output without increasing the scale of operations but an increase in the scale of operations always leads to an increase in output. Scale is fixed in the immediate future as it takes time and more of all resources to increase the scale of operations.

> **⊘ | Link**
>
> See Unit 5, topics 5.3 and 5.4 for further discussion on costs.

Economies of scale can come from internal sources – **internal economies of scale** or outside influences – **external economies of scale**. One objective of business is to produce the **optimum output**.

▼ **Table 4.6** Sources of economies of scale

| Economies of scale | Can come about because of: |
|---|---|
| Internal economies | • Bulk buying.<br>• Investment in technology.<br>• Managerial/specialist staff.<br>• Administration. |
| External economies | • Improved infrastructure.<br>• Research and development by outside agencies.<br>• Concentration of similar firms in one location. |
| Diseconomies | • As firms grow may be difficult to co-ordinate.<br>• Management can easily lose control of big businesses.<br>• Communication within the organisation becomes more difficult and may break down. |

**Key terms**

**Industrial inertia**: a business stays in its current location even though the factors that led to its original location no longer apply.

**Economies of scale**: advantages from the fall in costs per unit produced as the scale of output is increased.

**Scale of operation**: the size of production facilities of an operation.

**Average cost**: the total cost of production of all units ÷ by the number of units produced.

**Diseconomies of scale**: the disadvantages from the rise in costs per unit as the scale of output is increased.

**Internal economies of scale**: reduction in average cost arising from decisions made internally by the business in relation to its operations.

**External economies of scale**: reduction in average cost resulting from influences outside of the business.

**Optimum output**: this is when average cost is at the lowest point achievable in production known as the minimum efficient scale.

## Worked example

Butterfly Bakeries (BB) started out selling bread and cakes from a stall in the local market. Over the past ten years BB has expanded to one factory and three retail shops in different cities. Over that period BB's unit costs have fallen significantly, allowing a fall in prices, and this has driven the increase in demand for their baked products.

Explain how BB might have been able to reduce costs over ten years. [8 marks]

### Answer

BB has benefitted from economies of scale. ✓ [knowledge mark] As production has grown in size, BB can get bulk-buying discounts ✓ [knowledge mark] with larger orders for the ingredients, such as flour, used in the baked goods. ✓ [application mark] Administrative costs are spread over more output thereby reducing unit costs. ✓ [analysis mark] BB could have invested in machinery to batch produce output as baked goods are particularly suited to batch production, ✓ [application mark] bigger production runs cost less per unit so average costs fall. ✓ [contextualised analysis mark] When operating from a small market stall it is likely that BB baked in smaller ovens and smaller batches at a time. ✓ [application mark] Being able to produce higher quantities in batches would have reduced unit costs. ✓ [contextualised analysis mark]

## 4.3 Inventory management

This topic is concerned with:

➤ the purpose, costs and benefits of inventory

➤ inventory management.

### The purpose, costs and benefits of inventory

The **inventory** of a business consists of:

• raw materials

• components (parts needed for a product)

• partly made products (works in progress)

• finished products.

An efficient business will hold just enough inventory to meet its needs. A business needs a minimum level of inventory (known as **buffer inventory**) so that it does not run out of the items needed for production and to make sure there is enough finished goods to meet demand.

▼ **Table 4.7** Costs and benefits of holding inventory

| Costs of holding inventory | Benefits of holding inventory |
|---|---|
| • Storage costs such as rent, heating, lighting, security etc.<br>• Wastage costs if stock goes out of date/fashion or becomes damaged.<br>• Labour costs for monitoring and maintaining the stock.<br>• **Opportunity cost** is the cost of investing money in inventory instead of something more productive. | • The business will be able to meet expected demand.<br>• Prevent shortages of materials that could stop production.<br>• Discounts available for bulk-buying so holding materials can take advantage of this.<br>• Can guard against inflation by buying materials before price rises. |

**Key terms**

**Inventory**: stocks of goods, raw materials and component parts held by a business as needed to supply customer demand.

**Buffer inventory**: the products or raw materials of an organisation maintained on hand or in transit to stabilise variations in supply, demand and production.

**Opportunity cost**: the value of the next best opportunity that is lost by taking a particular decision.

**Link**

See Unit 1, topic 1.1 'Enterprise', for examples of opportunity costs.

 **Link**

See Unit 5, topics 5.1 and 5.2 on business finance for more detail.

## Inventory management

Many businesses hold inventory just in case they need it – buffer inventory. An **inventory control chart**, such as the one below, is used to help control the quantity held so that the cost of holding inventory is minimised whilst ensuring enough inventory to meet customer demand.

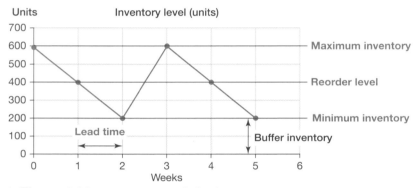

▲ **Figure 4.1** Inventory control chart

**Key terms**

**Inventory control chart**: shows the level of inventory held over time.

**Maximum inventory**: the highest quantity kept in stock.

**Reorder level**: the level of inventory at which more inventory will be ordered.

**Minimum inventory**: the buffer inventory quantity.

**Lead time**: the time taken for inventory to arrive from when it was ordered.

**Lean production**: using resources as efficiently as possible to minimise waste and improve quality.

**Just-in-time inventory control (JIT)**: managing inventories of raw materials, work-in-progress and finished products so that these are available exactly when they are needed and not before.

The decisions on all of the above will be determined by the production process, demand and time taken for orders to arrive. Using a chart helps businesses to analyse and control inventory levels e.g. the chart will indicate if reorders might have to be made earlier or later than usual. The chart will also ensure the correct size of regular orders.

Businesses can choose the quantities of inventory required or can choose to hold no stock. Some businesses use a **lean production** process known as just-in-time. Just-in-time can be a method of producing goods just-in-time for delivery to the customer, or a method of **just-in-time inventory control** (JIT). Just-in-time inventory control means that the business keeps a very low level of buffer inventory, or even none at all. This requires businesses to have:

✓ a good relationship with suppliers so that they can rely on materials arriving when needed

✓ the ability to accurately forecast demand

✓ an integrated production process from supplier → production → customer

✓ good planning and preparation.

★ **Exam tip**

You will not be asked to draw an inventory control chart and you will not be examined on the maths of the methods of inventory control. However, you should be able to interpret a chart and understand that the reorder level depends on production times, the level of buffer inventory and the lead time.

▼ **Table 4.8** Benefits and limitations of just-in-time inventory control

| Just-in-time inventory control | |
| --- | --- |
| **Benefits** | **Limitations** |
| • Reduces waste.<br>• Lower storage costs.<br>• Improves cash flow as less capital tied up in stock.<br>• Gives the business flexibility adapting to changing market conditions. | • Unreliable suppliers.<br>• Not suitable for small businesses that lack finance or space.<br>• Dissatisfied customers if orders are late.<br>• Not suitable if demand is unpredictable. |

## Revision checklist

**I can:**

➤ explain, analyse and evaluate the transformation process ☐

➤ distinguish between effectiveness, efficiency and productivity ☐

➤ show how marketing and operations are linked to value added ☐

➤ analyse and evaluate capital-intensive and labour-intensive production to enable a choice between them ☐

➤ evaluate the influence of marketing, resources and technology on operations decisions ☐

➤ explain the need for flexibility in volume, delivery times and specifications ☐

➤ analyse and evaluate the importance of process innovation ☐

➤ evaluate different operations methods and the difficulties of changing from one to another ☐

➤ evaluate location and relocation issues ☐

➤ analyse and evaluate the influences affecting the scale of operations ☐

➤ explain how economies and diseconomies of scale come about and relate to unit costs ☐

➤ discuss why businesses hold inventory ☐

➤ analyse and evaluate the costs and benefits of holding inventory ☐

➤ explain and interpret simple inventory control charts ☐

➤ recommend inventory control methods ☐

➤ evaluate the benefits and limitations of JIT inventory methods ☐

➤ apply all of the above to a range of businesses in different situations. ☐

**Raise your grade**

## Short answer questions

**1 (a)** Briefly explain the term 'value added'. [2]

The increase in value a business adds from one stage of production to another ✓ and can be calculated as the price – cost of bought-in goods and services. ✓

> **[2 marks]** It is important to explain both elements, i.e. 'added' – businesses add value at different stages of the production process – 'value' shown by the calculation. Always explain all parts of a term, don't just repeat one of the words.

**(b)** Briefly explain the term 'efficiency'. [3]

Efficiency measures the amount of resources ✓ in relation to the level of output produced. ✓

> **[2 marks]** It is important to consider the marks available. This question has three marks but the answer only includes two points. There needs to be a further explanation or an example. The answer could include an example of how to measure efficiency, e.g. One measure of efficiency is labour productivity. [1]

**2** Explain one way of improving effectiveness. [5]

Effectiveness is how well the product meets the needs of customers ✓ including availability, price, function and value for money. ✓ Effective market research ✓ can identify what customers want in a product ✓ so that the business can design products to meet customer needs. ✓

> **[5 marks]** A five-mark question does not need to have lots of writing but does need to focus on the question. This question only requires '**one** way of improving effectiveness' but does ask you to explain. The command word 'explain' (and the five marks available) implies that some analysis is required, not just knowledge or definitions. The explanation above shows an understanding of 'effectiveness' and some simple analysis of '**one** way of improving effectiveness'.

**3** Define the term 'industrial inertia'. [2]

Industrial inertia is when a business stays in its current location ✓ even though the factors that led to its original location no longer apply. ✓ Businesses stay in the original location for many reasons, especially if the cost of moving is greater than the cost of staying put. ✗

> **[2 marks]** While this is a full answer and well explained, there are only **two** marks available. The answer should stop at '… no longer apply'. You will incur an **opportunity cost** by writing too much for little reward – you will not have enough time to answer higher mark questions. Higher mark questions are often the last couple of questions, so don't waste time early on.

## Long answer question

**4** Gourmet Coffee Roasters (GCR) was set up by Henry Java five years ago. GCR roast coffee beans to supply to specialty coffee shops. The current roasting machine has the capacity to produce 240 kilos per 24-hour day. Henry operates the machine, by himself, for seven hours per day. He employs two other workers. One to package and label the roasted coffee beans and the other to deliver the bags of coffee to customers. Each kilo of roasted coffee beans produces four bags which are sold for $9.95 per bag. The cost of the beans Henry buys to roast is $3 per bag. Henry always sells out of coffee by the end of the week and cannot keep up with the demand for his coffee beans. This has resulted in some dissatisfied customers who now think Henry is an unreliable supplier. Henry fears that he might lose some very loyal customers. He is considering buying a bigger roasting machine which could produce 50 kilos of roasted coffee beans per hour. This would require a capital investment of $150 000.

**(a)** Calculate Henry's current productivity per day. [4]

The roasting machine can produce 240 kilos per day.

240/24 = 10 kilos per hour ✓

Henry is the only machine operator ✓ and he works 7 hours per day. ✓

7 hours x 10 kilos = 70 kilos per day ✓

> **[4 marks]** In calculation questions the marks often indicate the number of steps involved in the calculation. You will get full marks for just the answer '70 kilos per day' but it is easy to make a little mistake that results in the wrong answer. That is why it is always best to show all workings so that one error does not cost all four marks.

**(b)** Explain how Henry adds value to the coffee beans he buys. [6]

Value added is the increase in value a business adds from one stage of production to another ✓ and can be calculated as price – cost of bought-in goods and services, ✓ so the value added by GCR to the coffee beans is $9.95 – $3 = $6.95. ✓ Each stage of production adds value and at GRC this happens by roasting the beans, ✓ the packaging ✓ and the delivery to customers. ✓

> **[6 marks]** A concise answer which focuses on the context. Analysis of value added uses the information in the case study and gives examples from the case study. If you only define value added and give an example (unrelated to the context) you would only get 2–3 marks. Application to the particular business will get you the higher marks.

**(c)** Analyse how GCR might benefit from economies of scale by purchasing the new machine. [8]

Economies of scale occur when the scale of operation increases leading to a fall in costs per unit ✓ [knowledge mark]. Roasting larger volumes of coffee may mean that GCR can get bulk-buying discounts with larger orders ✓✓ [contextualised knowledge marks]. Administrative costs, such as transport, ✓ [knowledge mark] are spread over more output thereby reducing unit costs ✓ [analysis mark]. GCR could roast a higher volume of beans, in each production run, which reduces cost per unit so average costs fall ✓✓ [contextualised analysis marks]. Bulk-buying of coffee beans reduces the cost, per bag, of the raw materials [this repeats the earlier point] and fixed costs are spread over a higher amount of output ✓ [analysis mark]. However, some costs would rise such as the packaging and labour costs ✗ and Henry might need more employees to help with the packaging. ✗

> **[8 marks]** Some good analysis, in context, means that this answer quickly achieves full marks. There is some repetition of an earlier point – you cannot get another mark for repetition. The last sentence is unnecessary as the question only asks you to analyse the **benefits** of economies of scale, i.e. the fall in average costs, not whether costs might rise. If the question asked you to evaluate then you would include the last sentence and add more points – but then there would be more than eight marks available. Always use the command words and the marks available to guide your answer.

**(d)** Evaluate the factors that might influence Henry's decision to invest in the new coffee roasting machine. [18]

Henry should first review his current production process. ✓ [knowledge mark] As he is not using the old roasting machine to its full capacity. ✓ [analysis mark] If the roaster worked 24 hours a day then GCR could produce 240 kilos per day to make 60 bags of coffee. ✓ [contextual analysis mark] Henry only operates the machine for 7 hours a day, producing 70 kilos of coffee, 17.5 bags per day. ✓ [contextual analysis mark] If he employed another worker for 7 hours, so the machine runs for 14 hours, then he could double the output to 35 bags per day. ✓ [contextual analysis mark] This would mean that Henry would not need to find finance for an expensive new machine. ✓ [contextual analysis mark] Also, labour is more flexible than a machine ✓ [knowledge mark] as the amount of labour used can be varied according to customer demand. ✓ [analysis mark] If Henry invests in the new machine he could produce 50 kilos per hour, working 7 hours would increase output to 350 kilos, 87.5 bags per day, ✓ [contextual analysis mark] a five-fold increase. ✓ [contextual analysis mark] This could help Henry achieve economies of scale ✓ [contextual analysis mark] and reduce average costs. ✓ [analysis mark]

However, Henry must consider other factors before making a decision. As Henry is a sole trader, ✓ [contextual knowledge mark] he may not be able to raise the finance required to invest in the new machine. ✓ [evaluation mark] He should also compare the cost of employing another worker to the cost of capital. This is not a straightforward comparison because labour is more flexible it might be easier for Henry to change that resource if demand changes. ✓ [evaluation mark] Sales of coffee may be seasonal as more coffee is bought in cold weather, so demand could fluctuate during the year. ✓ [evaluation mark]

I would advise Henry to employ another worker so that he uses the capacity of existing machinery and adapt more easily to changing market conditions. ✓✓ [marks for an evaluative judgement based on a two-sided argument]

> **[18 marks]** Evaluation questions are always higher mark questions. Evaluation recognises different viewpoints, is critical of the evidence provided and/or the assumptions underlying the analysis. When you evaluate put forward a two-sided argument based on a chain of reasoning and conclude with a judgement based on your analysis. You will only get the evaluation marks if you have made connections through logical chains of reasoning and made informed judgements on the issues as they relate to the business context given in the question paper.

**Exam-style questions**

This section will allow you to practise writing answers for exam-style questions. Remember, it is useful to be aware of the mark schemes for the questions which can be found on relevant websites or from your teacher.

**Paper 1**

**Short answer questions**

1  (a) Briefly explain the term 'capital intensive'. [2]

   (b) Briefly explain the meaning of robotics. [3]

2  (a) Briefly explain the usefulness of an inventory control chart. [2]

   (b) Explain one cost, to business, of holding inventory. [3]

3  Explain the difference between internal and external economies of scale. [6]

**Long answer questions**

4  Analyse two methods that can be used to increase the productivity of labour. [8]

5  Evaluate the factors that influence the scale of a business. [12]

6  Discuss the difference between job production and batch production processes. [20]

**Paper 2**

 **Link**

Refer to Case study 2: Paul's Paper Supplies in Unit 14.

1  Briefly explain the difference between 'efficiency' and 'productivity'. [3]

2  (a) Calculate the growth in the size of market (measured in $). [3]

   (b) Briefly explain the significance of this result for Paul. [3]

3  Analyse two benefits of Paul changing his legal structure. [8]

4  Recommend whether Paul should change his legal structure when developing his business. [11]

## Key topics

➤ the need for business finance

➤ sources of finance

➤ costs

➤ accounting fundamentals

➤ forecasting and managing cash flows.

## 5.1 The need for business finance

This topic is concerned with:

➤ why businesses need finance to start up and grow

➤ why different needs for finance might mean different sources of finance are appropriate

➤ working capital

➤ the distinction between revenue expenditure and capital expenditure.

While there are many different sources of finance, different needs might mean that different sources of finance are required. Working capital is important for the day-to-day trading of a business.

Businesses need finance to start up the business and to buy **fixed assets**. Businesses also have to pay day-to-day costs such as wages.

### Why businesses need finance to start up and to grow

New businesses need funding to start up, as it will take some time to start earning any income. Most new businesses will need premises and equipment. Established businesses may want to grow, e.g. by increasing sales, capital assets or opening new branches, others may want to develop a new product. Sometimes a business may experience a fall in sales revenue and not have enough **current assets** to meet **current liabilities**.

The success of a business is determined by its ability to meet its objectives. In order to meet these objectives, a business must have sufficient finance to produce the good or service. In order to do this, **financial objectives** are created.

### Worked examples

1 Briefly explain the term 'current liability'. [3 marks]

2 Explain why a business needs finance. [3 marks]

**Answers**

1 A short-term debt, ✓ which a business has to pay within a year, ✓ such as a bill from a supplier. ✓

2 A business may need finance to start up, ✓ to buy equipment ✓ or to fund business growth. ✓

---

**✗ Common error**

Many candidates produce a list of reasons for business finance needs but do not consider the business context to which the question relates. For example, if the case study refers to a short-term need for finance then this is likely to arise from a temporary shortage of cash, not for long-term investment needs.

---

**Key terms**

**Fixed assets**: a tangible good that businesses purchase for long-term use, e.g. buildings and machinery. Cannot be converted to cash very quickly.

**Current assets**: assets owned by a business, which are either cash or can be converted to cash within a year, e.g. a bank savings account.

**Current liabilities**: short-term debts that the business has to pay within a year. Examples are bills from suppliers or creditors.

**Financial objectives**: financial goals that a business wants to achieve, which will specify a target and time period such as increasing sales revenue by 20% over the next five years.

## Why different needs for finance might mean different sources of finance are appropriate

A business may need short-term finance to pay a supplier; this type of finance will usually have to be paid back within a year. The purchase of new machinery requires long-term finance that would take over a year to repay. When choosing a source of finance, businesses have to consider **legal structure**; risk; the amount of finance required; the purpose of the loan and the time period for which the finance will be required. This links to topic 5.2 where sources of finance are considered in greater depth.

## Working capital

Working capital is a way of determining the **liquidity**, efficiency and financial health of a business. It is a business's **net liquid assets**. It measures whether a firm can meet short-term debts such as wages and supplier bills. Calculated as current assets minus current liabilities. It is an internal source of finance which enables a business to meet its day-to-day running costs such as paying bills and wages.

> 💡 **Remember**
>
> Consider the period of time for which the finance may be required, for example, a business may need short-term finance to pay a supplier; this type of finance will usually have to be paid back within a year. The purchase of new machinery requires long-term finance that would take over a year to repay.

**Key terms**

**Legal structure**: the legal definition of a business – sole trader, partnership, private limited company, public limited company, franchise, co-operative, joint venture.

**Liquidity**: the ability to meet day-to-day costs with cash or assets that can be quickly turned into cash.

**Net liquid assets**: current assets minus current liabilities.

## Worked examples

Lee Cai is a plumber and operates as a sole trader. He is worried about the business finance and is trying to calculate his working capital. He has drawn up a list of all his assets and liabilities:

| Assets | $ | Liabilities | $ |
|---|---|---|---|
| Office equipment | 6 000 | Bank loan | 20 000 |
| Tools | 3 000 | Supplier invoice | 5 000 |
| Van | 10 000 | Monthly rent | 3 000 |
| Cash | 1 000 | | |
| Bank | 4 000 | | |
| Stock | 5 000 | | |
| Debtors | 2 000 | | |
| **TOTAL** | **31 000** | **TOTAL** | **28 000** |

1 Calculate the working capital that Lee has available. [4 marks]

2 Analyse **two** reasons why it is important to Lee to know how much working capital is in the business. [8 marks]

**Answers**

1 To answer this question, you need to identify the current assets and current liabilities. Remember the definition of current assets – assets that are either cash or can be converted to cash within a year. In this question, the current assets are cash, bank, stock and debtors. Current liabilities are short-term debt so this includes the invoice and the rent.

Working capital = current assets – current liabilities ✓ [a correct formula]

Current assets = $12 000 ✓ [correct calculation of current assets]

Current liabilities = $8000 ✓ [correct calculation of current liabilities]

Working capital = $4000 ✓✓✓ [for the correct answer]

**2** It is important for Lee to know how much working capital is in the business, both to ensure good financial management of the business, ✓ [identifying a reason] and to make sure that he can pay his short-term debts. ✓ [identifying another reason] Good financial management includes management of current assets. The table shows that Lee has $5000 in stock. ✓ [putting the reason in context] This is nearly half of his current assets. ✓ [analysis of a reason] This is a high level of stock for a small business and perhaps Lee could free up some cash if he reduced stock levels. ✓ [good analysis as shown by a chain of reasoning]

If a business cannot pay its debts the business could become **insolvent**. ✓ [analysis of the other reason] As Lee is a sole trader this would mean he would be made bankrupt. ✓ [context for the other reason] ✓ Lee has unlimited liability and his personal possessions could be taken to pay the business debt. [good analysis of the other reason]

---

**✗ | Common error**

Sometimes candidates only state the final answer in calculations. If they make one mistake and end up with the wrong answer, they fail to get any marks. Including workings can mean that some marks are awarded even if the final answer is wrong. For example, in question 1 in the worked example above, a candidate may include all assets rather than just the current assets. The answer stated would then be $23 000 and the candidate would get 0 marks. However, if the answer was set out as:

Working capital = current assets – current liabilities

[1 mark for a correct formula]

Current assets = $31 000

[0 marks for the incorrect calculation of current assets]

Current liabilities = $8000

[2nd mark for the correct calculation of current liabilities]

Working capital = $23 000

[3rd mark for a correct calculation based on the candidate's own figures]

By showing the working out the candidate gets three of the four available marks, as they only made one mistake.

**⎿ Maths skills**

It is important to revise formulae and to apply the correct formula to set data. Marks are awarded for good maths skills.

**Key term**

**Insolvent**: means a business is unable to pay its debts. Sole traders or partners who become insolvent may become bankrupt.

**💡 Remember**

The distinction between capital expenditure and revenue expenditure is important when considering sources of finance. Usually finance for revenue expenditure should come from short-term sources of finance and for capital expenditure, long-term sources should be used.

### The distinction between revenue expenditure and capital expenditure

Revenue expenditure is spending on expenses necessary for the day-to-day running of the business, as is short-term spending.

Capital expenditure is long-term spending on either buying capital assets or improving an existing capital asset to make it last longer. This will be explored, in greater detail, in topic 5.2.

## 5.2 Sources of finance

This topic is concerned with:

➤ the different sources of finance

➤ the relationship between legal structure and finance sources

➤ the choice and appropriateness of each possible source of finance in a given situation

➤ factors influencing the sources of finance

➤ selecting the source of finance.

## The different sources of finance

Sources of finance can be internal or external. Internal is where the finance comes from within the business, such as **retained profit**. External finance comes from outside the business, e.g. a **bank overdraft**. A business may require short-term finance, usually repaid within a year, to cover a temporary shortage of cash or long-term finance for a long-term investment such as buying a machine. Repayments of long-term finance would be over more than 12 months, usually over three or more years.

## The relationship between legal structure and finance sources

Topic 1.2 considers legal structures in detail so this might be a good point to make sure you understand the legal structures of business. Legal structure determines the sources of finance available to businesses and helps to ensure that a source of finance is appropriate for the business. The table below explains the sources of finance you need to know. The explanation and analysis sections will indicate if a source of finance is only suitable for certain types of legal structure.

▼ **Table 5.1** Sources of finance

| Internal | Explanation | Analysis |
|---|---|---|
| Retained earnings | Profit earned and put back into the business. | • suitable for both short and long term<br>• no interest to pay<br>• not suitable for businesses that make little or no profit<br>• shareholders may object as this results in lower dividends. |
| Sale of unwanted assets | Selling assets, such a machinery, that are no longer used by the business. | • no interest to pay<br>• no longer own the asset<br>• can take time to sell so not usually for short-term finance<br>• may not get much as assets lose value over time. |
| Sale and leaseback of fixed assets | Selling assets that are still used by the business, such as a van, and then hiring the asset back. | • no interest to pay<br>• no longer own the asset<br>• leasing adds cost<br>• long term. |
| Working capital | The amount left in current assets after deducting all current liabilities. | • short-term financing<br>• no interest to pay<br>• not suitable for businesses that have little or no working capital<br>• may be unreliable if mostly in unsold stock. |
| **External** | | |
| Share capital | Public limited (plc) and private limited (Ltd) companies can sell shares. | • long-term financing<br>• only pay dividends if profit made<br>• only available to incorporated businesses<br>• dilutes ownership of a company. |
| New partners | A sole trader could become a partnership or an existing partnership could invite others to join if they contribute capital. | • short- or long-term financing<br>• no interest to pay<br>• means sharing control of a business<br>• profits have to be shared with the new partner. |
| Venture capital | Professional investors fund a high-risk business through either buying shares or providing a loan. | • long-term financing<br>• investor often provides advice as well<br>• long process<br>• may require a share of the business or a high rate of interest. |
| Overdrafts | Negative bank account balance. | • only suitable for short term<br>• higher interest than a loan<br>• can be arranged quickly<br>• flexible as can use when needed. |

| External | Explanation | Analysis |
|---|---|---|
| Bank loan | Businesses can borrow a fixed amount from a bank and pay back over a period of time with interest. | • long-term financing<br>• guaranteed the money<br>• can be difficult to keep up repayments<br>• may be a charge for early repayment. |
| Leasing | A business can rent an asset rather than purchase one. | • long-term source<br>• may be the only way business can get new equipment<br>• do not own the asset<br>• adds cost to the business. |
| Hire purchase | Buying an asset from another business and paying for it over a period of time. | • for long-term finance needs<br>• own the asset after all payments made<br>• can be expensive as might have high interest to pay<br>• can be taken back if payments missed. |
| Mortgages | A long-term loan secured on property. | • for long-term finance needs<br>• interest rates often lower than for a bank loan<br>• property at risk if payments not made<br>• adds to costs. |
| Debentures | A long-term loan to a company that guarantees a fixed rate of interest. | • long-term financing<br>• pay fixed amount of interest often lower than a loan<br>• only available to companies<br>• have to pay interest even if the firm makes no profit. |
| Micro-finance | Loans to small businesses where they cannot access other sources of finance. | • usually long term to help start-up a business<br>• only available to small businesses with no other source of finance<br>• usually only small amounts can be borrowed<br>• interest rates can be very high. |
| Crowd funding | Contributions made by a large number of people usually via the internet through organisations such as Kickstarter. | • long-term finance<br>• can be donations, loans or shares, depending on the business<br>• rewards for donations can be offered<br>• a portion of the money raised goes to the crowd funding organisation. |
| Government grants | Subsidy provided by a government to a business. | • long-term finance<br>• no interest and does not have to be repaid<br>• can take a long time to apply<br>• often requires a lot of research from the business. |

★ Exam tip

When a question asks for a recommendation for sources of finance, consider the business in terms of size, structure, sources available to the business, whether revenue or capital expenditure and the time horizon.

### The choice and appropriateness of each possible source of finance in a given situation

All businesses need finance but have to consider the factors that will influence the choice of sources of finance:

➤ Cost – How much will the finance cost? Can the business afford it?

➤ Flexibility – Does the business need the cash to be available at certain times? An overdraft is more flexible than a bank loan and, therefore, more suitable to meet a temporary need for cash. An example would be to pay a supplier's bill.

➤ Control – Would the source of finance dilute control of the business? Issuing shares or taking on a new partner would mean sharing control. Is this acceptable to the existing owners?

✗ Common error

Candidates will often just list sources of finance without considering the type of business and the finance needs. Not all sources of finance are available or suitable for all businesses in all situations. For example, if a business needs some temporary cash to pay wages you wouldn't suggest a long-term source such as debentures as this is a short-term finance need. An overdraft would be more appropriate in this situation.

➤ Level of existing debt – How much debt does the business have? Can the business take on more debt? Would lenders be willing to make a loan in this situation?

 **Maths skills**

It is important to be able to interpret and analyse quantitative information as shown in the answer to the worked example, where calculating the total cost of the investment helps to get context and analysis marks.

**Worked example**

Nabeel and Joanna have been business partners for a year. They provide cleaning services to local colleges. One of their employees has complained about the floor polishing equipment currently used. The business has five floor polishers that are wearing out. Because of the poor condition of the machines, it is taking a lot longer to clean the premises. As employees are paid an hourly rate this has increased the wage bill by 20 percent.

Joanna has suggested that they should buy new equipment and has researched the cost of replacing the five machines. The price of one new machine is $1950. Last year the business made a profit of $12 000.

Analyse **two** sources of finance available to Nabeel and Joanna. [8 marks]

**Answer**

The partners could use retained profits. ✓ [identifying a source] Five new machines cost $9750 and the business made a profit of $12 000, ✓ [using the context] so they should have enough profit to buy the machines. This would mean that they have no extra costs such as interest to pay ✓ [simple analysis] and they could increase future profits as the new machines will be more efficient. This means that the wage bill could be reduced as it is currently 20 percent higher than it should be. ✓ [good analysis shown by a chain of reasoning that uses the context provided] However, using retained profit might mean that they don't have enough capital for day-to-day expenses so another source of finance could be leasing ✓ [identifying another source] as the finance is for floor polishers which should be available to lease. ✓ [putting the source of finance in context] Leasing means that they would not own the asset; ✓ [simple analysis] but the cost of leasing may be offset by the savings made on the wage bill. Employees would be able to complete jobs more quickly therefore reducing the amount of hours they would be paid for. ✓ [good analysis shown by a chain of reasoning that uses the context provided]

**As you can see, the above answer would get full marks.**

★ **Exam tip**

Read the question carefully – if only '**two** sources of finance…' then only two sources will attract marks. To write about more than two is a waste of time and there is no reward for doing so.

## 5.3 Costs

This topic is concerned with:

➤ types of costs

➤ how cost information is used to monitor a business and inform decisions

➤ calculating the minimum level of production needed to break even or the profit made

➤ calculating the margin of safety

➤ uses and limitations of break-even analysis.

## Types of cost

For many businesses, profit is the most important objective. An understanding of costs is crucial to making a profit.

All businesses need accurate cost information to help in decision making, setting prices, monitoring and improving business performance. The following types of cost should be understood:

➤ fixed – fixed costs do not change with output

➤ variable – variable costs change directly with output

➤ marginal – marginal cost is the additional cost of producing one extra unit

➤ direct – direct costs can be assigned directly with output e.g. raw materials

➤ indirect – indirect costs cannot be assigned directly with output, e.g. office expense.

## How cost information is used to monitor a business and inform decisions

All businesses want to minimise costs, therefore it is important to know how to calculate the different types of cost. Once costs are calculated and understood businesses can use the information to calculate profit (see topic 5.4), check and improve the business, take decisions on future growth/investment and make pricing decisions (see topic 3.3).

> **X Common error**
>
> It is important to give precise definitions. Candidates often define fixed costs as costs that do not change. This is not precise enough, fixed costs do change, so this definition would not gain any marks. The precise definition is 'costs that do not change with output'.

> **💡 Remember**
>
> You will be expected to calculate cost, revenue, profit and break-even. It is important to know the correct formula for each and to understand what the figure means for the business. These calculations are useful as part of analysis or even evaluation.

▼ **Table 5.2** Calculations of costs

| Cost | Definition | Calculation |
|------|-----------|-------------|
| Total cost (TC) | All the costs of production added together. | Total cost = Total fixed costs + Total variable cost |
| Total variable cost (TVC) | All the variable costs of production. | Total variable cost = Variable cost per unit of output × quantity produced |
| Average total cost (ATC) | The total cost per unit of output. | Average total cost = Total cost ÷ output |
| Average variable cost (AVC) | The variable cost per unit of output. | Average variable cost = Total variable cost ÷ output |
| Average fixed cost (AFC) | The fixed cost per unit of output. | Average fixed cost = Total fixed cost ÷ output |
| Marginal cost (MC) | The extra total cost per extra unit of output. | Marginal cost = the change in total cost ÷ the change in output |

## Worked examples

Bandies Ltd manufactures wristbands used by concert venues when admitting people to a concert. They produce the bands using mainly labour. Each employee is paid $1 for every 25 wristbands produced, and can produce 250 wristbands per hour. The firm employs 120 people on production. Bandies Ltd is considering investing in a machine that can produce 5000 wristbands per hour at a cost of 1 cent per wristband. The machine will cost $100 000 and will require three people to operate. If the firm does invest in the machine, they would pay the operators an hourly rate of $10 each.

1  What is the average variable cost of producing one wristband:

   **a)** using only labour                                    [3 marks]

   **b)** producing by machine?                                [4 marks]

2  Analyse why it is important for Bandies Ltd to be able to identify and calculate its costs.                          [9 marks]

**Answers**

**1 a)** The variable costs are the wages paid to labour of $1 for 25 wristbands so:

Average variable cost = variable cost ÷ output ✓ [formula]

Variable costs are $1 for every 25 units produced ✓ [correct identification of the data]

So $1 ÷ 25 = $0.04 or 4 cents ✓ [A correct answer gets all 3 marks]

**b)** [No need to state the formula again.] In this situation the variable cost has two elements. We are told that the machine can produce each wristband for 1 cent. ✓ [correct identification of the data] However, we also know that three people are required to operate the machine at a cost of $10 per hour and the machine produces 5000 per hour. ✓ [correct identification of the data] The average labour cost will be $30 ÷ 5000 = $0.006 ✓ [calculation] 0.006 + 0.01 = $0.016 or 1.6 cents. ✓ [A correct answer gets all 4 marks]

**2** It is important for Bandies Ltd to be able to identify and calculate its costs as it is considering investing ✓ [identification of a reason] in a machine to increase the production of wristbands. ✓ [using the context] As the firm will want to minimise its costs of production, ✓ [identification of a reason] it needs to compare the costs of each production method. ✓ [simple analysis] If Bandies Ltd uses the labour production method, it would cost 4 cents per wristband, ✓ [context] whereas the machine can produce for 1.6 cents per wristband. ✓✓ [2 marks for analysis in context] This would suggest that it would be cost efficient to invest in the machine. However, the cost information is limited and the firm would need to identify and calculate other costs, such as redundancy costs, before making a decision. ✓✓ [2 marks for good analysis based on a chain of reasoning]

---

**Maths skills**

The ability to interpret and use the results of a calculation is as important as being able to remember formula and carry out calculation.

### Calculating the minimum level of production needed to break even or the profit made

Break-even analysis helps a business to calculate the minimum production level required to cover all costs and the profit made at different production levels. The break-even output is the level of sales required to cover all costs of production. At the break-even output **revenue** = costs. If sales are below the break-even output, then costs > revenue = loss; if sales are above the break-even output, then revenue > costs = profit. To calculate the break-even output a business needs to work out **contribution**:

- Contribution per unit = price per unit – variable cost per unit

- Total contribution = total revenue – total variable cost

OR

- Total contribution = contribution per unit × quantity sold

The break-even output is where contribution = total fixed costs. This is calculated as:

Break-even output = total fixed costs ÷ contribution per unit

**✗ Common error**

Some candidates get formulae the wrong way around. For example, in question 1 a) from the worked example, the answer might be given as quantity produced ÷ variable cost = 25 ÷ 100 = 25 cents. If we consider the answer of 25 cents, we can see that it seems a very high unit cost. This gives us a clue that something has gone wrong in the calculation.

**Key terms**

**Revenue**: the income earned by a business from sales. Calculated as price × quantity sold (P × Q).

**Contribution**: this is the contribution to fixed costs. When the revenue from selling a product is enough to pay the variable costs of production, then any revenue left over will be the contribution to fixed costs.

## Worked example

Rachel sells homemade luxury cupcakes for $5 each. The variable costs per cake (ingredients, energy, etc.) are $1. The fixed costs of the premises and kitchen equipment are $2000.

**a)** How many cakes does Rachel have to sell to break even? [4 marks]

**b)** Rachel produces and sells 2000 cakes. Calculate Rachel's profit. [4 marks]

**Answer**

**a)** Contribution per unit = price per unit − variable cost per unit ✓ [formula]

So contribution = $5 − $1 = **$4** ✓ [correct calculation of contribution]

Break-even output = total fixed costs ÷ contribution per unit ✓ [formula]

$2000 ÷ $4 = 500

Rachel has to sell 500 cakes to break even. ✓ [correct answer]

**b)** Once Rachel has sold 500 cakes, the remaining sales, minus the variable costs, will be profit. ✓ So:

2000 − 500 = 1500 ✓ [calculation]

1500 × $4 ✓ [correct data]

= $6000 ✓✓✓ [4 marks for the correct answer]

---

### Maths skills

There is often more than one way of calculating something. In 1 b) above, profit may be calculated as:

Profit = total revenue − total cost [1 mark for the formula]

Total revenue = $5 × 2000 = $10 000 [1 mark for the calculation]

Total costs = $2000 + ($1 × 2000) = $4000 [1 mark for the calculation]

$10 000 − $4000 = $6000 [4 marks for the correct answer]

Unless you are given instructions on using a specific method, you can choose the method best for you.

### X Common error

In calculations, you have to remember to include each step. In 1 b) above, candidates often forget about the variable cost and miss that step out of the calculations. Instead of multiplying the quantity of 2000 by $4 (price − variable cost per unit) they multiply by $5 (the price). Where an answer can be calculated by another method, if there is time, both methods could be used to check that the answer is correct.

## Calculating the margin of safety

The margin of safety is the difference between actual (or forecast) output and break-even output. If a business calculates its margin of safety then it will know by how much sales can fall before it loses money. In the example of Rachel's cupcakes, she needs to sell 500 to break-even. She actually produces and sells 2000. She can calculate her margin of safety as:

Margin of safety = actual output − break-even output

= 2000 − 500 = 1500

Rachel's sales can fall by up to 1500 before she makes a loss. If Rachel's output fell to 1000, her margin of safety would fall to 500. By calculating her margin of safety, Rachel can take action if she feels that it is too low. She could look at ways to increase sales revenue or reduce costs.

▼ **Table 5.3** Some decisions/issues that a business might consider
↑ higher ↓ lower

| Decision/issue | Effect on contribution | Effect on break-even output | Effect on the margin of safety |
|---|---|---|---|
| Increase price, costs and sales unchanged | ↑ | ↓ | ↑ |
| Decrease price, costs and sales unchanged | ↓ | ↑ | ↓ |
| Variable costs increase, price and sales unchanged | ↓ | ↑ | ↓ |
| Variable costs decrease, price and sales unchanged | ↑ | ↓ | ↑ |
| Fixed costs increase, price and sales unchanged | No Change | ↑ | ↓ |
| Fixed costs decrease, price and sales unchanged | No Change | ↓ | ↑ |

However, the above table assumes no effect on sales of, for example, changing price. Increasing the price might reduce sales to the extent that the unit contribution falls and lowers the margin of safety.

✓ **What you need to know**

All businesses need finance and all have to produce accounts. In the business syllabus the emphasis is on understanding finance – the need for finance, sources of finance and an ability to interpret published accounts.

## Uses and limitations of break-even analysis

Break-even is quick and easy to calculate. If break-even analysis indicates a low margin of safety, then the business owner/manager can take quick action to increase sales or reduce costs. Business owners/managers can use break-even analysis to forecast how changes in sales will affect revenue, costs and profit and how changes in price and costs will affect how much they need to sell. Break-even analysis can influence investment decisions such as launching a new product. If a business requires a loan, or wants to attract new investors, break-even analysis can help to persuade the bank to lend or the investor to invest.

However, all analysis has limitations and break-even analysis does have disadvantages. The assumption when calculating break-even is that variable costs rise in direct proportion to output. In the example of Rachel's cupcakes, looked at above, the assumption was that the unit variable cost of a cake is always $1, so 10 cakes = $10 total variable costs and 20 cakes = $20 total variable costs. This is not always true. Producers can sometimes get discounts for **bulk buying**. Break-even analysis is easy for one product but can be complex for a business producing many products. Break-even forecasts assume that all output is sold. But, for example, supermarkets end up throwing away fresh food that customers didn't buy. The data has to be accurate. If the data is incorrect then the results will be incorrect. Break-even analysis forecasts how many products a business needs to sell, not how many they **will** sell.

🔗 **Link**

The relationship between price and sales is explored in Unit 3, topic 3.3.

💡 **Remember**

Break-even forecasts are related to supply decisions, not demand for a product. For a business to break even, it will have to sell the forecast amount but there is no guarantee that this will happen.

**Key term**

**Bulk buying**: purchasing large quantities of a product, at one time, to get a discount.

## Worked example

### Ali's Festival Food (AFF)

Ali is planning to sell sandwiches at a local festival. Ali wants to know how many sandwiches he needs to sell to cover all his costs and make a profit. He has estimated the following:

| Average price of a sandwich | $6 |
|---|---|
| Average variable cost of a sandwich | $1.50 |
| Fixed costs | $900 |
| Forecast sales | 600 sandwiches |

**a)** Calculate:

    **i)** Ali's break-even output                                                     [4 marks]

    **ii)** the margin of safety.                                                          [2 marks]

**b)** What would happen to the margin of safety if fixed costs rise by 10%?     [4 marks]

**c)** What would happen to Ali's break-even output if he increased price to $6.50?     [3 marks]

### Answer

**a) i)** Contribution per unit = price per unit − variable cost per unit ✓ [formula]

    So contribution = $6 − $1.50 = **$4.50** ✓ [correct calculation of contribution]

    Break-even output = Total fixed costs ÷ contribution per unit ✓ [formula]

    $900 ÷ $4.50 = 200 Ali has to sell 200 sandwiches to break-even. ✓     [4 marks for the correct answer]

    **ii)** Margin of safety = actual output − break-even output ✓ [formula]

    600 − 200 = 400 ✓ [2 marks for the correct answer]

**b)** Fixed costs would rise by $900 × 10% = $990 ✓ [correct calculation]

Break-even output = 990 ÷ $4.50 = 220 ✓ [correct calculation]

Margin of safety = 600 − 220 = 380 ✓ [correct calculation]

Ali's margin of safety would fall to 380 ✓ [4 marks for the correct answer]

**c)** So contribution is now = $6.50 − $1.50 = **$5** ✓ [correct calculation]

Break-even output = $900 ÷ $5 = 180 ✓ [correct calculation]

Ali's break-even output falls to 180 ✓ [3 marks for the correct answer]

---

**✗ Common error**

In question b) above, it is easy to do the calculation but forget to answer the question: 'What would happen to the margin of safety if fixed costs rise by 10%?' The answer, of course, is that the margin of safety would fall to 380. If the question had been 'Calculate the margin of safety' then 380 would get full marks, but this question is slightly different. The calculation is still required but also an indication of the direction of the change. Always read the question carefully, underline the key command words.

**Maths skills**

It is easy to see maths skills tested in calculation questions. However, finance affects all aspects of a business such as production and marketing. When answering questions on other areas it is important to give some consideration to the financial aspects of any decision. There is often an opportunity for you to apply maths skills to analyse and interpret business issues.

## 5.4 Accounting fundamentals

This topic is concerned with:

➤ contents of financial statements

➤ ratio analysis

➤ practical use of ratio analysis

➤ users and limitations of published accounts.

### Contents of financial statements

▼ **Table 5.4** An example of an income statement

| First Development Ltd | | |
|---|---|---|
| **Income statement** | 2017 | 2016 |
| Year ended 31 December | $'000 | $'000 |
| | | |
| Revenue | 3 880 | 2 945 |
| *Less* cost of sales | 1 455 | 1 170 |
| Gross profit | 2 425 | 1 775 |
| *Less* expenses | 1 226 | 1 050 |
| Operating profit | 1 199 | 725 |
| *Less* finance costs | 98 | 72 |
| Profit before tax | 1 101 | 653 |
| *Less* tax | 275 | 163 |
| **Profit** (attributable to shareholders) | 826 | 490 |

▼ **Table 5.5** An example of a statement of financial position

| First Development Ltd statement of financial position as at the 31 December 2017 | | |
|---|---|---|
| | $'000 | $'000 |
| Non-current assets | | 2 580 |
| | | |
| Current assets | 2 355 | |
| *Less* current liabilities | 1 362 | |
| **Net current assets (working capital)** | | 993 |
| | | |
| *Less* non-current liabilities (long term) | 255 | |
| **Net assets** | | 3 318 |
| | | |
| **Financed by** | | |
| Reserves | 2 492 | |
| Retained profit | 826 | |
| **Equity** | | 3 318 |

**Income statement**: a historical statement of the financial position of a business over a specific period (normally one year). It shows the profit or loss made by the business – which is the difference between the firm's total income and its total costs.

**Cost of sales**: direct cost of output/sales (see topic 5.3 above).

**Gross profit**: revenue less cost of sales.

**Expenses**: indirect cost of output/sales (see topic 5.3 above).

**Operating profit**: a key measure of profit. Operating profit records how much profit has been made in total from the trading activities of the business before taking account of interest paid on loans.

**Finance costs**: interest paid on loans.

**Profit before tax**: operating profit less interest paid on loans.

**Tax**: an estimate of the corporation tax payable on profit.

**Profit**: (attributable to shareholders): profit left after tax that can be paid to shareholders and/or used as retained earnings (see topic 5.2 above).

**Statement of financial position**: a document describing the financial position of a company at a particular point in time. It compares the value of what it owns (assets) with the amount it owes (liabilities). Topic 5.1 explains assets and liabilities in more detail. You will see, from the example below, that **net assets = equity (capital employed)**. This is always the case, because the equity is the amount of long-term money put into the business and the net assets employed how it is used. The statement is sometimes referred to as a 'snapshot' of a business as it is put together on one specific day. The statement could be different a day later, for example, non-current assets, included on the statement, may be sold the next day.

**Non-current assets**: fixed assets such as premises, machinery and office equipment.

## Ratio analysis

Businesses use percentages changes, fractions and ratios to analyse figures. They are all related.

 **Maths skills**

To convert from fractions to percentages, multiply the fraction by 100. For example, $\frac{1}{2} \times 100 = 50\%$

To convert from percentages to fractions, divide by 100. For example, $\frac{50}{100} = \frac{1}{2}$

You can also convert from fractions to ratios. A ratio is a way of comparing one part to another. For example, $\frac{1}{2}$ is 1 part for every 2. If profit is $\frac{1}{2}$ of revenue, then the ratio of revenue to profit is $2:1$

Businesses calculate percentage increases or decreases in figures like gross profit, profit, sales etc. This is a way of monitoring business performance over time or to compare different businesses. Calculating percentage changes over time can help to detect trends.

 **Maths skills**

The formula for calculating a percentage change is:

$$\text{Percentage change} = \frac{(\text{new figure} - \text{previous figure})}{\text{previous figure}} \times 100$$

▼ **Table 5.6** Ratios you should know

| Ratio | Calculation | Explanation |
|---|---|---|
| **Liquidity Ratios** | | |
| Current ratio | Current assets ÷ current liabilities | The current ratio estimates whether the business can pay debts, due within one year, out of the current assets. A ratio of less than one is often a cause for concern, as it may mean that the business cannot pay its debts. |
| Acid test ratio | (Current assets – inventory) ÷ current liabilities | The acid test ratio removes inventories from the current assets total. It is more difficult to turn inventories into cash quickly. |
| | | |
| **Profitability ratios** | | |
| Gross profit margin (%) | (Gross profit ÷ sales revenue) × 100 | Measures gross profit as a percentage of sales. A good gross profit margin depends on the type of business, but the higher the better. |
| Profit margin (%) | (Profit for the year ÷ sales revenue) × 100 | Measures the profit for the year as a percentage of sales. A high profit margin for the year can attract potential shareholders as it may be a sign of high dividends. |

## Practical use of ratio analysis

Ratios are a useful way of monitoring business health. They can be used to compare business performance over time or between businesses. Businesses can also try and improve ratio results such as reducing working capital problems.

## Worked example

Super Appliances plc has produced the following information.

Sales Revenue $40m

Gross Profit $28m

Profit for the year $10m

Current assets $20m

Inventories $8m

Current liabilities $16m

Calculate:

a) the gross profit margin [3 marks]

b) the profit margin [3 marks]

c) the current ratio [3 marks]

d) the acid test ratio. [4 marks]

### Answers

a) Gross profit margin = (Gross profit ÷ sales revenue) × 100 ✓ [formula]

($28m ÷ $40m) × 100 ✓ [use of the correct data]

= 70% ✓ [3 marks for the correct answer]

b) Profit margin = (Profit for the year ÷ sales revenue) × 100 ✓ [formula]

($10m ÷ $40m) × 100 ✓ [use of the correct data]

= 25% ✓ [3 marks for the correct answer]

c) The current ratio = current assets ÷ current liabilities ✓ [formula]

($20m ÷ $16m) ✓ [use of the correct data]

= 1.25 ✓ [3 marks for the correct answer]

d) The acid test ratio = (current assets − inventories) ÷ current liabilities ✓ [formula]

($20m − $8m) ÷ $16m ✓ [use of the correct data]

= $12m ÷ $16m ✓ [use of the correct data]

= 0.75 ✓ [4 marks for the correct answer]

★ **Exam tip**

It is important to be careful in answering a question about improving business performance. For example, a question which asks how gross profit margin could be increased could be answered as increase price or reduce costs. This is imprecise. A better answer would be increase price whilst costs remain the same (or fall), or decrease costs whilst price remains the same. The aim is to increase the percentage of sales revenue, so we need to make sure all elements are included in the answer.

✗ **Common error**

When calculating percentages, candidates often forget to multiply by 100. So in part a) of the worked example above, the answer might be given as 0.7, rather than the correct answer of 70%. This would mean getting only two of the three marks available.

## Users and limitations of published accounts

**Stakeholders** such as owners/shareholders, potential investors, etc. would be interested in the published accounts of a business. Competitors would also find the information useful as a way of comparing performance. However, published accounts are historical and may not reflect the future. By the time they are published they are already out of date. Businesses may '**window dress**' the results to show the company in a favourable light. Financial accounts do not reflect the qualitative aspects of a business such as being a good employer, producing safe and reliable products, etc. The accounts may not detail the performance of individual parts of a company – especially a company producing many products.

## 5.5 Forecasting and managing cash flows

This topic is concerned with:

➤ purposes of cash flow forecasts

➤ cash flow forecasts in practice

➤ methods of improving cash flow.

### Purposes of cash flow forecasts

Cash flow is all the money coming in or going out of a business over a period of time, calculated at the precise time it enters or leaves the business. Profit includes all the transactions that will lead to cash flowing in or out of the business, now or in the **future**. Profit is calculated when things are bought and sold rather than when they are paid for. For example, a business may provide credit to customers and a profit would be recorded, but no cash has changed hands so does not change the amount of cash in the business.

A cash flow forecast is the amount of money **expected** to flow in and out, over a period of time, in the future. Businesses need cash to survive so cash flow calculations are the most important thing to help achieve short-term objectives. In the long term, making a profit is the main objective (for more detail on business objectives see topic 5.1 above and topic 1.4). Businesses need to pay out money for the costs of producing output or for buying assets such as machinery. The money is often paid out before the business receives income from the sale of its output. The delay between money going out and money coming in is called the cash flow cycle. It is important that a business has enough money to pay suppliers, employees, etc. otherwise the business could become insolvent. The money available to a business for day-to-day running costs is called working capital.

### Cash flow forecasts in practice

Businesses can use cash flow forecasts to ensure that there is always enough cash to pay suppliers and employees. If the forecast predicts a shortage of cash, then the business can arrange some temporary finance in time to meet payments out. Cash flow forecasts can show that a business plans for the future, which will be of interest to banks, potential investors and shareholders. The business can also check that it does not have too much cash. Cash is a liquid asset but does not attract any interest. A business with too much cash might be wiser to invest in the business, e.g. buying more stock, purchasing some machinery or employing more labour – things to help the business grow.

▼ **Table 5.7** Example of a cash flow forecast for a start-up business

| Quarter | 1 | 2 | 3 | 4 |
|---|---|---|---|---|
| **Cash inflows ($000s)** | | | | |
| Opening balance – a new business will not have an opening balance in the first quarter. | 0 | –8 | –10 | –6 |
| Sales | 0 | 6 | 12 | 20 |
| Other cash in (initial start-up finance, e.g. from a loan). | 20 | 0 | 0 | 0 |
| **Cash outflows ($000s)** | | | | |
| Set-up costs – start-up costs of a new enterprise | 20 | 0 | 0 | 0 |
| Wages | 5 | 5 | 5 | 5 |
| Rent | 3 | 3 | 3 | 3 |
| Closing balance = (opening balance + cash inflow) – cash outflow | –8 | –10 | –6 | 6 |

As can be seen from the cash flow forecast above, some assumptions have been made in predicting cash flow over the coming year. For example, the business expects sales of $6000 in quarter 2, and for sales to double in quarter 3. If these assumptions are false, then the forecast is inaccurate. There is also an assumption that wages and rent don't change over the course of the year, but costs may go up. Staff may need training (not shown in the forecast above), landlords may put up rent or competitors may reduce prices and affect the sales of this business. An inaccurate forecast can cause many problems for a business. If there is no early indication that the business is running out of cash, the business could become insolvent. In the cash flow forecast above, the business can see that it will need some temporary finance in quarters 1–3 but that the balance is positive in quarter 4. Also, does the business have to pay back the start-up loan and when? This is not shown in the forecast. If the assumptions made are wrong, or if the business needs to buy more supplies (not included in the forecast), or pay back some of the loan, then the business could run out of cash and become insolvent.

**Worked example**

Samson Enterprises Ltd are about to launch a new product. Annette, the finance manager, expects sales of $5000 in quarter 2, and for sales to double in quarter 3 and to double again in quarter 4. She estimates that an initial investment of $15 000 will be required, which will come from existing capital in the company. Annette has identified the following costs:

- Equipment – $12 000 in quarter 1 and another $12 000 in quarter 3.

- Advertising – $2000 at launch in quarter 1.

- Wages – $3000 per quarter.

- Materials – $1000 in quarter 1, $2000 in quarter 2, $4000 in quarter 3 and $5000 in quarter 4.

Construct a cash flow forecast for the launch of the new product. [9 marks]

**Answer**

Samson Enterprises Ltd cash flow forecast for new product to December 2018

| Quarter | 1 | 2 | 3 | 4 | Mark |
|---|---|---|---|---|---|
| **Cash inflows ($000s)** | | | | | |
| Opening balance | 0 | –3 | –3 | –12 | ✓✓✓ |
| Sales | 0 | 5 | 10 | 20 | ✓✓ |
| Investment | 15 | 0 | 0 | 0 | |
| **Cash outflows ($000s)** | | | | | |
| Equipment | 12 | 0 | 12 | 0 | |
| Advertising | 2 | 0 | 0 | 0 | |
| Wages | 3 | 3 | 3 | 3 | |
| Materials | 1 | 2 | 4 | 5 | |
| Closing balance | –3 | –3 | –12 | 0 | ✓✓✓✓ |

## Methods of improving cash flow

Businesses can use various methods to improve cash flow but all have their disadvantages.

▼ **Table 5.8** Advantages and disadvantages of methods for improving cash flow

| Method | Explanation | Advantages | Disadvantages |
|---|---|---|---|
| Reduce costs | Cost reductions could come from looking for cheaper suppliers or hold less stock so less cash tied up in stock. | Will also help improve gross profit and profit.<br><br>Should be easy for the business to analyse costs. Can calculate if have too much stock. | Cheaper supplies could be lower quality. Less stock held may mean the business cannot meet orders, especially if there is an unexpected increase in demand. |
| Manage trade receivables and trade payables | Try to reduce the time between paying suppliers and getting money from customers. Ask suppliers for a longer credit period or give customers a shorter credit period. | Credit from suppliers is usually interest-free.<br><br>Customers paying more quickly reduces risk of debt default. | Can be difficult to balance the need to manage cash flow with the need to keep customers and suppliers happy. If competitor businesses offer better credit terms then the business could lose customers. |
| Debt factoring | Banks and other financial agents give about 70–80 percent of the debt value, in instant cash. The agent then gets the customer to pay back the debt. | Can be a quick way of raising cash. Also, the business no longer has to chase the customer to pay back the debt. | Only suitable for large businesses with a lot of cash tied up in debtors. This is because the agent takes a fee from the repaid debt or the business loses some of the cash. |
| Sale and leaseback | A business sells an asset, such as a machine, to raise cash. Then rents the asset back from the company. | Releases a big sum of money from the sale and pays a small amount, each month, to rent the equipment. | The business no longer owns the asset unless they get enough cash to buy it back. Also increases monthly cash outflows in the form of rent. |

| Method | Explanation | Advantages | Disadvantages |
|---|---|---|---|
| Leasing | Rather than buying an asset, such as a vehicle, the business rents for a monthly sum. | No need to find a large amount of capital to buy. Instead the asset is rented for a fixed period of time. At the end of the lease period there is an option to hand it back or to buy it from the lease holder. | The business never owns the asset unless they buy it at the end of the period. There can be strict conditions regarding the use and maintenance of the asset. |
| Hire purchase | Buying a capital asset such as machines and vehicles, over a specific period of time. Usually a small deposit is required and then monthly payments. | A way of buying capital equipment that the business will eventually own. No need to pay out a high amount of cash in one go. The equipment is available to use immediately. | Can be expensive as often high rates of interest charged. The asset remains the property of the supplier until all money has been paid. If payments are missed the supplier could take the asset back. |

## Revision checklist

**I can:**

➤ understand the need for business finance ☐

➤ understand sources of finance ☐

➤ understand costs ☐

➤ understand financial statements ☐

➤ understand ratios ☐

➤ understand working capital ☐

➤ understand cash flow forecasts. ☐

## ⬆ Raise your grade

This section will help to ensure answers to **finance** questions are answered fully and maximise the chances of achieving higher grades.

**Short answer questions**

1 (a) Briefly explain the term 'venture capital'. [2]

Venture capital is finance ✓ provided to a business by professional investors. ✓

**[2 marks]** It is important to explain both elements, i.e. 'venture' – provided by professional investors, and 'capital' – business finance. If the answer given said 'capital ✗ provided by professional investors ✓' only 1 mark would be awarded.

**(b)** Briefly explain the term 'current asset'. [3]

Assets owned by a business, ✓ which are either cash or can be converted to cash within a year. ✓

> **[2 marks]** It is important to consider the marks available. This question has 3 marks but the answer only includes 2 points. There needs to be a further explanation or an example. The answer could include an example such as 'cash' or 'bank account'. ✓

**2** Explain the difference between cash and profit. [5]

Cash is money in a business which flows over a period of time, ✓ calculated at the precise time it enters or leaves the business. ✓ Profit is the money ✗ a business makes when it sells its goods.

> **[2 marks]** A five-mark question does not need to have lots of writing but does need to answer the question which asks about 'the difference'. The answer above explains cash so gets a knowledge mark and an explanation mark. However, the definition of profit is incorrect so no knowledge or explanation marks here. The 5th mark is for an explanation of the **difference between the two elements.** The second part of the answer could have been: Profit is the difference between total revenue and total cost. [1] Profit is calculated when things are bought and sold rather than when they are paid for. [1] Profit may be in the form of cash and other assets. [1]

**3** Define the term 'break-even output'. [2]

Break-even output is the level of sales required to cover all costs of production. ✓ At the break-even output revenue = costs. ✓ If sales are below the break-even output, then costs > revenue = loss. ✗ If sales are above the break-even output, then revenue > costs = profit. ✗ To calculate the break-even output a business needs to work out contribution. ✗

> **[2 marks]** While this is a full answer and well explained, there are only two marks available. This is wasting valuable time which often leads to the high mark questions at the end being briefly answered due to running out of time.

**4** Marisa, a keen skateboarder, is setting up her own business. She estimates that she can sell her skateboards for $80. She has also forecast the following costs for her first year of trading:
- Rent – $3000 per year
- Marketing – $400 per year
- Machine hire – $1500 per year
- Raw materials – $30 per skateboard
- Artwork – $10 per board

**(a)** Calculate the contribution per board. [3]

Contribution = selling price per unit – variable costs per unit ✓

= $80 – $30 ✗

= $50 ✓

> **[2 marks]** The formula is correct but the cost of artwork has not been included in the variable costs per unit so the final answer of $50 is incorrect. However, the **'own figure rule (OFR)'** means that the calculation has been applied correctly even though there is a mistake, so 2 marks are possible. This highlights the importance of always including formulae and step-by-step workings in answering calculation questions. If this answer just stated $50, no marks would be gained as the examiner cannot see how you got to the answer so cannot award marks for steps in the calculation. The answer should be $40.

**(b)** Calculate Marisa's break-even output. [3]

Break-even output = fixed costs ÷ contribution ✓

= $4900 ÷ $50 ✓

= 98 ✓

> **[3 marks]** This answer has used the incorrect contribution from the calculation in (a). The answer of 98 is wrong but full marks are awarded! The reason is the **OFR**. The calculation has been applied correctly and the mistake already cost 1 mark in the previous question and would not lose another mark **for one mistake. The correct answer, of course, is $4900 ÷ $40 = 122.5**

**(c)** Calculate Marisa's gross profit margin if she makes and sells 450 boards. [8]

Gross profit = Revenue – cost of sales ✓

Sales Revenue = 450 x $80 = $36 000 ✓

Cost of sales = $40 x 450 = $18 000 ✓

Gross profit = $36 000 – $18 000 ✓ = $18 000 ✓

Gross profit margin = (Gross profit ÷ sales revenue) X 100 ✓

= $18 000 ÷ $36 000 ✓

= 0.5 ✗

> **[7 marks]** There are several steps in carrying out this calculation. The answer has all the correct formulae and has identified the correct data. At the last step multiplying by 100 has not been carried out. However, 7/8 marks have been achieved for the correct calculations before this point. The correct answer is 50%.

**(d)** State two methods that Marisa can use to increase her gross profit margin. [5]

Marisa could increase her revenue from sales of her skateboards ✓ or reduce her expenses. ✗

> **[1 mark]** It is important to read the question carefully and consider the marks available. One knowledge mark can be gained by simply identifying factors affecting the gross profit. A change in revenue can impact gross profit but a change in expenses affects **profit** (make sure you know the difference between gross profit and profit). The other 4 marks are available for explaining two methods which can change the gross profit **margin**. Therefore, a better answer would have identified an increase in price whilst direct costs remain the same (or decrease) or a decrease in direct costs whilst price remains the same.

**Long answer question**

1  Evaluate the usefulness of ratio analysis of a business's financial information to its stakeholders. [12]

Ratio analysis is comparing one figure with another. ✓ The main ratios are profitability and liquidity ratios. ✓

> At this point, the candidate shows understanding of ratio analysis and has achieved the maximum marks available for Level 1. Therefore, no more knowledge marks are available.

Ratio analysis means that stakeholders (banks, employees, managers, etc.) can measure and compare changes in sales/profits/liquidity over time. ✓ Some stakeholders might want to compare businesses in the same sector, e.g. comparing two car producers. ✓

> At this point, Level 2 has been achieved as there is 'some explanation/application of ratio analysis to stakeholders'.

The owners are the most important stakeholders. In incorporated companies, such as Ltd and plc firms, the owners are the shareholders. Shareholders usually want high dividends and a high share price. Incorporated firms are required to publish their accounts each year. This would allow shareholders to use ratios, such as the gross profit ratio and profit ratio, to compare a company's performance over time. ✓

> At this point, Level 2 analysis has been achieved as there is now 'some analysis of the usefulness of ratio analysis to a stakeholders'. If the answer was to stop here, this would achieve 6 marks out of a possible 12.

If the analysis showed a declining trend in the profit ratios, a shareholder might be concerned that this would lead to lower dividends in the future, and might decide to sell the shares to invest in another company showing rising profitability. The shareholders might not be happy with the Board of directors and, therefore, not vote them back in at the next AGM. ✓

> At this point, good analysis, Level 3, is shown as evidenced by a chain of reasoning. The answer explains why profit ratios are important to a shareholder and then goes on to explain how this might affect shareholder actions towards the business.

Managers are another stakeholder group. As employees of the company they will want good salaries, job security and promotion. But also, managers might be blamed if things go wrong. Managers will use both profitability and liquidity ratios to help decide a course of action. For example, if the difference between the current ratio and the acid test ratio is quite high, then maybe the firm's inventory level is too high. They could then take action to reorganise the management of inventory, reduce the amount of cash tied up in it, and improve the acid test ratio.

> Another piece of good analysis, Level 3, is shown as evidenced by a chain of reasoning. Two good pieces of analysis will achieve the top Level 3 mark. It is important to realise that it is not the quantity of evidence; it is the quality of the evidence. Eight marks so far. Now it is time to evaluate, as all the knowledge, explanation and analysis marks have been achieved. The last four marks are for evaluation and judgement.

However, ratio analysis may be of limited value to some stakeholders whilst other stakeholders might have more information. Shareholders usually have to rely on published accounts. By the time they are published the accounts are historical. ✓

> Some simple evaluation, enough to take this answer into Level 4. Some further explanation of this point is required.

This means that the current financial information could be very different. Managers are more likely to have access to up-to-date information which will be more useful than historical data. ✔

> Further explanation of the previous point, as well as showing that ratio analysis might be more useful to some stakeholders than others, i.e. managers rather than shareholders.

Ratio analysis is useful to stakeholder groups but may have limitations. Businesses may 'window dress' the results to show the company in a favourable light. ✔ Financial accounts do not reflect the qualitative aspects of a business such as being a good employer, producing safe and reliable products, etc. Also, the published accounts may not detail the performance of individual parts of a company – especially a company producing many products. ✔

> Great conclusion. There is a developed argument regarding the usefulness of ratio analysis. Note that as the question is about 'usefulness' there is no need to give lengthy explanations or calculations of ratios.

## ❓ Exam-style questions

This section will allow you to practise writing answers for exam-style questions. Remember, it is useful to be aware of the mark schemes for the questions which can be found on relevant websites or from your teacher.

### Paper 1

#### Short answer questions

1  (a) Distinguish between 'internal' and 'external' sources of finance.  [2]

   (b) Briefly explain **one** liquidity ratio.  [3]

2  (a) Define the term 'cash flow'.  [2]

   (b) Briefly explain the term 'profitability'.  [3]

3  Explain why banks might be interested in a business's cash flow statement.  [5]

#### Long answer questions

4  Analyse **two** sources of finance available to a public limited company.  [8]

5  Evaluate the usefulness of break-even analysis to a sole trader.  [12]

6  Discuss the methods a manufacturer of farm machinery could employ to improve cash flow.  [20]

## Key topics

➤ business structure

➤ size of business

➤ external influences on business activity.

### 6.1 Business structure

This topic is concerned with:

➤ local, national and multinational businesses

➤ multinationals

➤ privatisation.

### Local, national and multinational businesses

Although candidates should know the different classifications from the AS syllabus, candidates may now be examined on the definitions and effects different sizes of businesses may have.

**X Common error**

Many candidates mistake a public organisation such as the government water board for a public limited company. This may lose marks as the candidate's answer may not have a suitable example.

| Local | National | Multinational |
|---|---|---|
| Family businesses, cooperatives | Chains located in more than one area/region | Groups of businesses under one overall name in many countries |
| Sole traders; Partnerships; Ltd companies | plc's | plc's |

▲ **Figure 6.1** Main differences between local, national and multinational businesses

**✓ What you need to know**

There are many reasons for the growing importance of international trading links, however, you must focus on a limited number and explain them fully, rather than listing and explaining each to a basic level.

**Key terms**

**Local business**: a business which provides goods and/or services to a limited and specific area of one country. It could be a village or town depending on the business.

**National business**: a business that provides goods or services to many different regions of one country.

**Multinational business**: a business that has its headquarters in one country but operates in at least one country other than its home.

**💡 Remember**

Candidates may be expected to give examples of national and multinational businesses to support their answers – do not try to be clever, stick with well-known businesses.

▼ **Table 6.1** The growing importance of international trading links and their impact on business activity

| Reason 1: | Increase in international trade agreements. |
|---|---|
| Importance: | Increases state security and national interests such as access to raw materials and up to date knowledge and technology. |
| Consequence: | Increased GDP and standard of living for citizens. |
| Impact on business activity: | Increased access to raw materials and cheaper labour. |
| | Increased cost savings due to state incentives such as tax breaks and lower cost of production. |

| Reason 2: | Reductions in trade barriers. |
|---|---|
| Importance: | Increases reciprocal trade and the flow of foreign products and services without the need for direct government financial intervention. |
| Consequence: | Increased GDP and access to foreign and luxury goods and services. |
| Impact on business activity: | Increase in new markets and customer base, leading to increased demand and production levels. |

## Multinationals

Many governments try to attract multinational businesses to set up production facilities in their countries. Although there are many benefits for the host country, there are also many disadvantages.

▼ **Table 6.2** Benefits and disadvantages that a multinational might bring to a country and possible relationships between multinationals and the state

| Benefits a multinational might bring to a host country: | |
|---|---|
| Availability of products and services that cannot currently be produced. | Increases the satisfaction of citizens that can cause a stable government. |
| Knowledge, expertise and training brought into the country. | Increases the skill level of the country that can lead to independent innovation. |
| Investment and creation of jobs. | Increases the level of purchasing power in a country which increases the living standards. |
| **Disadvantages a multinational might bring to a host country:** | |
| Local industries undercut and overwhelmed. | Can cause a lack of national output and reliance on a limited number of multinational employers. |
| Multinationals can exert undue power over a host country. | Can lobby governments for favourable tax/legal/environmental/breaks which are damaging for the host country. |
| Decreases competition and increases monopolies. | May lead to a reliance on a single business which can lead to an increase in prices and decrease in quality. |
| Skilled employees and management may be brought from home countries. | The jobs created may be unskilled/low level which limits the social advantages and creates resentment and/or cultural problems. |

## Worked example

Analyse the benefits of SG entering a joint venture with a multinational business (NRG Autos).                                      [10 marks]

 **Link**

Refer to Case study 3: Sohail's Garage in Unit 14.

### Answer

If SG enters a joint venture with NRG, then the new company will benefit from the expertise of both companies, ✓ while each company keeps its original business separate from the other. ✓ As SG is only national, they may also benefit from NRG as they may be bringing cars with technology which is new to the country ✓ and may have a global brand image which may help boost desirability. ✓

*At this point, the candidate has 4 out of 10 marks without any analysis. The candidate must now focus on analysis to gain additional marks and will more than likely pick up the additional application mark organically.*

As SG only has experience of selling used vehicles, their reputation for quality ✓ may not be sufficient for them to start selling more profitable premium cars. ✓ Therefore, the merger with a recognised multinational brand such as NRG may allow SG to create a new business venture ✓ highlighting the established customer service and trust of SG, and the brand awareness of a much larger brand which is renowned for its premium products worldwide. ✓

This merging of the best elements of each business would then create a customer-focused package that would target a new market for both businesses and would expose each business to less risk and a quicker route to market. ✓ ✓

**X** Common error

Many candidates read questions such as these incorrectly and may formulate an answer which, while correct, focuses on the incorrect point of view.

## Privatisation

### Advantages and disadvantages of privatisation in a given situation

While there are very few instances of nationalisation, limited to when businesses with national importance, such as banks, are failing, privatisation is much more likely within the current global economy.

There are a number of advantages and disadvantages that a candidate may be expected to show knowledge of and apply to a given situation:

**Key terms**

Nationalisation: the process of converting a private sector business into a public corporation.

Privatisation: the process of converting a public corporation (owned and managed by the government) into a private sector business, usually a plc due to the size of the business.

**Remember**

Privatisation and nationalisation is usually a political decision and depends on the political views of the ruling party.

### Advantages

- Less regulation and market forces can reduce overheads.
- Freedom to diversify and introduce new products which may be luxury rather than necessity goods and services.
- Greater freedom for investment into machinery which may not be financially viable for a government.
- Greater competition and a downward pressure on prices.

### Disadvantages

- The process can be expensive and may lead to accusations of favouritism and a lack of opportunity for all.
- Loss making services such as found in rural districts may be reduced/withdrawn.
- Natural monopolies may occur and may have a negative influence on the population and the economy.

▲ **Figure 6.2** Advantages and disadvantages of privatisation

## 6.2 Size of business

This topic is concerned with:

➤ external growth.

### External growth

The AS module focuses on the internal methods a small business may use to grow that are usually limited and rely on the business owner's ability to generate capital in a slow and orderly fashion. The A Level module, however, focuses on the ability of a business to generate capital quickly and via external means.

### The different types of merger and takeover

A business can grow quickly via two main methods: by merging with another business, often a competitor, supplier or customer; or by taking over another business. A takeover can be hostile or friendly.

> **✗ Common error**
>
> Many candidates confuse the terms merger and takeover, and take them to mean the same thing; this is not true and must be avoided. A merger is when there is equality between the two businesses, while in a takeover there is a dominant partner.

| Merger | Hostile takeover | Friendly takeover |
|---|---|---|
| Mutual benefits/agreements between Business A and B. | Business A assumes control of Business B without consent. | There is agreement for Business A to buy Business B between both parties. |
| Both businesses contribute their resources without much financial input. | Occurs by the purchasing of shares and can be costly. | While costly, there may be better staff relationships. |
| There is now only one legal entity. | The businesses may remain separate entities. | The businesses may remain separate entities. |

▲ **Figure 6.3** Differences between merger, hostile takeover and friendly takeover

**Key terms**

**External growth**: the growth of a business by buying or acquiring other businesses instead of relying on its own operations.

**Merger**: when two or more businesses agree to combine into a single business entity, rather than remaining two separately owned businesses; usually to achieve greater business efficiencies.

**Takeover**: when one business acquires the ownership of another company by purchasing a majority stake through the purchase of shares.

**Hostile takeover**: a business being taken over without consent who wants to remain independent.

**Friendly takeover**: a business taken over with the agreement of both parties.

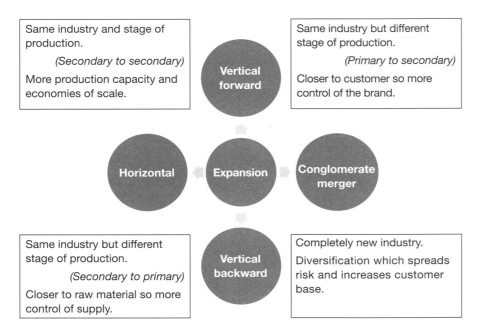

**Vertical forward**
Same industry and stage of production.
*(Secondary to secondary)*
More production capacity and economies of scale.

Same industry but different stage of production.
*(Primary to secondary)*
Closer to customer so more control of the brand.

**Horizontal** — **Expansion** — **Conglomerate merger**

Same industry but different stage of production.
*(Secondary to primary)*
Closer to raw material so more control of supply.

**Vertical backward**

Completely new industry.
Diversification which spreads risk and increases customer base.

▲ **Figure 6.4** Impact of a merger/takeover on the various stakeholders

Each stakeholder in the business will be affected in a different way; impacts may be both positive and negative.

▼ **Table 6.3** Positive and negative impacts on stakeholders

| Stakeholder | Positive | Negative |
|---|---|---|
| **Customer/ consumer** | • Cheaper prices due to economies of scale.<br>• Closer relationship with customers. | • Customer choice may be reduced.<br>• Monopolies may occur limiting innovation. |
| **Employee** | • New opportunities for training and promotion.<br>• Access to new work practices and ideas. | • Reduced job security as redundancies may occur.<br>• Changes in work practices may cause dissatisfaction. |
| **Shareholder** | • Increased economies of scale increase profits.<br>• Greater share of the market increases the customer base. | • Diluted share ownership.<br>• Increased risk of investing in a business in flux. |
| **Government** | • Increased investment into key/growing industries. | • Reduced employment increases welfare payments.<br>• Increased (monopolistic) power of individual businesses. |
| **Competition** | • Less competition leads to more focused marketing.<br>• Streamlined product portfolios with less diverse options. | • Increased strength of single competitor.<br>• Larger competitor may have a larger brand presence and investment into product development. |
| **Suppliers** | • Larger orders due to the increased business size.<br>• Less capital expenditure on administration due to simpler buying channels. | • More risk of losing customer to competitor.<br>• Increased customer power reduces unit prices reducing unit profits. |

## Worked example

Recommend to Sohail which of the three existing divisional managers he should promote to manage the new joint venture if this is chosen.    [16 marks]

Refer to Case study 3: Sohail's Garage in Unit 14.

### Answer

Umar is an autocratic leader who seems to follow McGregor's Theory X view of workers, which is that they do not like working and need to have close supervision. Steven is a democratic leader who believes that McGregor's Theory Y style of including employees is more productive, while Sara is very laissez-faire and trusts her employees. ✓✓✓✓

As the joint venture is working with a multinational company that might have a different working culture, it is important to promote the right person. While Umar's style of leadership would ensure that there was tight control of the new venture and has got consistently good results working in PVS, he might seem to be too direct and rude to the employees from NRG Autos. They would more than likely be senior or experienced, as NRG would want the new venture to have the best chance of succeeding. This means that an autocratic leadership style might annoy others and cause the business to have a bad morale problem. ✓✓✓

Sara, on the other hand, might also not be able to control a new business, as her team of sales people must be highly specialised in their industry to be able to recommend the correct products, and can therefore be trusted. She also has a very small team, which means that managing them isn't as difficult as a large team such as Umar's team.

Steven, however, has proved that he can take a new department and build it into a successful business. He is respected by his team who feel included and responsible, although Steven has the final responsibility for all decisions and has shown he can manage a large team effectively. This may be useful when managing a larger team of people from two different organisations and might help to integrate the two styles of working. ✓✓✓✓

I would therefore recommend Steven as the most suitable manager for the joint venture ✓ (although this is a decision, only one mark is awarded as there is no judgement) because he is most likely to be able to manage the two different organisational cultures and as the new business would be targeting higher value customers, would need to have motivated and happy staff who knew their roles and responsibilities and would feel a part of the new organisation, while Umar may demotivate staff and Sara might not give enough direction, therefore the new business wouldn't have a clear objective. ✓✓✓

## Why a merger/takeover may or may not achieve objectives

To answer a question based on mergers and takeovers it is necessary to identify the objectives a business may have for the merger or takeover. One of the main reasons for a merger is to achieve the objective of **synergy**, however, this may not always happen; some main reasons for failure to achieve objectives are listed in Figure 6.5.

**Key term**

**Synergy**: combining two businesses to lead to a benefit/benefits greater than the sum of the two parts.

| Compatibility and culture | • Are the moral and ethical views similar?<br>• Are organisational cultures integrated and exploited? |
| --- | --- |
| Focus on objectives | • Are core strengths and competencies protected?<br>• Identification and implementation of organisational change. |
| Workforce dissatisfaction | • Are the needs of the workforce identified and considered?<br>• Is the workforce informed and consulted on the change process? |
| Customer acceptance | • Do the new brand values meet customer expectations?<br>• Does the company identify and minimise any impacts on the customer? |
| Exploitation of opportunities | • Are opportunities quickly identified and exploited efficiently?<br>• Is there a professional approach from management towards progress? |

▲ **Figure 6.5** Why a merger may not achieve objectives

### The importance of joint ventures and strategic alliances as methods of external growth

Often businesses will identify common areas of interest with competitors or businesses with similar objectives. While there is an opportunity to gain synergies through working together, both businesses may lose brand appeal or lose focus through a merger. For this reason, businesses may enter into joint ventures or strategic alliances to work together for a project or business venture.

Some key reasons why joint ventures and strategic alliances are important for external growth are:

➤ Cost and risk of investment are shared – lower risk of business failure in the event of product failure.

➤ Exploitation of key strengths – each business will have a strength which complements the other and the final product is more valuable than the sum of the two parts.

➤ Protection of the overall brand – a joint venture may minimise the parent companies' risk of brand failure.

➤ Incompatible management styles – minimises the risk of organisational failure due to the businesses focusing only on their areas of expertise.

## 6.3 External influences on business activity

This topic covers:

➤ political and legal influences

➤ economic constraints and enablers

➤ social

➤ technological (including the internet)

➤ other businesses

➤ demographic

➤ environmental factors.

**Remember**

Candidates must always identify whether the case refers to a merger or a hostile or friendly takeover, as this will greatly affect the chances of success.

**Key terms**

**Joint venture**: a business agreement between two or more organisations who develop a new business but retain their own separate identities.

**Strategic alliance**: agreements between organisations to commit resources to achieve agreed, common objectives.

**Remember**

Even though they are similar, joint ventures and strategic alliances are different and have their own uses. Candidates must choose the most appropriate from the two options if asked.

## Political and legal influences

### How a government might use the law to seek to control business activity

Governments seek to control business activity to manage the economy. If the economy is strong, then governments will have the finances available to look after other aspects of the country.

Each country has its own specific laws and regulations; however, most countries will have laws to protect the following:

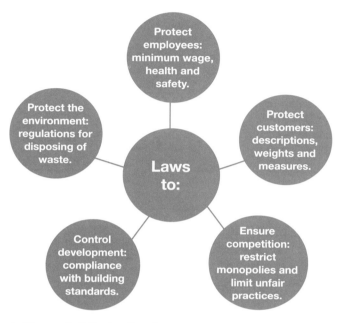

▲ **Figure 6.6** Protection laws

### How international agreements might have an impact on businesses

There are many international agreements on trade, such as the WTO and GATT, environmental agreements such as the Kyoto agreements in addition to trading standards such as the ISO regulations and many more. They have different impacts in businesses.

▼ **Table 6.4** The impact of international agreements on business

| International agreement | Positive impact | Negative impact |
|---|---|---|
| Carbon emissions | More energy efficiency which reduces costs. | Increases cost of alternative methods of energy production. |
| International trading opportunities | Larger markets across the world leads to larger revenue streams. | Increased competition from multinational businesses. |
| Accounting standards | Allows for comparison of accounting records globally. | Interpretation may vary between countries and may not reflect local practices. |
| Labour issues | Increases the mental and physical safety of employees which increases motivation. | Increases the cost associated with health and safety and other labour issues. |

## Economic constraints and enablers

Another way in which multinational businesses are affected is by the economic constraints often imposed by governments and trade organisations in addition to natural competition.

This section will mainly focus on the state's influence on business economic activity.

**Remember**

It is not necessary to have detailed knowledge of law for the Business A Level, however, it would be useful to be able to describe some key laws and what they are used for.

X **Common error**

Candidates often see laws only as a constraint, however, laws can also be a benefit as they can stop businesses from making poor products with disastrous consequences.

✓ **What you need to know**

Each individual agreement will have both positive and negative impacts and they may vary according to the size of the business and their individual objectives. The candidate must focus on one argument and ensure the argument is relevant for the business or industry highlighted.

## How the state might intervene to help and constrain businesses (small and large)

The state has many influences on business and might intervene based on the objectives of the government at that time. Ways the state might intervene include:

▼ **Table 6.5** How the state might intervene to help and constrain businesses

| Methods of intervention | Helpfulness | Constraints |
|---|---|---|
| Taxation | Can be lowered to increase investment and profitability. Tax breaks can be offered for start-up businesses. | Can be used to constrain the sales of demerit goods or services. Can be used to limit inflationary business practices. |
| Laws including environmental, employee and consumer protection | Can be relaxed to within international constraints to give an advantage to key industries. | Minimum standards increase business costs which can decrease productivity and profit. |
| Information support | Organisations to enable start-up advice, growth and export. | May be difficult to access or may be too generic for all industries. |
| Grants and subsidies | Direct financial support to essential services or key industries with poor initial cash-flow. | Strict rules and regulations to the awarding of grants and subsidies, may exclude smaller businesses with less experience. |
| Awarding government contracts | Capital investment into infrastructure projects awarded to 'local' businesses. | Often require long term investment and strict adherence to profit reducing regulations. |

## How the state might deal with market failure

**Market failure** has many negative outcomes that governments may try to minimise depending on the government in power. Some outcomes of market failure may be:

➤ increased unemployment

➤ decreased tax revenues

➤ reduction in essential good and/or services.

▼ **Table 6.6** Methods the state may use depending on the issue and their objectives

| Market failure | Solution | Possible consequences |
|---|---|---|
| Fluctuating prices | Set quotas. Increase/reduce taxation. | + reduced volatility<br>– increased speculation<br>– reduction of suppliers if costs rise/profits fall |
| Shortage of appropriate labour | Increase training opportunities/grants for training. Offer favourable packages for skilled immigrants. | + long term increase in skilled labour pool<br>– short term fix only<br>– may cause social unrest due to changing demographics |
| Shortages of goods/services | Import products/services from abroad. Reduce laws or restrictive economic barriers. | + reassured customer and businesses<br>– long term issues due to reduction of domestic produce |
| Market dominance (monopoly power) | Legislation and regulation of monopoly power. Restriction of takeovers/mergers. | + more consumer choice<br>– businesses may relocate to states with less restrictions<br>– reduction in business investment |
| Extreme market failure | Businesses taken into state ownership. | + short term stability and confidence<br>– shareholders lose investment and financial costs of support |
| Inefficiency | Reduction in laws, control and regulation to minimise costs. | + increased productivity and profitability<br>– longer term problems associated with deregulation and business self-regulation |

## The key macroeconomic objectives of governments

Although governments have many **macroeconomic objectives**, the main objectives include:

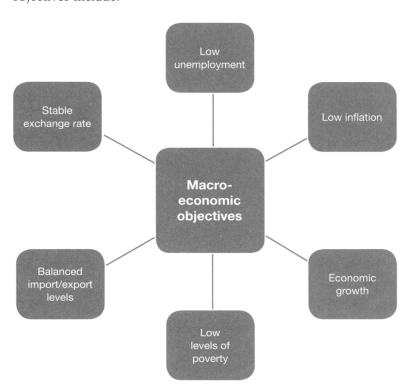

▲ **Figure 6.7** The key macroeconomic objectives of governments

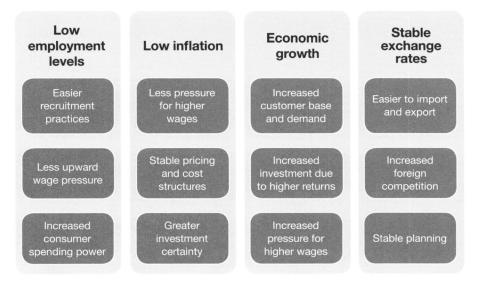

▲ **Figure 6.8** How these macroeconomic objectives can have an impact on business activity

## How a government might place a different emphasis on macroeconomic objectives from time to time

Depending on the most important macroeconomic objective at a particular point, the government may put emphasis on objectives in the following ways:

➤ reducing or increasing corporation taxes or **VAT/GST** – reduces or increases the selling prices and demand, which may influence the rate of inflation and also economic growth

> reducing or increasing government regulations – restricts or enables businesses, such as reducing labour laws may increase employment therefore reaching the macroeconomic objective of increasing employment levels

> joining/leaving trading blocks – can increase the ability of the country to meet international markets and increase exports and possibly decrease imports.

## Policy instruments used to achieve macroeconomic objectives

Governments have a number of policy instruments they may use to achieve their objectives. Candidates will be expected to identify the most appropriate instrument and justify the reason for their choice.

> Fiscal policies – altering the amount and rate of government spending and taxation.

> Monetary policies – alter interest rates and restrict the ability to lend money by financial institutions.

> Exchange rate policies – altering interest rates can affect the value of a currency in relation to another. Governments can also link their currency to a stronger currency, i.e. the US Dollar.

> **Remember**
>
> Fiscal policy relates to the supply of money and can be directly managed, while monetary policy can only influence the demand for money.

> **X Common error**
>
> Candidates often have generic ideas regarding the effects of policies on business. Every business and business sector will react and be affected in a different manner to a specific economic condition depending on their objectives and their most important external influences.

> **X Common error**
>
> Candidates who misread a question about low unemployment levels may well answer the wrong question and severely limit their marks.

> **Key terms**
>
> **Policy instrument**: a way in which government can manage the macro-economy: fiscal, monetary and exchange rate policies.
>
> **Fiscal policy**: the management of spending levels and tax rates to influence an economy – influences the supply of money.
>
> **Monetary policy**: the management of money supply and interest rates – influences the demand for money.
>
> **Exchange rate policy**: the management of a currency in relation to other currencies. Closely related to monetary policy and is dependent on similar factors.

▼ **Table 6.7** How changes in macroeconomic performance and policies may affect business behaviour

|  | ME performance | ME policy | Possible impact on a business | Possible business response |
|---|---|---|---|---|
| **Fiscal** | High inflation levels. | Increase VAT/sales tax. | Reduction of demand due to increased selling price. | Seek new markets. Reduce cost of production. |
|  | Low employment. | Increase spending on training opportunities. | Increase in trained employees and less direct training expenditure. | Employ more staff. Utilise government training schemes to upskill existing staff. |
| **Monetary** | High inflation levels. | Increase interest rates. | Increased cost of borrowing will limit investment and expansion. | Cut back on borrowing. Repay existing loans. Increase innovation. |

## Social

In many countries social aspects are very important. It is important for all countries who wish to export products that they are aware of the social and ethical values of their customers.

▲ **Figure 6.9** The impact of, and issues associated with, corporate social responsibility (CSR)

The impact of issues related to CSR is increasing due to the increased access of communications technology and the desire of customers to provide a 'fair' standard of living to the workers who produce their goods and services. Impacts on business could include:

➤ increased costs due to social auditing

➤ transparency of accounts due to social scrutiny

➤ the promotion of women and ethnic minorities to positions of power.

Pressure groups are able to create negative publicity for businesses, especially if the needs of the community are not met. There are many examples of businesses altering their impact on the community due to widespread negative publicity.

### Technological (including the internet)

Technology is influencing businesses in many ways and it is difficult to escape the effect of modern technology.

▲ **Figure 6.10** Problems of introducing technological change

**Key terms**

Corporate social responsibility (CSR): a business approach that contributes to sustainable development of economic, social and environmental benefits for all stakeholders.

Social auditing: a business approach that reviews and accounts for the impact of its operations on society and the environment.

Pressure group: a group that tries to influence public policy on behalf of a particular cause.

**X Common error**

Many candidates fail to identify important social issues and focus only on economic issues. Some business practices may be illegal in some countries (such as discrimination or paying a wage lower than the minimum wage), as well as being against social and ethical considerations.

**💡 Remember**

Technological change affects different stakeholders in different ways, and what may be a benefit for one stakeholder will be a disadvantage for another.

## Other businesses

No business works in a vacuum and must take into consideration other competing businesses as well as suppliers of their raw materials.

▼ **Table 6.8** How businesses are constrained by and rely on other businesses

| Suppliers | May only be able to provide a limited quantity of products and prices may be affected by market conditions, e.g. scarcity. |
|---|---|
| Business customers | May have particular demands which increases costs and time of production and quality of product. |
| Financial institutions | May place restrictions on the amount and uses of the finance offered. |

## Demographic

**Demography** is the way in which the population is made up in terms of age, gender, sex, religion or race. These distinguishing features are influenced through births, deaths, migration and social change.

### How a business might react to a given demographic change

Below are some of the main influences that may cause businesses to react.

▼ **Table 6.9** How a business might react to a given demographic change

| Demographic change | Impact | Reaction |
|---|---|---|
| Increasing age of population | Change in focus from fashionable to family related products. | Changing product line to focus on quality and practicality. |
| Increasing role of women in the workforce | Increased need for flexible working and maternity leave. | Greater product focus on female market with disposable income. |
| Increase in multiculturalism | Change in demand for food, fashion styles and working patterns. Increased workforce with lower (or higher) financial expectations. | Change in the product line to reflect the multicultural mix of the population and a change in workforce remuneration and conditions. |

## Environmental factors

There are many factors which can cause environmental issues, from governmental regulations to pressure groups. These must be taken into account when considering the future outcomes of the business.

| Governmental | • Sets laws regulating disposal of waste and use of natural materials.<br>• Can impose fines and restrictions on those who ignore laws. |
|---|---|
| Pressure groups | • Highlights positive and negative ethical and social issues that can influence customer behaviour.<br>• Can be used for marketing and promotional activities if positively reviewed. |
| International targets | • Targets such as carbon emissions can affect the use of polluting methods of power generation.<br>• Increases the manufacturing costs. |

▲ **Figure 6.11** How environmental issues influence business behaviour

**Key term**

**Demographic change:** describing the changes in the makeup of the population of a region or a country.

**X Common error**

Candidates may identify demographic changes but then use cultural stereotypes which negates the understanding of the issue and the likely effects, such as 'women like cooking, so will need to change the style of cooking pans'. This is a business exam so must therefore focus on the changing impact of women on business.

**X Common error**

Candidates often categorise pressure groups as negative influences which hinder business activity, however, they can also have positive impacts by promoting businesses that are ethically and environmentally concerned.

## Worked example

Discuss the extent to which external factors such as those shown in Table 3 in the case study could influence the future success of SG. [18 marks]

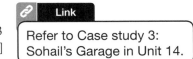

**Link**

Refer to Case study 3: Sohail's Garage in Unit 14.

### Answer

SG is a motor sales company that is planning to expand its business. There are many external factors that could influence the success of SG, however, I believe that the most important are the change in annual salary, the interest rates within the country and the exchange rate index. ✓

As SG is planning on investing into a joint venture with a multinational business or expanding through a takeover, interest rates will be very important. If SG takes over PPL Garages, then they will have to arrange finance, possibly through a large bank loan of up to $100m in order to complete the takeover. This would mean that a stable interest rate (a rate that doesn't change) would allow SG to plan effectively and be confident in their ability to pay the interest and repayments. ✓✓

If SG enters into the joint venture, then their customers are likely to be aspirational customers who are buying luxury cars. Therefore, the change in annual salary within country X means that although people's incomes are increasing, people are likely to need to borrow money from financial institutions to buy new luxury cars and therefore interest rates will be important as their customers will be happy to borrow what they feel is affordable. ✓✓ SG will also have a competitive edge as their currency is relatively strong in comparison to other countries which means that the imported cars are going to be more affordable for residents of country A.

However, it is also important to take into account the government's objectives. As GDP is positive and within a similar range to current interest rates and salary rises, then the external factors identified are favourable to SG Motors as they are constantly and steadily improving. ✓✓✓

Therefore, the external factors are likely to be very important and will have a positive influence on the future of SG, as not only do the constant interest rates allow for accurate budgeting for both SG and its potential customers, but the currency index is also a positive factor when importing cars from NRG. This is likely to either reduce the selling price of the cars, making them more affordable, or will allow for a higher gross profit margin which will allow for earlier repayment of loans. ✓✓✓✓

However, these external factors are only one aspect of the success of the organisation, and internal factors such as choosing the correct manager and the success of the joining of two business cultures will also be critical for the success of the business. ✓✓✓✓✓

## Revision checklist

### I can:

➤ discuss how the state may help and constrain businesses ☐

➤ explain market failure ☐

➤ discuss the impact of macroeconomic objectives on business activity ☐

➤ explain how CSR influences business activities and objectives ☐

➤ discuss why the needs of the community need to be considered ☐

➤ explain the ways in which macroeconomic objectives are achieved ☐

➤ discuss how businesses could respond to demographic change ☐

➤ discuss how environmental issues influence business behaviour ☐

**Raise your grade**

Each of these questions will rely on the exemplar case study and the case study will need to be utilised to score more than a passing grade.

🔗 **Link**

These questions refer to Case study 3: Sohail's Garage in Unit 14.

## Paper 3

1    Analyse the likely impact of a weakening exchange rate in country A.    [10 marks]

SG is a private limited company that is looking to enter a joint venture with NRG, a multinational plc which will import cars into country A that SG will sell on their behalf. A joint venture is when two companies set up a new business and each invest their own specific skills but keep the original businesses separate. This means that both businesses keep their core businesses separate which is a good idea if you want to retain control of your business. A plc is a company that is owned by shareholders and is traded publicly on the stock market. Anyone can buy the shares and will hopefully get a return on their investment. Exchange rate means the value of one currency in relation to another. If the value of the currency in the home country is weak, this means that exports will be cheaper for foreign markets to purchase. If the home currency is strong, this means that it is cheap to buy imports, but harder to export. ✓✓✓

> At this point, the candidate has described every element that has been identified in the question, and got full marks for the knowledge section. However, this has wasted a lot of time and the amount of information given for three marks is not worth the time spent. Remember, this is an A Level paper and therefore knowledge is the least awarded skill.
>
> The candidate has not mentioned the case study once so there is no application to the case study. The first sentence is a repetition of the case study and not linked to the answer, therefore an easy mark has been missed.

Because NRG is a multinational company and is considering importing cars in a joint venture with SG, a weakening exchange rate would make the cost of importing NRG's cars more expensive for the citizens of country A to buy, which may reduce demand for premium cars as people focus more on needs than wants so may be more likely to purchase second-hand cars which will not be directly affected by the change in interest rates. ✓

However, SG and NRG are planning on importing premium cars, so potential customers might not be so price conscious and may be more influenced by the luxury aspect of owning an expensive imported car and may see the ability to purchase as a status symbol, which means that demand for premium cars may not alter significantly. There are also other factors such as the level of profit that NRG may be aiming to make per unit, which means that NRG may sell cars with low profit margins just to gain an initial market share which would negate the effects of the weakening exchange rate. ✓✓✓✓

> At this point, the candidate applied the case study effectively by highlighting relevant aspects to the question. The candidate has also earnt the maximum analysis marks through identifying a relevant point and analysing the potential effects, both positively and negatively. Note that only one factor, the changing cost of the car, has been analysed. This is all that is needed as it effectively provides the answer to the question. The last internal factor is ensuring a balanced, reasoned argument is present.

**2** Recommend to SG whether he should invest in the joint venture or the merger. [12 marks]

If SG invests into option A, then his payback period is 1 year and 5 months, which is 10 months faster than option B which will take 2 years and 3 months. However, the net present value for option A is only $442m, while the NPV for option B is $680m, which is over 50% greater. ✓✓✓✓

> The candidate has identified two relevant influences using relevant points, clearly applying data in both instances, and has then compared the results and made some use of theory to answer the question, analysing the difference in payback and NPV. Candidates often get these marks and then spend a long time further analysing different points, which is wasted time as no further marks are available. The candidate must focus on these two points and analyse them well.

If SG is risk averse and would rather pay off the money he would need to borrow to finance further expansion, then option A would be most suitable as the joint venture would start making a profit sooner than option B, which would be in a riskier financial position for a much longer time, and if interest rates went up could cost him more money in the long run in interest payments. However, in the 5 years calculated, option B would earn over 50% more profit than option A which would be the preferable option for stakeholders as the return on their investment would potentially be 50% more. ✓✓✓✓

> The candidate has now achieved all of the available marks for knowledge, application and analysis. The only marks that need to be achieved now are evaluation marks.

I would recommend that SG should invest in the merger with PPL, as although the payback is longer and the risk is higher, the rewards of a predicted 50% higher profit yield would make the investment more attractive, and would also be in a tried and tested market that SG is comfortable in and would be more likely to make a success, especially as there are less variables such as building relationships with multinational businesses who may try to interfere with SG's current winning formula ✓✓✓✓.

> Evaluations do not need to be long for a 12-mark question as only 4 marks are available, however they do need to be structured well to show good judgement, buy using command words such as 'however' and 'although' as well as a clear answer to the question.

**3** Discuss the extent to which external factors, such as shown in Table 3 in the case study, could influence the future success of SG. [16 marks]

There are two types of factors; internal and external factors. Internal factors are those that a business can control and affect and can manipulate to affect their own business performance. Examples of internal factors are salary levels, levels of training and management styles. SG has three different management styles in each of its three departments; an autocratic, democratic and laissez-faire. The advantages of these are... ✓✓

> While all of the information above is true, the candidate is going to waste a lot of time and get no marks. The question asks about 'external factors' and the paragraph above is not answering the question. This common mistake happens due to a lack of planning. A candidate will stray off the question and keep on writing without checking the question is answered. The above is irrelevant, a better beginning is shown below.

External factors, such as interest rates and inflation rates ✓✓ could influence the future success of SG due to their expansion plans which would probably require external investment from a financial institution. This means that interest rates would have to be considered and on a loan of at least $100m would be considerable. Inflation, which is at a low rate of 1.5%, means that the NPV of the loan would also need to be calculated to ensure the return is viable over the 5-year investment period. ✓✓✓

> The statement above meets all of the requirements of the knowledge and application marks. There is now no need to spend any more time explicitly identifying or applying data to the answer. There is also some use of argument to explain the influence of external factors, however these need to be developed.

If SG chooses to takeover PPL, then they will have to find investment of $600m. As they made a gross profit of around $80m in 2016, then they would have to find external investment from either selling shares through private investors, or gaining a loan from a financial institution. This could cause SG to have high interest payments which could minimise profit, so it is very important that interest rates are stable and inflation remains low so they are able to plan effectively and ensure the stability of the business.

However, other factors such as the gradual increase in annual salary could also influence the future success. As people have more disposable income, they may prefer to buy newer cars, which SG would not be concentrating on, which may change the long-term objectives of SG. ✓✓✓✓

> The statement above shows good use of reasoned argument to explain the influence of external factors, which means that an L2 answer has been achieved. As all the marks for analysis have been achieved, then all is needed is the evaluation.

Using the information above, I believe that external factors such as the interest rate and the inflation rate would be very significant in influencing the future success of SG, as the biggest risk for SG at this time is the financial investment. The SG group will need to also consider their overheads and consolidate all of their businesses to reduce overheads where possible, which is an internal factor which will reduce the risk.

Another internal factor that is important is that with either choice there will be significant internal issues such as the integration of two business cultures that could influence the future success.

Therefore, even though external factors are very important and need to be carefully monitored, SG will need to choose the best manager to take control to minimise internal issues to focus on meeting financial commitments that could force the business to close ✓✓✓✓✓.

> The evaluation makes a judgement to the extent to which external factors would influence the future success of SG, which is supported by evidence from the case study. There is also mention of internal factors that are important in determining the future success that balances the importance of focussing only on external factors.

**Exam-style questions**

This section will allow you to practise writing answers for exam-style questions. Remember, it is useful to be aware of the mark schemes for the questions which can be found on relevant websites or from your teacher.

On Paper 3, the only short answer questions are related to financial questions. Therefore, all exam-style questions for this unit are worth 10 marks and above.

> **🔗 Link**
>
> These questions refer to Case study 3: Sohail's Garage in Unit 14.

**Paper 3**

1 Analyse the benefits for SG of choosing to enter a joint venture with a multinational such as NRG. [10]

2 Analyse the likely impact of a change in exchange rates for SG. [10]

3 Using financial results from calculating Net Present Value and payback, recommend to the Board of Directors which option should be chosen by SG. Justify your answer. [12]

4 Evaluate the extent to which external influences should influence the activities of SG. [16]

## Key topics

➤ human resource management

➤ organisational structure

➤ business communication.

## 7.1 Human resource management

This topic is concerned with:

➤ approaches to HRM

➤ labour legislation

➤ cooperation between management and workforce

➤ workforce planning

➤ role of trade unions in HRM.

### Approaches to HRM

Candidates should be aware of the two main ways in which businesses approach their human resources: 'hard' HRM and 'soft' HRM. Human resource management is an important issue and is often linked to business strategy.

| Hard HRM | Soft HRM |
|---|---|
| Employees are resources to be used | Humanistic approach |
| No difference between machinery and premises | Individuals rather than groups of workers |
| Trained, recruited and dismissed according to business needs | Appraisal used to identify training and development for employee benefit |
| Close monitoring and supervision leads to high productivity and achievement of targets | A trained and happy employee leads to productivity and loyalty |
| No emotion or consultation | Emotional links lead to feelings of fairness |

▲ **Figure 7.1** The difference between 'hard' and 'soft' HRM

### Flexibility

Regardless of which method of HRM is used, businesses need to have a flexible workforce. There are three main types of contracts businesses will use to ensure they can meet their organisational needs:

> **Key terms**
>
> **Hard HRM**: the treatment of employees as homogenous groups of resources to be used in achieving business objectives.
>
> **Soft HRM**: the treatment of employees as individuals, with priority given to individual development.

> **X Common error**
>
> Many candidates mistake a soft approach to HRM as being less strict – this is not true, there are still rules and regulations, however, the approach to development and trust is different.

> **💡 Remember**
>
> There are opportunities to bring in management theories such as McGregor's Theory of X and Y that can strengthen the arguments and analysis offered.

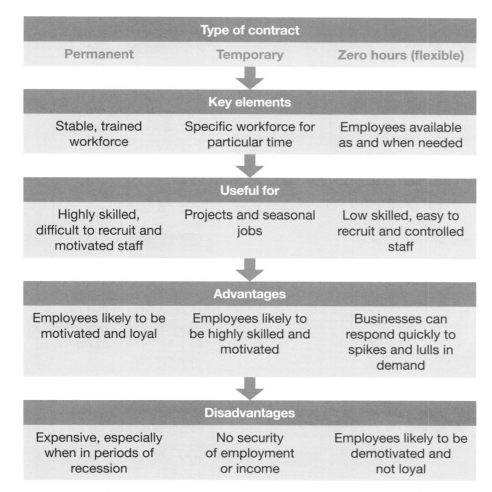

▲ **Figure 7.2** Main types of contracts to ensure organisational needs are met

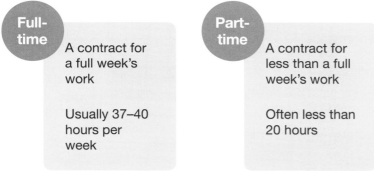

▲ **Figure 7.3** Differences between full- and part-time contracts

### The measurement of employee performance

**Staff appraisal** is a vital tool that businesses use to ensure organisational objectives are met.

Different methods of measuring employee performance are:

➤ Planned interviews – discussion with managers regarding targets, training or other issues.

➤ Observation – managers observe employees and measure against pre-set targets and benchmarks.

➤ Productivity – similar to observation, however, the rate of work output is measured against pre-set targets.

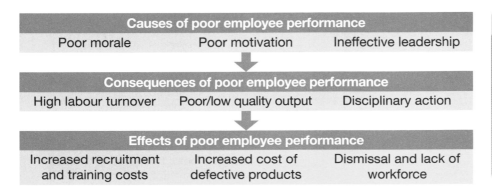

▲ **Figure 7.4** The causes and consequences of poor employee performance

## Strategies for improving employee performance

Employee performance can be improved in many ways.

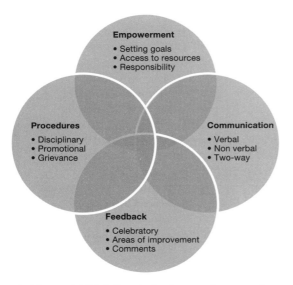

▲ **Figure 7.5** Methods for improving employee performance

## Management by objectives (MBO)

When appraising staff, **MBO** is commonly used as a way of consistently setting and measuring objectives. The objectives set should be **SMART** objectives.

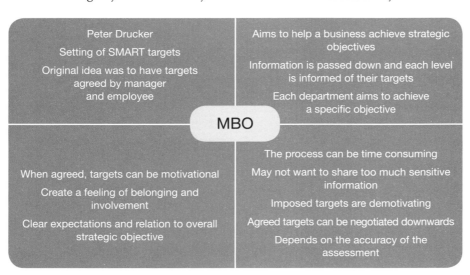

▲ **Figure 7.6** Management by objectives

## Labour legislation

Most countries have specific labour laws that aim to govern how employees are treated, to protect employees from exploitation. The HRM department is responsible for meeting all applicable laws to ensure exploitation does not occur.

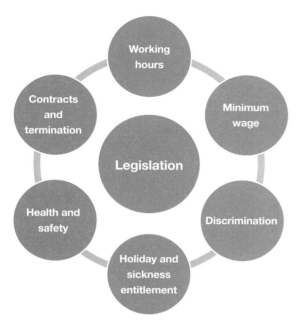

▲ **Figure 7.7** The need for labour legislation and the broad principles that often underlie it

## Cooperation between management and workforce

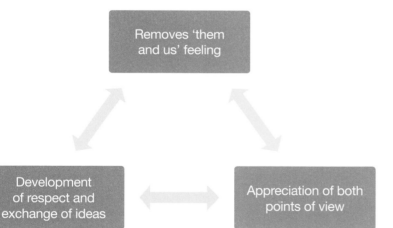

▲ **Figure 7.8** How cooperation between management and the workforce can be of benefit to both

> **Remember**
>
> Candidates do not need to know specific legislation, nor do candidates need to know specific details other than the broad outline. Legislation differs between countries and trading blocs and may be effectively linked to multinational businesses and the effects of growth.

> **X Common error**
>
> Candidates often mention that employees may fight against managers; managers are also employees, but in a different position with different priorities. It is important to make this distinction.

> **Remember**
>
> There are many different levels of management and senior managers consider junior managers to be a part of the workforce.

## Workforce planning

It is important to remain focused on the objectives of a business; the main objectives are to make a profit and reward investment. Employees are often the biggest financial outlay and staffing levels and contracts need to be managed carefully.

Reasons for and the role of a workforce plan:

➤ clear focus on strategic objectives

➤ appropriate methods of increasing and reducing workforce

> developed workforce plan to meet current and future need

> training schemes to ensure that future plans can be actioned efficiently.

## Role of trade unions in HRM

| Benefits to employees | Benefits to the employers |
| --- | --- |
| Skilled representation with negotiating experience.<br><br>More power than on an individual level.<br><br>Legal representation when in dispute with management.<br><br>Up-to-date information regarding employment legislation. | External bodies can mediate when in dispute with employee bodies.<br><br>Ensure members follow legislation and intervene when infractions made.<br><br>Employers can discuss issues with a few impartial representatives, saving time due to not meeting all employees. |

▲ **Figure 7.9** The benefits to employers and employees of trade union involvement in the workplace including their role in collective bargaining

Trade unions often work on the employee's behalf as legislation may be difficult and a layperson may not know or understand specific rights and responsibilities. Trade unions are also able to bargain collectively on the behalf of groups of employees which adds strength to the power of the employee.

**Key terms**

**Trade union**: an organised association of workers within a similar trade or trades, formed to protect and enhance worker rights and interests.

**Collective bargaining**: negotiation of one person on behalf of many from a position of strength.

▲ **Figure 7.10**

---

### Worked example

Analyse the benefits to SG of using trade unions to communicate with their employees. [10 marks]

 **Link**

Refer to Case study 3: Sohail's Garage in Unit 14.

**Answers**

Trade unions are organisations that are able to represent individual workers within a particular business sector and bargain collectively on their behalf, to ensure that employee rights are respected and to ensure that any information provided by a business is passed accurately to all those concerned. ✓✓✓

As SG has grown into a large business with three separate sectors with three different styles of management, there may be some resentment between departments of the favourable treatment of some workers at the expense of others. Employees could contact their trade union representative who could approach Sohail directly to make him aware of any negative feelings that may be causing dissatisfaction and a poor working environment. ✓✓✓

In addition to this, Sohail could also contact the trade union himself to ask them to disseminate information to all their members, to keep them aware of potential future strategic plans and the likely impact on the employees. This could reduce feelings of concern regarding their jobs in a potential merger or takeover and lead to suggestions for improvement to be returned directly via the trade unions to Sohail. ✓✓✓✓

## 7.2 Organisational structure

This topic is concerned with:

➤ relationship between business objectives, people and organisational structure

➤ types of structure

➤ formal and informal organisations

➤ control, authority and trust

➤ centralisation

➤ line and staff management.

### Relationship between business objectives, people and organisational structure

A business is usually created to meet the objectives of the investor. These strategic business objectives are achieved by the employees who are controlled and managed by one of a number of organisational structures that will be investigated in this section.

Purpose and attributes of an organisational structure such as flexibility, meet the needs of the business, permit growth and development.

| Flexibility | Responsive to growth and development of the business |
|---|---|
| Achievement of business needs | Allows the matching of resources to organisational needs |
| Growth and development of the business and the employee | Separates areas of the business to allow for sustainable management |

▲ **Figure 7.11** Relationship between business objectives, people and organisational structure

> **X  Common error**
>
> Candidates often refer to business structures without referring to the constituent parts. Organisational structures exist to organise and manage employees to achieve strategic objectives.

> **Key term**
>
> **Organisational structure:** the framework of a business, highlighting chain of command, and lines of communication.

## Types of structure

Businesses have many different types of structure. Each has its own advantages and disadvantages and may use more than one structure depending on the stated objectives. It is important to understand the **chain of command**, **levels of hierarchy** and **lines of communication**.

▼ **Table 7.1** Advantages and disadvantages of the different types of structure

| Type of structure | Definition | Advantage | Disadvantage |
|---|---|---|---|
| **Hierarchical** | Various levels presented in order of authority and responsibility from top to bottom. | Allows a clear view of the importance of each member of staff. | Is very rigid and can stifle creativity and innovation due to the inability to assume responsibility. |
| **Tall (narrow)** | Many levels, usually in bureaucratic and traditional organisations with a **narrow span of control**. | Clear understanding of superiors and juniors and less chance of confused instructions. | Very slow decision-making as many levels of authority required. |
| **Flat** | Fewer levels with a **wide span of control**, often in newer business or those who have **delayered** to save time or cost. | Faster decision-making and staff have more authority at lower levels. | Less senior management oversight and a wide span of control may make monitoring all staff difficult. |
| **Functional** | Management is separated into specific business activities or departments such as R&D or marketing. | Customer needs easily identified as all team members are specialists. | May reduce the uniformity of the business and each department may follow different objectives. |
| **Matrix** | Management crosses departmental boundaries and can manage staff both junior and senior from many departments. | Allows the best employees to complete a task regardless of rank and encourages cross department cooperation. | There may be more than one 'boss', which may confuse employees and cause communication difficulties. May also work on more than one project and can be difficult to determine priority. |

## Why some organisations are structured by product and others by geographical area

The A Level syllabus focuses on multinational corporations, which have different ways of structuring their businesses to ensure that their organisational aims are met. Candidates will have to be able to apply the following structures:

| Product | Geographical region |
|---|---|
| • Useful for businesses that have a large variety of products each with its own specific needs.<br>• Costs and revenues can be clearly allocated.<br>• Can be duplicated effort as each department completes similar functions. | • Useful for businesses who provide products for different regions.<br>• Customer needs can be easily recognised and specialised products produced/provided.<br>• Variations in brand image, quality and perceptions which may detract from an overall premium brand or standard. |

▲ **Figure 7.12** Different business structures used by multinational corporations

Organisational structures do not stay the same; they change according to a variety of factors both internal and external.

> 💡 **Remember**
>
> Businesses often use more than one functional structure depending on a variety of factors, such as product, aim or type of department. Candidates must apply the most appropriate structure and justify their view.

▼ **Table 7.2** The reasons and ways structures change

| Internal | Reason | Methods of change |
|---|---|---|
| Change in the style of management | Changing to a more democratic style to increase worker input and motivation. | Delayering is one method, as well as a change in lines of communication. |
| Delayering | Decrease costs and increase speed of communication. | Reducing the number of supervisory managers and increasing the **autonomy** of workers. |
| Expansion into new geographical markets | An increase in the number of departments and products leads to an increase in the scale of operation. | Increasing the layers of management and changing the structure from a matrix to a geographical structure. |
| **External** | | |
| Growth of market | Increase in demand leads to an increase in production to maximise profit opportunities. | Changing to a product orientated or geographical structure or to maximise product availability and suitability. |

## Formal and informal organisations

Organisations can be classed as **formal** and **informal**: formal structures are more often found in traditional businesses where there is clear delegation and responsibility and there is a need for order; informal organisations tend to be in newer and innovative businesses where creativity and trust is essential to achieve organisational aims.

**Key terms**

**Formal structure**: strictly defined levels of authority and channels of communication and a fixed set of rules which cover most eventualities.

**Informal structure**: a social network for communication and authority where people work together regardless of levels of seniority and relationships and ability are most important.

Features of a formal structure:

➤ clear and distinct levels of hierarchy, responsibility and authority

➤ processes and procedures in place to ensure consistency and order

➤ reduced responsibility at lower levels of hierarchy

➤ delegation of tasks whilst retention of control and responsibility

➤ high levels of control and authority in lieu of trust.

## Control, authority and trust

All organisations have processes and procedures for the control of operations, which delegate authority and manage trust to enable organisations to reach their aims and objectives. How this control, authority and trust manifests itself depends on the organisational setting, however, there are common features:

➤ the higher a person is in the level of hierarchy, the more responsibility he or she will have

➤ while a junior manager may have the authority to assign resources, the responsibility often lies with more senior managers

➤ when delegating tasks, a superior must trust their junior as the final responsibility lies with the senior manager. Without trust, there may be conflicts including:

   ○ a slow and inefficient management process

   ○ over-management of the junior's activities

   ○ wastage of resources

   ○ jealousy of better skills or knowledge of a junior

   ○ inappropriate delegation can lead to accusations of favouritism and a lack of motivation.

▼ **Table 7.3** Formal structures have specific features

| Levels of hierarchy | Clearly defined titles with specific responsibilities; manager, supervisor etc. |
| | Many levels of hierarchy are found in tall organisations and have narrow spans of control. |
| | Fewer levels of hierarchy are found in flat organisations and often have wider spans of control. |
| Chain of command | The path that information and instructions follow; often clearly specified and followed. |
| Span of control | The number of employees each manager or supervisor is responsible for; can be a wide or narrow span of control. |
| Responsibility | Clear accountability for tasks regardless of who carries out or gives orders for the task. |
| Authority | The power to give orders and make decisions regarding tasks. |
| Delegation and accountability | The process of passing responsibility for a task down the chain of command to the person who ultimately has responsibility for the final action. |
| | The employee is accountable to the manager who delegated the task, therefore it is important that managers delegate responsibility to reliable employees, which can increase empowerment and motivation. |
| | Delegation allows for a more efficient use of time and resources. If tasks are delegated to the right people this can motivate, however, it means that the manager with final responsibility has to depend on the ability of the employee, and if employees are delegated work they are unqualified for or unable to do in the time frame, it can demotivate staff and reduce productivity. |
| Centralised and decentralised structures | A centralised structure is where all decision making is kept with senior managers – there is limited opportunity for decision making at departmental or product level. |
| | Decentralised structures delegate responsibility to individual departmental or product centres and trust the decision making of each department manager. |

## Centralisation

Centralisation is often associated with tight control and larger organisations that have rigid levels of hierarchy.

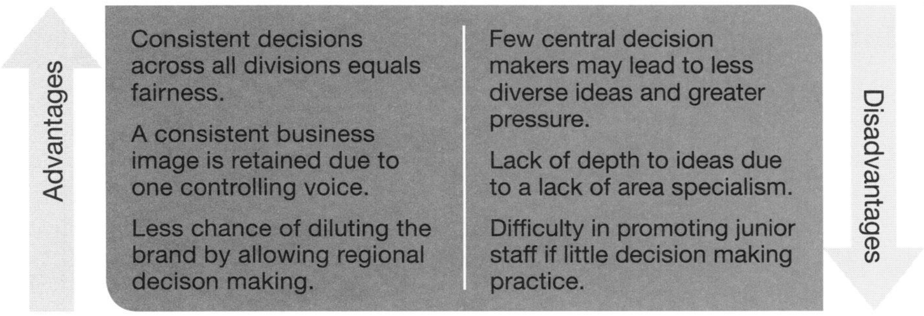

Advantages →
- Consistent decisions across all divisions equals fairness.
- A consistent business image is retained due to one controlling voice.
- Less chance of diluting the brand by allowing regional decison making.

Disadvantages →
- Few central decision makers may lead to less diverse ideas and greater pressure.
- Lack of depth to ideas due to a lack of area specialism.
- Difficulty in promoting junior staff if little decision making practice.

💡 **Remember**

Whether centralisation is an advantage depends on not only the stakeholder but the objectives of the stakeholder. It is important to read the exam case study carefully to identify key objectives.

▲ **Figure 7.13** Advantages and disadvantages of centralisation for stakeholders

## Line and staff management

Employees are either directly managed within a department or profit centre, or have autonomy and offer specialist advice to any department, product group or division within a business.

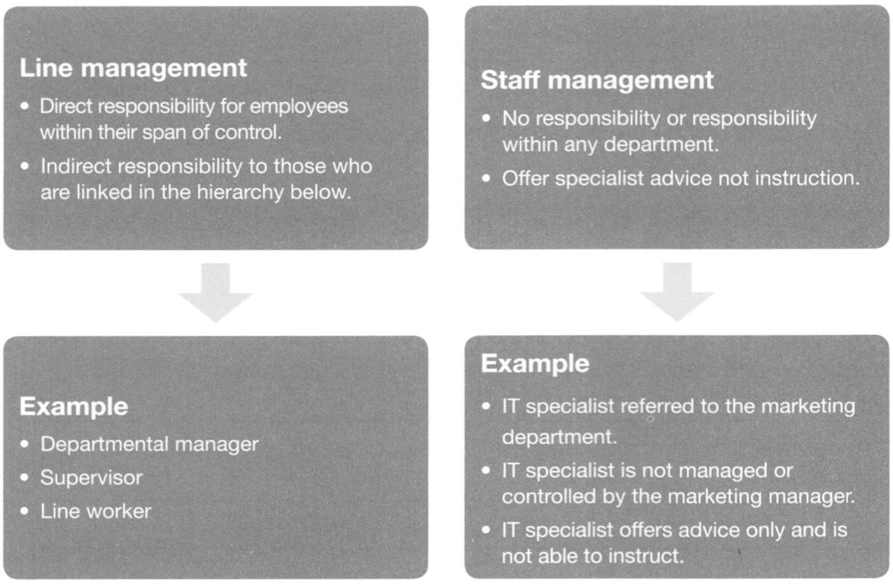

**Example**
- Departmental manager
- Supervisor
- Line worker

**Example**
- IT specialist referred to the marketing department.
- IT specialist is not managed or controlled by the marketing manager.
- IT specialist offers advice only and is not able to instruct.

▲ **Figure 7.14** Examples of and distinctions between line and staff management

**Worked example**

Analyse the benefits to SG of using hierarchical structures to communicate with their employees. [10 marks]

**🔗 Link**

Refer to Case study 3: Sohail's Garage in Unit 14.

**Answer**

As SG has three different divisions that specialise in different areas, ✓ the hierarchical structures will allow information to be disseminated to the relevant employees in specific language that may reduce the interpretation of the data and could allow employees to ask questions to their direct manager regarding the communications. Not only this, but the hierarchical structure will allow information to be transmitted to all divisions equally, managers will be given instructions on what and when to make information public. ✓

This may reduce the fear or worry of employees of changes in the organisational structure or objectives, ✓ and this is a benefit for SG as they are considering expanding which would affect employees in many ways. ✓

Without motivated and engaged staff, the business might experience a reduction in revenue as selling cars, which is the main aspect of the business, is heavily customer facing and worry and fear for jobs may be transferred to customers who may choose to buy their cars elsewhere. ✓

## 7.3 Business communication

This topic is concerned with:

➤ purposes of communication

➤ methods of communication

➤ channels of communication

➤ barriers to communication

➤ the role of management in facilitating communication.

### Purposes of communication

Effective communication is necessary for businesses to prosper. Effective communication needs to occur both internally and externally.

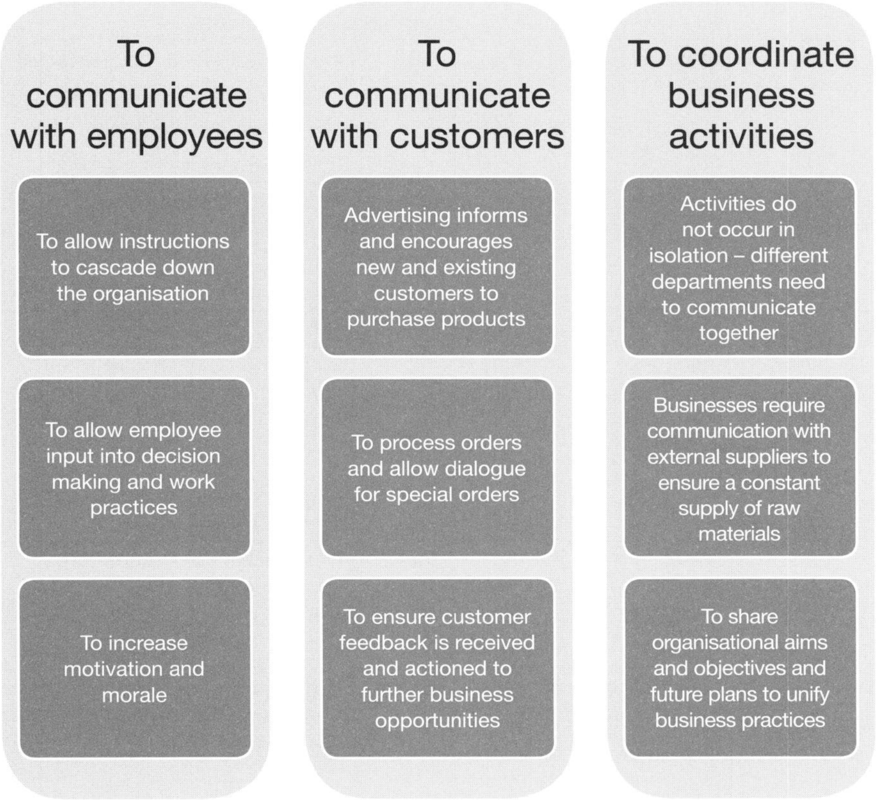


▲ **Figure 7.15** Situations in which communication is essential

✗ **Common error**

Candidates often identify methods of communication without any focus on whether the communication channels are appropriate for two-way communication.

## Methods of communication

Candidates must identify appropriate methods of communication for businesses. Appropriate methods include:

▼ **Table 7.4** Strengths and weaknesses of the different methods of communication

| Method | Business use | Strengths | Weaknesses |
|---|---|---|---|
| **Spoken** | | | |
| **Personal** | One-to-one meeting. | Direct and clear information.<br>Two-way communication. | Takes time to have personal meetings with multiple employees. |
| **Group meetings** | Staff meetings. | Quick method of passing detailed information with many employees.<br>Allows for limited two-way communication. | Time consuming and unexpected issues raised.<br>Verbal communication increases opportunities for misunderstanding. |
| **Telephone/mobile** | Communication between departments or divisions. | Quick form of communication.<br>Allows for two-way communication. | No guarantee of effective two-way communication.<br>No record of conversation.<br>Body language is not visible. |
| **Written** | | | |
| **Letters** | Specific instructions to individuals. | Clear instructions which can be reread.<br>Permanent records. | Slower method of communication.<br>Handwritten letter may be difficult to read.<br>Information can be misinterpreted. |

| Method | Business use | Strengths | Weaknesses |
|---|---|---|---|
| **Notice boards** | Less important general interest information. | Information is available to many people for a period of time.<br><br>Quick and cheap method of disseminating information. | No guarantee all recipients will see information.<br><br>Reactions are unknown.<br><br>Information is not targeted. |
| **Reports** | Formal communication to a wide number of recipients. | Detailed, often with diagrams and illustrations.<br><br>Well-structured and presented in a logical way. | Important information can be lost or hidden in long reports.<br><br>Sensitive information may be disclosed. |
| **Electronic** | | | |
| **Emails** | Quick method of written communication. | Quick and cheap method of written communication worldwide.<br><br>Complex documents can be attached. | May be an overload of information due to the ease of sending to multiple recipients.<br><br>Data protection issues.<br><br>Less actual conversation and easy to ignore emails. |
| **Websites** | To convey information to a wide audience e.g. customers. | Complex and detailed information may be shared quickly and cheaply.<br><br>Projects a business image. | Data protection issues and security issues due to the accessibility. |
| **Social media** | Communication with customers. | Fast communication with external stakeholders.<br><br>Immediate reaction can be monitored and allows a responsive reaction. | No control of communication once sent may be detrimental to a business image.<br><br>Relies on junior employees to be the electronic voice of the organisation. |
| **Video conferencing** | Host meetings between managers in various geographical locations. | Saves time and cost due to no travel requirements.<br><br>Regular meetings can be held between geographical divisions.<br><br>Allows for body language and tone to be observed. | Difficult to monitor if a large meeting.<br><br>Depends on the technological abilities of the business and the country. |

## Channels of communication

### One-way communication

➤ Bureaucratic businesses with tall structures generally rely on **one-way communication**: decisions are made at the top of the organisation and cascade down to the employees at the bottom of the structure.

➤ Employee involvement, responsibility and trust is minimal.

### Two-way communication

➤ Often found in flatter structures which rely on the skills and ability of their employees, **two-way communication** allows for decisions to be made at any level of the organisation and can be cascaded both up and down in the hierarchy of the business.

➤ Employee involvement, trust and responsibility is critical within this type of organisation.

### Vertical communication

➤ **Vertical communication** is found between different levels of hierarchy.

➤ Communications are likely to stay within one functional area.

➤ Typically found in organisations that have separate costs centres and operations.

**X Common error**

Candidates often list methods of communication without selecting the most appropriate. Unless a list is asked for, a list is irrelevant.

**Key terms**

**One-way communication**: information moves in one direction only, usually from the top to the bottom of the organisation.

**Two-way communication**: information moves both up and down the organisation and originates at all levels.

**Vertical communication**: communication between different levels of the hierarchy.

## Horizontal communication

➤ Horizontal communication is found within the same level of hierarchy.

➤ Communications are likely to cross between different functional areas.

➤ Typically found where there is close cooperation and collaboration between all departments.

Channels of communication depend on the organisational culture of the business. While each channel has it benefits, there are also problems associated with each:

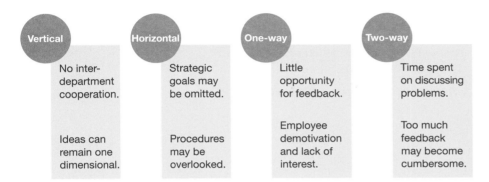

▲ **Figure 7.16** Problems associated with different channels of communication

## Barriers to communication

Communication can fail due to barriers. These barriers can be due to the sender, the receiver or the medium used. It is important for businesses to minimise barriers to ensure communication is effective.

| Using the wrong communication method | Information overload | Too many stages of communication |
|---|---|---|
| • Problem with the medium.<br>• May not allow all intended recipients to access information. | • Problem with the sender.<br>• Relevant information may be hidden in excessive quantities of information. | • Problem with the sender/medium.<br>• Distortion of the message during the journey. |
| **Noise** | **Language** | **Emotions** |
| • Problem with the medium/sender.<br>• Vital information may be misheard or misunderstood due to distraction or excessive noise. | • Problem with the medium, sender and recipient.<br>• Techical information or information in a foreign language may not be understood. | • Problem with sender/medium and/or recipient.<br>• Attitude and perception influences the understanding of the message content. |

▲ **Figure 7.17** Barriers to communication

## The role of management in facilitating communication

Management has a vital role in the facilitating of communication: if managers do not have the skills required or choose incorrect methods there could be negative consequences for the business.

The role of management is to:

➤ decide on the method and channel of communication

**Remember**

Vertical and horizontal communication may both be one- or two-way or a mix of both. Each have their own specific advantages and uses.

**✗ Common error**

Candidates often select an appropriate method of communication, however, when analysing suitability only focus on the positive aspects – all methods of communication have drawbacks which must also be considered.

**✗ Common error**

Candidates often discuss informal communication as a negative aspect, however, this is not correct. While informal communications can have a negative impact if used incorrectly, it is a vital part of the communications network.

➤ decide the information to be disseminated

➤ ensure communication is received by all intended recipients.

## The role of informal communications within a business

Businesses use formal methods of communication, as highlighted within this topic, to disseminate and collect information, however, employees within businesses use informal communications when formal methods may not be suitable.

The role of informal communications is to:

➤ discuss rumours, often called the 'grapevine'; often when formal communications are lacking and employees discuss eventualities

➤ ask favours from other team members; often done when records are not wanted of conversations and the jobs done are irregular.

## Ways in which communication can influence the efficiency of a business

The impact of effective communication:

➤ Efficiency in completing tasks – clear communications ensure fewer mistakes are made that lead to a decrease in time, or an increase in wastage and cost.

➤ Decisions can be made quickly and made available to interested stakeholders – a clear direction can increase the belief of investors and increase investment opportunities.

➤ Communication between departments reduces duplication and coordinates activities throughout the business – this leads to streamlined operations and efficient use of resources.

---

### Worked example

Evaluate the extent to which the organisational structure influences the success of SG. [10 marks]

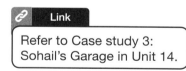

**Link**

Refer to Case study 3: Sohail's Garage in Unit 14.

### Answer

Although SG is one overall business, each of its functional divisions is run by a manager in their own style, and Sohail has identified the differences in leadership styles may be affecting profitability within the organisation.

Because of the leadership styles, each division is likely to have the following structures:

Umar follows the McGregor Theory X of leadership, where employees should be kept under tight control and monitored closely. This is more than likely to have a strict hierarchical style where information flows in one direction only and instructions are meant to be followed closely.

Steven however thinks like a Theory Y manager and trusts his staff. While he may still have a hierarchical structure, it is likely to be flatter and have more of a two-way communication.

Sara however has a different approach and trusts her division to work collaboratively, possibly in a matrix structure and with a lot of informal communication. ✓✓

Sohail, however, has identified that each division works independently of each other. This lack of horizontal communications means that SG may not be as successful as it could be due to two main reasons; work is being duplicated in all three departments, which means money is being wasted on repetition. This could lead to long term issues especially if SG merges with PPL Garages and brings a fourth organisational structure. If SG is able to improve its structure, it could remove duplicated activities, reduce costs and increase profits.

The other negative influence on success is that as horizontal communications are poor, the managers are unlikely to share ideas or best practice, which means that one division may have excellent ideas and methods but does not share these ideas with the other divisions. Not only does this reduce the effectiveness of the business as a whole, but if a customer does business with two divisions they would have a completely different service, and this means that SG does not have a unified organisational goal.

However, each department is still profitable, ✓ and profits have increased in each of the divisions over the year as seen in Table 1 in the case study, ✓ which means that the organisational structure allows the business to be successful. ✓ This means that the organisational structure of SG allows for each division to meet the needs of its customers ✓ and the fact that Sohail is considering expanding the business ✓ indicates that the business is indeed successful. ✓

Although the business is currently successful, the evidence suggests that the organisational structure of SG is limiting the success and should be improved. ✓ Sohail has already identified that the infrastructure is in need of improvement and horizontal communication is poor leading to communication problems. If Sohail is able to reorganise the functional organisational structure and implement a matrix structure which would increase the horizontal communications, the business may well become more successful due to the streamlined nature of the business and the shared ideas and experiences of all of the managers. This would also unify the business aims which would improve the customer experience thereby improving the success of SG. ✓

## Revision checklist

### I can:

- ➤ analyse the appropriateness of different methods of communication ☐
- ➤ discuss the benefits of different channels of communication ☐
- ➤ recognise potential barriers to communication and recommend ways of overcoming them ☐
- ➤ assess the importance of informal communication methods ☐
- ➤ analyse and evaluate the impact of effective communication on business activity. ☐

## ⬆ Raise your grade

🔗 **Link**

These questions refer to Case study 3: Sohail's Garage in Unit 14.

Each of these questions will rely on the exemplar case study and this will need to be utilised to score more than a passing grade.

1  Analyse the benefits to SG of effective workforce planning. [10 marks]

SG currently uses a functional structure in which each division works as an individual business. ✓✓ Due to this, back office roles such as finance and marketing are replicated which adds to the cost of SG which reduces the profitability of the business. ✓

If Sohail plans his workforce effectively, he will be able to streamline the organisation and reduce duplicated roles. ✓ This will ensure that there is a standardised system that operates throughout the organisation. A benefit of this is that a matrix structure will be utilised to allow specialists to work across divisions, ✓ and create a standard system throughout the organisation that will allow for easy analysis of business performance ✓ and monitor the profitability levels of all three businesses, as this is something that he has currently identified as an issue. ✓

Not only this, but if the workforce is planned effectively, then Sohail will be able to identify any training needs that will be required ✓ if and when SG relocate to a new centralised head office. ✓ If new systems and procedures are to be implemented and decisions made centrally, it is important that SG has employees with the specific skill levels and qualifications to effectively manage the transition between the old and the new systems. Without effective workforce planning, uninformed decisions could be made which may jeopardize the future success of the new, enlarged and centralised business. ✓

> **[10 marks]** It is important that candidates are aware of the mark schemes used in previous examination periods to identify exactly where marks are awarded and how many marks are available for each section.
>
> Marks at A Level are awarded for the quality of the argument rather than the quantity of knowledge. Remember, once a candidate has been awarded one Level 2 mark, then any other Level 1 marks are irrelevant.

2   Recommend to Sohail the most appropriate communication methods SG should utilise to inform the employees of the proposed organisational changes.                    [14 marks]

As SG's business structure is organised by product and there is little communication between the departments, it is important to ensure that the method of communication allows the employees to receive the same information at the same time, or else there will be a lot of informal communication between friendship groups, which could lead to a demotivated, worried and defensive employee base which could in turn affect customer relationships and sales as the business is in the tertiary sector. Not only will information 'off the grapevine' not be complete, but it may be incorrect or misunderstood which may lead to skilled and valuable employees to seek new, more secure employment based on rumour, which is another disadvantage of using the incorrect communication method.

> There is no mention yet of the communication methods that you could recommend, however the initial paragraph has knowledge of communication, which is a Level 1 response, clear application to the case by using data regarding the functional structure and the tertiary service business which is Level 2 application as two separate pieces of data is used. There is also Level 1 analysis as the paragraph analyses the disadvantages of using an inappropriate communication method. Most importantly, it shows to the exam marker that the candidate understands communication methods and the effects of inappropriate methods. The examiner will therefore be looking now for the specific answers to the question.

Sohail could therefore choose to use the internal email system to share relevant information between divisions and different levels of management. Emails have the advantage of being an inexpensive method of communication, quick to reach all recipients and the sender is able to attach any relevant documents to the email. This will allow all of the employees to have the relevant data regarding the two proposed options and if Sohail wanted to hear employee opinions, employees could reply with comments, suggestions and observations regarding the changes which may add a different perspective to the decision-making process. However, there is a chance that there may be information overload with an email, with too much information and too many attachments or options that may either confuse employees or might not even be read. As there is no way to have direct two-way communication, especially if there are a number of different employees asking questions, employees may use informal methods of communication to discuss what they have understood and this may cause the demotivation issues highlighted above.

> There is good use of theory here to analyse the advantages and disadvantages of one appropriate method of communication in context, however, this will not be sufficient for maximum marks as the question asks for the most appropriate methods – more than one.

Sohail could therefore use a group meeting with each division to ensure that every member of staff is present and receives the information. A register can be taken and any staff members who are absent can be given the information by managers when appropriate. Although this method takes more time and not all of the employees can be given the information at the same time, the face to face contact means that Sohail can give all the relevant information and employees can then ask questions directly and receive answers immediately. This may reduce the chance of misunderstanding, however, staff meetings don't allow all employees to ask questions and answers could also be misunderstood. Sohail could also cascade the information down the levels of hierarchy so the line managers who may have better staff relationships could give the information to smaller groups and have more discussion, however, this does depend on the manager, and as mentioned in the case, Umar does not share information easily and Sara does not seem to lead her division with much authority, which means Sohail is dependent on others to convey the correct message.

> Only two methods of communication have been used; meetings and emails, however this is appropriate and meets the assessment guidelines. Each method is analysed effectively and there is a relation to the case study. There is no need to list all the methods of communication you know as there are only two marks available for knowledge.

My recommendation to Sohail would be to start off with divisional group meetings to give the basic and necessary details; departmental and divisional managers could then take smaller groups and use prepared notes and presentation materials to explain the finer details and allow for two-way communication. I would also recommend that Sohail sends an email with any further details so anybody who has any further questions may have them answered and may stop gossip. Using the different methods will negate most of the weaknesses of each method and allow the best chance of accurate information to be spread. As SG is likely to expand, it is vital that employees have as much information as possible to allow them to feel secure at work and continue providing the service customers expect.

> While the evaluation is not very long, the paragraph answers the question and justifies the reasons for the methods of communication selected. Note that although the question is asking about methods of communication and this is the main part of the answer, additional knowledge in the form of channels of communication and hierarchy is also added to strengthen the answer.

**3** Recommend a suitable organisational structure for the expanded SG business if the merger with PPL occurs. Justify your recommendation. [16 marks]

At the moment, the organisational structure is organised according to the product, and each division works almost individually. Sohail is concerned that the current system is unsuitable as there is little horizontal communication and office jobs such as accounting and marketing are duplicated, using different computing systems and procedures.

> Within this introductory paragraph there is L1 knowledge of organisational structure and application the case study. It also provides a clear base for the answer.

Although each division has a slightly different focus, the core business is selling vehicles, therefore there is likely to be ways in which Sohail can streamline the organisation and make it more efficient. There are two organisational structures that may be suitable for the expanded organisation.

One organisational structure is the matrix structure. As Sohail wants to centralise the administrative functions in a new headquarters, all of the functional teams will be able to work together which, for example, will reduce the need for three different marketing departments. Within the matrix structure there is an opportunity for functional areas to work across divisions and this will also unify the systems so Sohail will be able to more effectively monitor the levels of profitability. However, as there are currently three different systems and a potential fourth system that is used for PPL, there will be a need for redundancy within the workforce that will demotivate the workforce as they will be worried for their jobs. In addition to this, it will take time to train all the members of staff in the new systems and not all staff may want to relocate to a central location which may lead to increased staff turnover that could reduce the short-term efficiency of the organisation. In divisions such as Umar's, which do not have much autonomy, they may not be used to making decisions so may be hesitant and cause delays in their decision making and operations.

Another organisational structure that could be used is the functional structure. This will allow for all of the different functional areas to have individual managers, and as SG has proposed a new headquarters, each department could have purpose built office space created. As, for example, four different sets of finance teams would be brought together, this would decrease the employee cost which is often one of the biggest costs to a business. Each division manager would then have reduced responsibility and could focus on their area of expertise which is managing the sales teams. However, even though the functional areas would all be close to each other in the new head office, as each department would have its own hierarchical structure, there may again be a lack of horizontal communication which could lead to management inefficiencies that could lead to missed opportunities to add value to the product and the service.

> There is a clear two-sided analysis of two different organisational structures. Note that only two have been identified and there have not been any formal definitions. These are not needed as the knowledge is shown within the answer.

I would recommend that SG chooses a matrix structure as there are more benefits to the newly formed business. While there may be some initial problems in implementing the new system, there will be more cooperation between the different functional areas that will allow for innovative ideas and methods that take into consideration factors outside of the specific functional requirements. The matrix structure may also allow more two-way as well as horizontal communication as functional departments tend to have tall hierarchies that may reduce the speed of decision making and innovation, something Sohail may be keen on in a new headquarters.

> There is a clear recommendation based on the evidence within the analysis. Although there is a link to the case study, this evaluation could be strengthened by making the evaluation more relevant to the case study and gauging the relative importance of various factors.

## ? Exam-style questions

This section will allow you to practise writing answers for exam-style questions. Remember, it is useful to be aware of the mark schemes for the questions which can be found on relevant websites or from your teacher.

 **Link**

These questions refer to Case study 3: Sohail's Garage in Unit 14.

**Paper 3**

1 Analyse the disadvantages of ineffective delegation for SG. [10 marks]

2 Discuss the likely impact of internal communication problems on SG with the takeover of PPL. [12 marks]

3 Recommend appropriate methods of measuring employee performance at the different levels of hierarchy within SG. [14 marks]

4 Discuss the impact of a strong trade union on SG if the proposed takeover of PPL Garages occurs. [16 marks]

## Key topics

➤ marketing planning

➤ globalisation and strategies for international marketing.

## 8.1 Marketing planning

This topic is concerned with:

➤ elasticity of demand

➤ product development

➤ forecasting

➤ coordinated marketing mix

When **planning marketing** operations it is vital to have a systematic approach to developing objectives and activities to achieve business objectives. There has to be a detailed **marketing plan** to highlight the actions that need to be completed within a particular time period to all stakeholders involved.

| Analysis of current environment | • Organisation, market and competition.<br>• Ability to identify starting position. |
|---|---|
| Setting marketing objectives | • Dependent on corporate objectives.<br>• Provides a target for all stakeholders. |
| Deciding target markets | • Identifies specific market segments.<br>• Reduces wastage on advertising spend. |
| Implementing marketing strategy | • Related to budgets and existing abilities.<br>• Minimises risk of costs exceeding revenue and failure. |
| Monitoring and measuring progress | • Identifies any areas of strength or weakness to be exploited or fixed.<br>• Ability to measure progress of campaigns. |

▲ **Figure 8.1** The detailed marketing plan

### Elasticity of demand

**Price elasticity of demand** (PED), which is most commonly used, refers to the responsiveness of the demand or revenue in relation to the change in price of the product. Candidates may be asked or may be able to utilise **income elasticity** (YED) and **promotional elasticity** (PrED) to support answers to questions related to marketing. Just as important is the **cross elasticity of demand** (CrossED).

### Key terms

**Market planning**: a systematic approach to developing marketing objectives, setting out specific activities to achieve business objectives.

**Marketing plan**: outlines the activities associated with achieving marketing objectives.

**Price elasticity of demand**: measures the responsiveness of the quantity demanded in relation to the change in price. Calculated as a ratio.

**Income elasticity of demand**: measures the responsiveness of the quantity demanded in relation to the change in income. Calculated as a ratio.

**Promotional elasticity of demand**: measures the responsiveness of the quantity demanded in relation to the change in advertising expenditure. Calculated as a ratio.

**Cross elasticity of demand**: measures the responsiveness of the quantity demanded in relation to the change the price of a competing product. Calculated as a ratio.

### Remember

A marketing plan is not a static document; it is responsive to the external environment and can change if market conditions alter.

| PED | YED | PrED | CrossED |
|---|---|---|---|
| • Determines the effect a price change will have on revenue.<br>• Helps to set a price that will gain maximum revenue. | • Determines the effect a change in income will have on revenue.<br>• Allows a business to be responsive to market conditions. | • Determines the effect a promotion will have on revenue.<br>• Allows a business to maximise return on marketing expenditure. | • Determines the effect a competitor's price change will have on revenue.<br>• Allows a business to select the most appropriate pricing strategy. |

▲ **Figure 8.2** Price elasticity, income elasticity, promotional elasticity, cross elasticity

PED: $\dfrac{\text{Percentage change in quantity demanded}}{\text{Percentage change in price}}$

YED: $\dfrac{\text{Percentage change in quantity demanded}}{\text{Percentage change in income}}$

PrED: $\dfrac{\text{Percentage change in quantity demanded}}{\text{Percentage change in promotional spending}}$

CrossED: $\dfrac{\text{Percentage change in quantity demanded of Product A}}{\text{Percentage change in price of Product B}}$

## Product development

All **products** go through stages of **development** from the original idea to the launch. The finished product is developed by testing and refining the original concept.

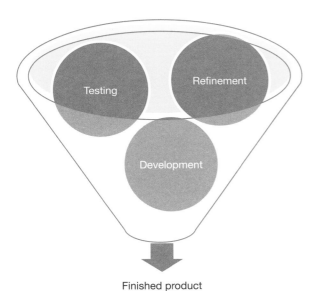

Finished product

▲ **Figure 8.3** Usefulness of the concept

💡 **Remember**

Elasticities of demand are predictions – they are not fact.

✗ **Common error**

Many candidates put the formula upside down; if candidates have written the formula down they may gain marks for identifying the figures, however, an incorrect answer on its own will receive 0 marks.

Many candidates complete the calculations but fail to effectively analyse the possible effects of external changes which are unrelated to price or promotion – such as economic conditions or social changes.

**Key term**

**Product development**: the creation of products with new or different characteristics; may include modification of an existing product or an entirely new product.

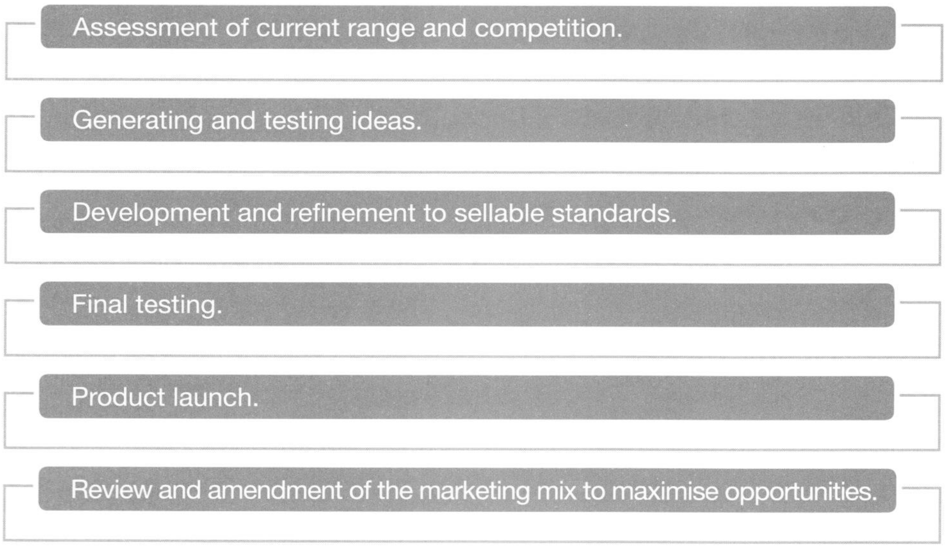

Assessment of current range and competition.
Generating and testing ideas.
Development and refinement to sellable standards.
Final testing.
Product launch.
Review and amendment of the marketing mix to maximise opportunities.

▲ **Figure 8.4** Product development as a process from original conception to launch and beyond

**Remember**

Product development is a cyclical process and often repeats itself. A product does not always manage to go through all the steps and may be terminated if research suggests the product will be unprofitable.

Customers
Blue sky thinking
Production teams
Sources of new ideas
Existing products
Market research

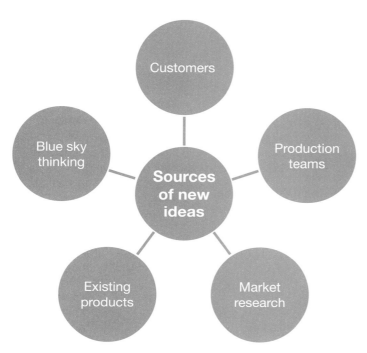

▲ **Figure 8.5** Sources of new ideas for product development

**Remember**

Most 'new' products are usually developments of existing products – each source may add one piece of data to an overall idea. It is very rare for one source to develop a new idea without any external influence.

### The importance of research and development

Without research and development (R&D) a business will encounter many problems when the products are sold:

- Design faults can lead to a business being taken to court.
- Persistent poor quality can ruin a business's reputation.
- Falling behind competitors who invest in new products and technology.
- No unique selling point in comparison to competitors.

## Forecasting

### The need to forecast marketing data

Without effective forecasting, a business will be vulnerable to external influences that have not been anticipated or planned for and can cause a business or product to fail. Methods of forecasting can be quantitative and qualitative and use both internal and external data. Marketing relies heavily on the ability to predict potential customer behaviour.

When forecasting for marketing purposes, businesses often focus on market trends. One of the most common is the moving average method.

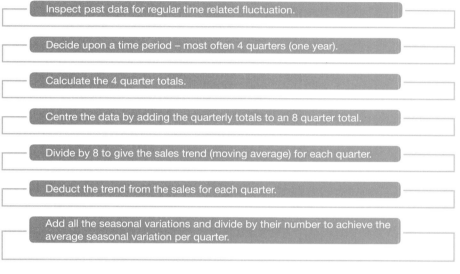

▲ **Figure 8.6** Calculation and use of moving average method to forecast sales

## Coordinated marketing mix

The marketing mix, which consists of the 4 Ps, requires coordination to ensure that each of the elements of the marketing mix complement each other while still achieving the specific marketing objectives.

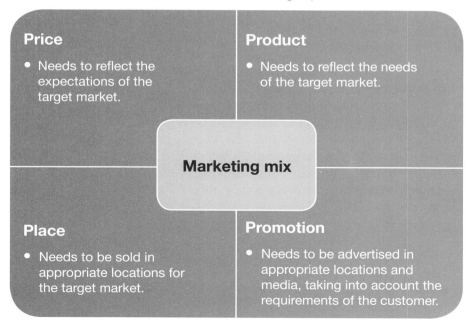

▲ **Figure 8.7** The need for and development of a coordinated marketing mix

**Key terms**

**Forecasting**: a method that businesses use to predict the future.

**Trends**: the average change (increase or decrease) within a time period.

**Moving average**: a consecutive set of average sales figures over a set time period.

**✗ Common error**

When asked to forecast or predict future events, some candidates use their own personal knowledge or opinions to justify a prediction: without using the text, candidates will limit their potential marks.

**💡 Remember**

The moving average doesn't take into account seasonal trends or random, unpredictable events. Without factoring in these events the moving averages will be of less use.

You are unlikely to be asked to calculate a moving average, however, you may be asked to complete a table of calculations or comment on the results.

**✗ Common error**

Candidates often use the marketing mix independently of any external factors, such as the stages of the product life cycle or the economic environment, which limits analysis marks.

**💡 Remember**

Although the marketing mix will try to influence the customer, it is unlikely to change the perceptions of the customer to a great degree – the marketing mix must be focused on a particular segment of the market.

## Worked example

Discuss how SG may change its marketing plan if it decides to enter a joint venture with NRG Autos. [16 marks]

 **Link**

Refer to Case study 3: Sohail's Garage in Unit 14.

### Answer

As SG currently focuses on second-hand cars for its core business, its marketing plan will need to be altered to take into account the change in the product range and the higher price and the likely methods of promotion. ✓✓

Current promotion is likely to focus on the range and affordability of the vehicles that SG sell and possibly their price in relation to competition. If a customer is buying a second-hand car, they are less likely to have specific and non-negotiable demands, and may choose a car which is not quite perfect due to its price point. However, customers who are buying a new, premium car are less likely to choose the next best option as the price is already significant for a new car, and customers expect their demands to be met if they are paying a premium price. ✓✓

The promotion, which currently may be geared towards the mass market, will need to change focus towards a narrower target market, such as premium magazines which cater for the lifestyle conscious customer who is willing to buy premium and prestige brands. Although advertising in specialist magazines may be more expensive, the new joint venture would need to spend a large sum of money at the beginning of the project to build on their brand name, as NRG are currently unavailable and may be unknown in the country. Without appropriate promotion to build customer awareness, the joint venture may not succeed. ✓✓

The pricing strategy will also have to be amended, depending on the objectives of the new joint venture. ✓ If NRG and SG want the product to remain exclusive, then they may choose a price skimming strategy. ✓ This would reduce the number of customers in the short term, but would strengthen the premium brand image. ✓ However, if the new company wanted to penetrate the market and gain a large customer base within the target market, then the pricing strategy would have to be based on current competitor prices in order to entice potential customers. ✓

Therefore, the marketing plan would change from a mass market, value based strategy to a strategy which is more selective in its target market and chooses more appropriate channels of promotion, ✓ such as high class magazines and suitable radio stations in the target markets. ✓ Although SG and NRG may decide upon the pricing strategy that best fits the organisational goals, ✓ they will need to monitor the pricing strategy ✓ and the promotion activities carefully as part of the marketing mix, ✓ as they will need to be responsive not only to the activities of the competitors but also the perception of the target customer. ✓

## 8.2 Globalisation and strategies for international marketing

This topic is concerned with:

➤ globalisation

➤ strategies for international marketing.

### Globalisation

Technology has enabled distant communities to trade and communicate with each other. Globalisation has increased competition and has been responsible for the integration and interdependence of economies. It has also affected marketing strategies.

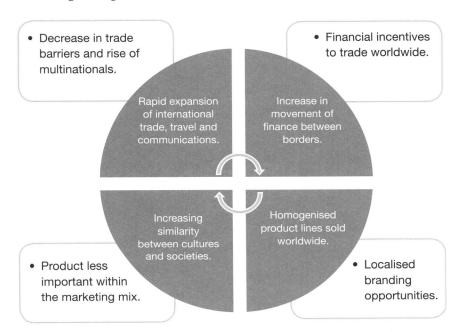

- Decrease in trade barriers and rise of multinationals.
- Financial incentives to trade worldwide.
- Product less important within the marketing mix.
- Localised branding opportunities.

Rapid expansion of international trade, travel and communications.

Increase in movement of finance between borders.

Increasing similarity between cultures and societies.

Homogenised product lines sold worldwide.

▲ **Figure 8.8** Economic globalisation within the context of the broader concept of 'globalisation'

Increasing importance of global brands and reduction in **tariffs**.

Increasing financial investment into branding and brands.

Increased competition from international low cost suppliers and **FDI**.

▲ **Figure 8.9** The implications for marketing of increased globalisation and economic collaboration

> **Remember**
>
> Globalisation is very important for marketing as social and cultural aspects of different societies affect the cognition and impact of generic marketing messages.

> **Key terms**
>
> **Tariffs:** a tax on imported products and services.
>
> **Foreign Direct Investment (FDI):** a foreign business investing into manufacturing or services in another country.

> **Remember**
>
> Globalisation has many benefits and drawbacks depending on the stakeholder and the business objectives. While globalisation may drive some small businesses into bankruptcy, it has also allowed many small businesses to prosper with the advent of the internet.

## Strategies for international marketing

Depending on the business and the target country, there are many important variables that need to be taken into consideration.

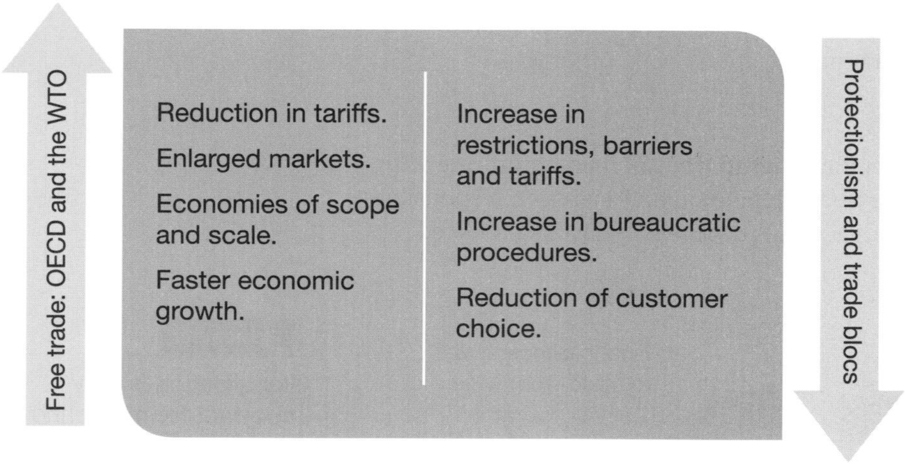

**Free trade: OECD and the WTO**

Reduction in tariffs.

Enlarged markets.

Economies of scope and scale.

Faster economic growth.

Increase in restrictions, barriers and tariffs.

Increase in bureaucratic procedures.

Reduction of customer choice.

**Protectionism and trade blocs**

▲ **Figure 8.10** The importance of international marketing for a specific business/situation international markets

As globalisation is increasing the availability of products and services from international businesses, international marketing is becoming of increasing importance to:

➤ increase brand awareness and loyalty

➤ expand into new markets

➤ exploit growth in emerging markets.

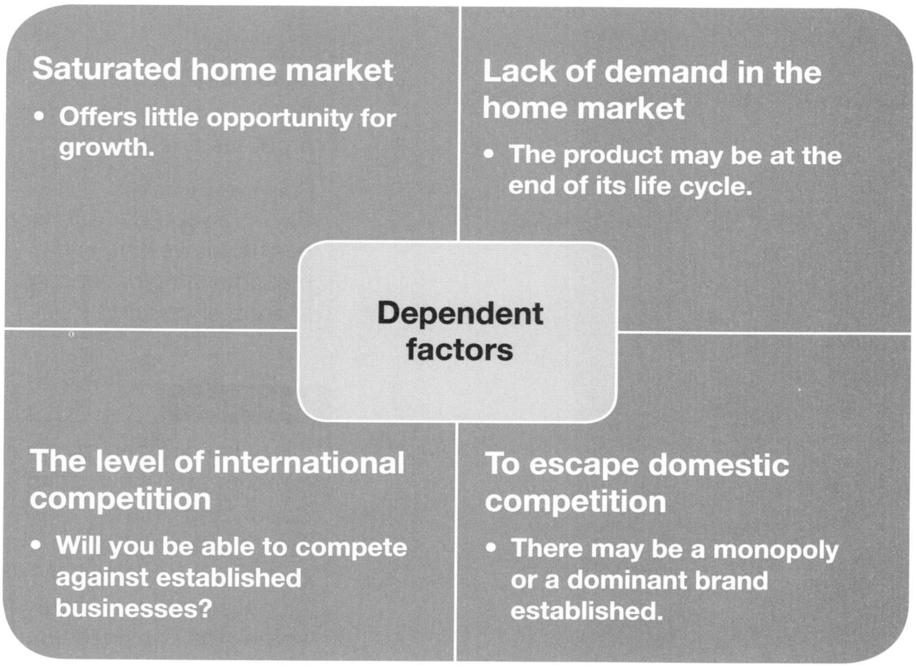

**Saturated home market**
- **Offers little opportunity for growth.**

**Lack of demand in the home market**
- **The product may be at the end of its life cycle.**

**Dependent factors**

**The level of international competition**
- **Will you be able to compete against established businesses?**

**To escape domestic competition**
- **There may be a monopoly or a dominant brand established.**

▲ **Figure 8.11** Factors influencing the method of entry into international markets

> **Remember**
>
> International marketing is important to keep abreast with existing and new competition.

> **X Common error**
>
> Candidates are expected to utilise the case studies provided, which will include all the relevant factors. Candidates who do well identify and use these, candidates who fare poorly either try to be original or fail to use examples from the case study.

> **Remember**
>
> Businesses will never be able to factor in all the variables and in an exam you will not be expected to; you must choose and give justification for the variables you believe are most important; in an exam case study there will be obvious variables offered – use them.

When planning an international strategy, it is important to factor in the variables that are likely to influence the outcome.

## Identification, selection and entry

Once a business has made the decision to enter the global market, the business has to identify the most appropriate country or region to enter; thorough research will be needed by exploring the following factors.

| Product factors | Organisational factors | Market factors |
|---|---|---|
| • The position on the product life cycle.<br>• The compatibility with local cultures and tastes. | • The level of knowledge of the intended market.<br>• The ability to manage operations in multiple locations. | • Size of relevant market segments.<br>• Growth and sales opportunities.<br>• Stength and size of competiton.<br>• Cost of start up.<br>• Cultural and political factors. |

▲ **Figure 8.12** Factors of identification, selection and entry

Once a country has been identified and selected as suitable for expansion, a decision has to be made on the methods of entry. Four main methods could be utilised.

> **X Common error**
>
> Candidates may in exam situations recommend or analyse unsuitable methods of entry – such as franchising for a secondary sector business – this would be incorrect as franchising is considered to be suitable for the tertiary sector.

▼ **Table 8.1** Methods for entry

| | Definition | Advantages | Drawbacks |
|---|---|---|---|
| **Foreign direct investment** | | | |
| **Acquisition of an existing foreign business** | Purchasing the majority of the shares in an existing business to gain control. | The brand is established and should be trusted.<br><br>Initial marketing budgets may be reduced. | Managers and employees may not agree with a new business culture.<br><br>Merging costs (i.e. administration) may be high. |
| **Investment into establishing new business operations and facilties** | Investing capital into the creation of an entirely new business structure operating within the laws and regulations of the country. | Bypass trade barriers, access country specific expertise and may attract governmental aid. | Start-up costs are high.<br><br>Time is needed to establish the brand. |
| **Franchising** | Authorising a third party organisation to carry out specific activities using the brand name and resources of the business for a fee. | Low investment cost – franchisee invests into the business.<br><br>Ability to open mutiple locations quickly. | Strict oversight needed to maintain standards.<br><br>Most useful for the service industry. |
| **Joint ventures** | An agreement with another business to develop a new corporate identity separate to the existing businesses for a period of time. | Brings two complementary skill sets together.<br><br>Keeps the original business separate and safe from takeover. | Potential loss of control or information.<br><br>Difficulty in merging two organisational structures and cultures. |

When a business expands globally, it must decide whether to market its products via a pan-global method or via altering marketing to account for local differences.

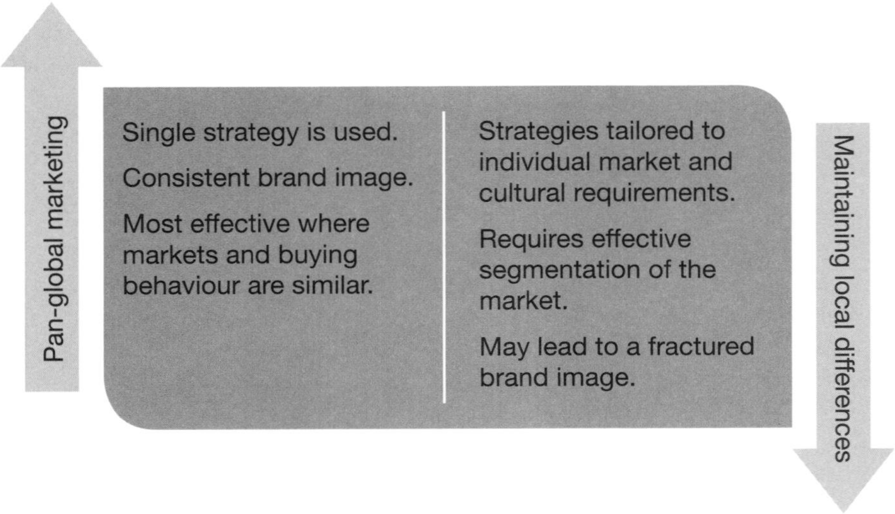
Pan-global marketing
Single strategy is used.
Consistent brand image.
Most effective where markets and buying behaviour are similar.
Strategies tailored to individual market and cultural requirements.
Requires effective segmentation of the market.
May lead to a fractured brand image.
Maintaining local differences

▲ **Figure 8.13** Whether a business in a given situation should develop an international market through pan-global marketing or maintain local differences

**Common error**

Not all multinational businesses use pan-global marketing, even brand leaders take into account local cultural differences.

**Remember**

There is no one single 'best strategy'. Whichever strategy is chosen will be assessed based on the strength of the evidence and analysis.

When choosing a strategy, businesses often follow a checklist to ensure it meets not only the customer requirements but also fulfils the organisational requirements.

Whichever strategy is chosen it must:

- develop effective long-term relationships
- incorporate service and **aftersales service** to develop a sustainable business.

**Key term**

**Aftersales service**: help, information and assistance after the product has been purchased.

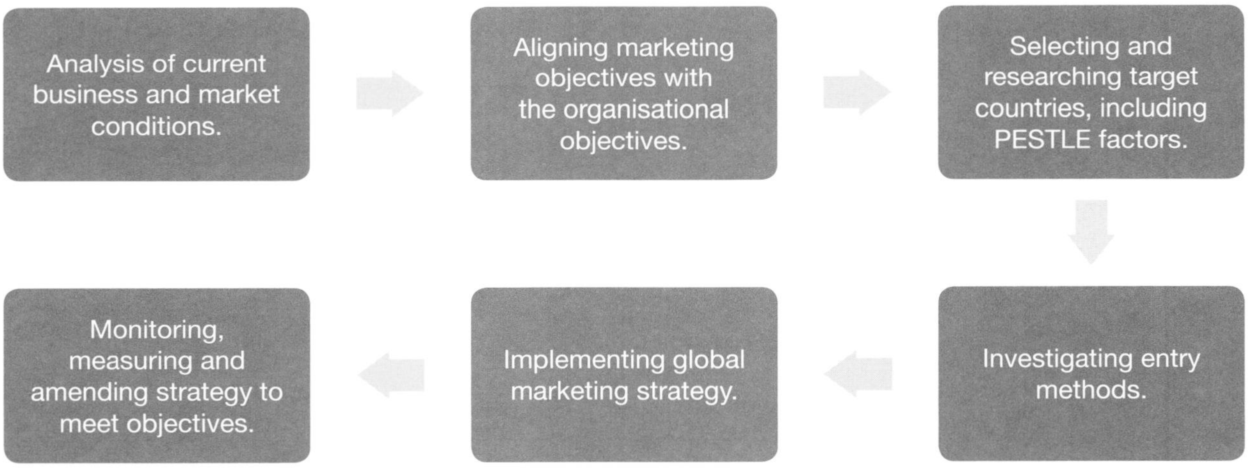
Analysis of current business and market conditions.
Aligning marketing objectives with the organisational objectives.
Selecting and researching target countries, including PESTLE factors.
Investigating entry methods.
Implementing global marketing strategy.
Monitoring, measuring and amending strategy to meet objectives.

▲ **Figure 8.14** Choosing a strategy to develop a global market

## Worked example

Analyse the benefits of effective market planning for SG if they choose a joint venture with NRG Autos. [10 marks]

**Link**

Refer to Case study 3: Sohail's Garage in Unit 14.

### Answer

If SG engages with the joint venture, they will be targeting a new premium market which they currently have no knowledge of. While their current marketing strategy targets low to middle income customers who require second-hand cars, the new strategy will be focusing on higher income customers who want to purchase a premium car. ✓✓

If SG are able to complete an effective analysis of the organisation, market and potential competitors, they will be able to identify the specific market needs and create a marketing strategy that utilises their strengths while remaining committed to the organisational objectives which in the case study is mentioned as excellent customer service. ✓✓

Incorporated into the marketing plan will be the income, price and cross elasticity of demand, which will enable SG to set an appropriate selling price for the car that will maximise either profitability or quantity sold depending on their business objectives. As long as SG are aware of any external factors that might influence the various elasticities, this could enable the long-term success of the new joint venture. ✓✓✓

An effective market plan will also enable SG to have a coordinated marketing mix, ensuring that the price of the premium cars is relative to the promotional activities and the quality of the premium cars, as well as creating new sales rooms which are separate from the existing SG brand to ensure customers don't receive mixed messages which could harm the brand in the longer term. If this is budgeted effectively, then although the expenditure may be large as the brand is new to country A, it may achieve the organisational objectives of building a reputable brand in the long term which will enhance the chances of a successful joint venture. ✓✓✓

## Revision checklist

### I can:

➤ explain globalisation, international marketing and the increasing importance for business ☐

➤ assess how increasing globalisation and economic interdependence might impact on how a business markets its products and services ☐

➤ evaluate the influences on businesses considering entering international markets ☐

➤ recommend whether a business should adopt a pan-global or localised marketing strategy. ☐

## ⬆ Raise your grade

Each of these questions will rely on the exemplar case study and this will need to be utilised to score more than a passing grade.

**Link**

These questions refer to Case study 3: Sohail's Garage in Unit 14.

1 Analyse the benefits to SG of using current market research. [10 marks]

If SG invests in effective market research, then SG will be able to identify the correct market segment and maximise the chances of making their business more successful. SG are currently aiming to either expand by taking over a competitor or investing into a joint venture with a foreign car manufacturer aiming to enter a new market.

If SG conduct primary research, then they will be able to gather up-to-date information about the current needs of their existing and potential customers. SG would then be able to determine whether there actually is a market for the premium imported cars, because if there isn't a large enough market then the business is likely to fail.

SG also need to research the current laws, political influences and social views on importing products into the country. If the current situation is very nationalistic and the government is encouraging customers to buy domestic products, then the business is going to have to spend a lot of money on promotion which will reduce the overall profits.

SG could also use secondary data, which has been collected by another organisation for a different purpose but is able to be used by SG. This secondary data will be able to show past trends and what people have actually been purchasing in the past. This could be used to predict future sales and could be used to base current marketing campaigns, however secondary data isn't always useful as it may be out of date or the analysis that has been completed has been slanted to show the results that were favourable for the company who first did the research.

> Although this answer starts off well, the knowledge shown is only likely to gain Level 1 as there isn't detailed knowledge of primary research. The candidate could have given some examples and shown how the information would be used. Application and analysis is also likely to be Level 1 as the second point is only vaguely related to SG if they invest in a joint venture. However, this is implied and not explicit and the analysis is undeveloped and weak.
>
> Where this answer goes wrong is where the candidate begins talking about secondary data. The questions asks for 'current market research' and secondary is historical, therefore all of the candidates work from this point is wasted and does not gain any marks.

**2** Discuss a suitable marketing strategy that Sohail could use for the joint venture in country A.

[14 marks]

A new joint venture would need a new marketing strategy to target the new types of customer the joint venture would be hoping to attract.

Sohail could complete a review or an investigation into the current strengths of the business, the customer requirements and the vehicles that the competitors offer. This could then influence the 4 Ps and Sohail could ensure that the price of his product would match the expectations of the customer. If Sohail identifies a specific target customer, he would then be able to pay for more expensive methods of promotion as he would be able to target the customer and the cost per potential customer could be less.

Sohail also needs to consider the method of distribution. If he uses his existing locations, then the new product may not have the brand image required to establish effective relationships with the target customer. He may also need to invest in training his staff to act in a way that is expected by the target customer.

Sohail would need to ensure that the strategy is integrated and consistent. He must market the new venture at the level that customers would expect and in a separate setting so that SG's current image does not tarnish the image of the new business.

Although the answer seems to have a lot of theory and analysis throughout, there are some key errors that are commonly seen that severely limit the marks awarded. Although the answer refers to Sohail throughout and the joint venture at times, this is not enough to award application marks as the candidate is simply repeating information found in the question. If the candidate is lucky the candidate will gain one mark for the mention of vehicles.

Regarding analysis, the theory used to answer the question is basic, for although the answers given are correct, they are undeveloped and are generic. Each piece of analysis needs to have a series of linked consequences using connecting words such as 'this leads to' or 'however'. Without expansion, candidates will remain in the lower level category of answer.

Again, there is some judgement shown as to what a suitable marketing strategy should be, however, the judgement does not take into account the need for up-to-date research or how the marketing strategy would be related to the joint venture.

This answer would be lucky to score half marks.

**3** Discuss the changes that SG might need to make to its current marketing strategy if they decide to merge with PPL Garages. [16 marks]

The marketing strategy is the plan of how the marketing objectives are going to be achieved and includes identifying the current marketing strategy, what the businesses key objectives are and how best to attract potential customers to buy your products. The marketing strategy looks at the 4 Ps.

SG are currently looking at ways to make demand less sensitive to price increases as they are in a very competitive market. If they merge with PPL Garages then they will be reducing the competition as PPL is the biggest competitor for SG, so this will be a benefit for SG.

SG may be able to change its current focus from relying on low profit margins and their low prices to becoming more upmarket. They already have an excellent reputation for customer service and this could be used within their promotional strategy to highlight the fact if you buy a car from SG then you will be looked after and will feel happy with your purchase. This may succeed as GDP and salaries are increasing at a steady rate, the country and the citizens have more money available to spend which may mean they have more disposable income.

This could turn the focus away from low prices as people may be more likely to pay a higher price for a better service and could meet Sohail's aim of reducing price sensitivity.

The place where vehicles are being sold could also be upgraded. If SG and PPL merge, then there may need to be time and money spent on rebranding the two businesses to create a unified brand and make sure customers get the same service in all of SG's garages. As they are already rebranding, SG could invest in new showrooms, or upgrade the facilities to move the brand away from a low cost or budget market.

Sohail will need to make sure that if he changes one of the 4 Ps then he also changes the other Ps to complement the change and provide a unified message to the customer.

Rebranding and upgrading the new facilities would be a good way of changing the marketing strategy as first impressions matter to customers, and if the garages don't have a budget look any more customers may be willing to pay higher prices, especially if the excellent customer service is included in new promotional activities.

> Level 2 knowledge is achieved as the candidate clearly knows about marketing strategies and has applied his knowledge throughout the answer to the case study, ensuring Level 2 application has been achieved.
>
> Analysis is likely to be just within the Level 2 boundary, but could be improved by giving further detail about how the rebranding or promotion could be changed to fit in with current objectives and the changing market strategy. Negative effects of the changing strategy could also be discussed and developed.
>
> Evaluation is likely to be Level 1 as there are no potential effects from external factors, nor are there any limits to the changes that could be made; SG will spend a large amount on the merger – will the business have enough capital available to upgrade its garages? It may also help to show which would be the most important factor/s to focus on.

 **Exam-style questions**

This section will allow you to practise writing answers for exam-style questions. Remember, it is useful to be aware of the mark schemes for the questions which can be found on relevant websites or from your teacher.

 **Link**

These questions refer to Case study 3: Sohail's Garage in Unit 14.

**Paper 3**

1   Analyse the advantages of NRG Autos carrying out pan-global marketing.   [10 marks]

2   Evaluate the benefits to SG of preparing a thorough marketing plan before it decides to sell cars from NRG Autos for the first time in country A.   [14 marks]

3   Evaluate a marketing strategy SG/NRG Autos could use when selling their cars in country A for the first time.   [16 marks]

4   Discuss to what extent revising the marketing plan would contribute to the success of either the joint venture or merger.   [16 marks]

## Key topics

➤ operations planning

➤ capacity utilisation

➤ lean production and quality management

➤ project management.

## 9.1 Operations planning

This topic is concerned with:

➤ enterprise resource planning (ERP).

### Enterprise resource planning (ERP)

**ERP** is a method of automated integration of production systems from product planning to delivery. ERP requires major investment; the average cost is $15m so only big businesses would be able to implement this system. The major effect of ERP is to make production quicker, cheaper, more efficient and management decisions better informed.

▼ **Table 9.1** How ERP can improve efficiency

| Process | Benefits to efficiency |
|---------|------------------------|
| Inventory control | • All departments know exactly how much inventory is held.<br>• Customer orders can be linked to inventory to minimise inventory costs.<br>• ERP system keeps track of the order and can inform the customer.<br>• Products delivered as soon as they are produced. |
| Costing and pricing | • Precise costs of each order can be calculated.<br>• Prices can be customised for each individual order.<br>• Reduces the administrative costs of pricing. |
| Capacity utilisation | • Enables planning of production to ensure that operations are working at or close to full capacity.<br>• By ensuring efficient use of all equipment production costs fall. |
| Responses to change | • Indicates changes in orders so all departments know simultaneously.<br>• Management can react quickly and flexibly to changes.<br>• Reduces the cost of identifying and reacting to change. |
| Management information | • Management know about events as they happen.<br>• Decisions can be based on accurate, up-to-date information.<br>• Reduces the cost of obtaining information. |

### Key terms

**Enterprise resource planning (ERP):** a software-based system that integrates management information from all functions in a business into a single computer system that serves all those functional needs.

**Capacity utilisation:** the current level of output in a situation compared with the maximum possible with existing resources. Calculated as (Current output ÷ maximum output) × 100.

A Level

## 9.2 Capacity utilisation

This topic is concerned with:

➤ measuring capacity utilisation

➤ outsourcing.

### Measuring capacity utilisation

There are risks associated with working close to maximum **capacity** such as breakdowns occurring. Inability to meet an unexpected increase in demand, difficult to schedule machine maintenance and staff may feel under pressure to maintain that level of working. If capacity utilisation is too low, then resources are idle and unit costs will be higher.

Short-term capacity utilisation problems such as seasonality or a competitor's marketing strategy, can be planned for by changing production or inventory levels or finding new markets. Long-term capacity utilisation problems will need greater measures. Businesses may need to act if, in the long-term, there is too much (over-), or too little (under-) capacity.

▼ **Table 9.2** Over- and under-capacity long term measures

| Over-capacity long-term measures | Under-capacity long-term measures |
|---|---|
| Rationalisation <br><br>• close production lines <br>• reduce premises <br>• reduce staff numbers. | Re-organise way resources are used <br><br>• can be quick and low cost <br>• will need support of employees <br>• may not work. |
| Produce new products <br><br>• will require changes to existing processes <br>• may take a long time <br>• employee changes such as redundancy or retraining may be required. | Employ more resources <br><br>• new equipment <br>• more employees <br>• could be expensive <br>• takes time. |
| Find new markets for existing products <br><br>• overseas <br>• other regions of the same country. | Subcontract <br><br>• no new equipment required <br>• flexible and quick <br>• some loss of quality control <br>• may increase unit costs. |

⭐ **Exam tip**

Capacity utilisation applies to services as well as goods. You may be asked to calculate capacity utilisation from data given (see topic 9.1 above), to interpret the results and comment on how to improve it.

**Key terms**

**Capacity**: the maximum output of goods produced, or services provided, in a specified time period, using all resources available – 100% capacity utilisation means that the maximum output is produced.

**Rationalisation**: organising resources and working methods in a better way so that the result is greater efficiency. This often involves reducing capacity by cutting overheads, for example by closing a factory or a production line.

**Subcontract**: paying another business to undertake part of the tasks required to produce a product or service.

## Outsourcing

**Outsourcing** is a type of subcontracting where functions such as accounting, IT and training are transferred to another business. Sometimes the public sector outsources to private sector organisations – indirect **privatisation**. If a business outsources overseas this is known as **offshoring**. Outsourcing can help a business focus on its core activities, react flexibly and quickly to changes, reduce unit costs and benefit from outside expertise. However, it does mean that the business has to give up some aspects of the outsourced functions – such as quality control, data confidentiality and employees. Businesses need to carefully consider a decision to outsource as it can be difficult and expensive to reverse the decision. Some factors which should be considered are:

➤ The strategic importance of the function in giving the business a competitive advantage.

➤ The impact on operational performance – how significant the function is in ensuring the smooth operation of the business.

➤ The impact on costs – would it cost significantly more to outsource?

➤ Could the external business perform the function better?

### Worked example

Explain two problems a business might face when offshoring a call centre. [6]

#### Answer

Offshoring means the relocation of functions is to a business in a different country. ✓ One problem could be language and cultural barriers ✓ businesses located overseas may lack the cultural knowledge, fluency and communication skills necessary to provide excellent support. ✓ Another problem might be that the host business will have less control over business functions. ✓ It may be difficult to monitor for quality assurance ✓ and put policies in place to help increase customer satisfaction. ✓

## 9.3 Lean production and quality management

➤ the nature and importance of lean production

➤ tools to help businesses implement total quality management (TQM)

➤ methods and importance of quality assurance

➤ the importance of benchmarking.

### The nature and importance of lean production

**Lean production** is not another production process but an approach to the 'way things are done' – a systematic method to minimise waste without decreasing productivity. It also takes into account waste created through overburden and waste created through unevenness in workloads. **Quality** is an important feature of lean production which requires the implementation of **total quality management (TQM)**.

Lean production requires businesses to thoroughly review all activities and processes and to look for ways to continually improve on all methods used. The aim is to increase efficiency in all processes.

---

**X | Common error**

Candidates may think that lean production only refers to the production of goods. This would be incorrect. Lean production is a way of 'doing things' so applies as much to the provision of services as to the production of goods.

---

▼ **Table 9.3** Lean production and …

| Process | Explanation | Example |
|---------|-------------|---------|
| Inventory control | Inventory management can affect the efficiency of all business processes so it is important to have an efficient system. | Reduce waste caused by excessive stock holdings in the case of goods or, in services, the means to supply the service. |
| Quality | Improved quality reduces waste and increases customer satisfaction. | Reduce quantities of defects in products or services that do not meet customer expectations. |
| Employees roles | Developing and improving roles can make the whole business process more efficient. | Reduce waste caused by excessive movement of people. |
| Capacity management | If under- or over-utilisation can be eliminated the business can be leaner and more cost-effective. | Reduce waste caused by too much capacity. |
| Efficiency | Improved efficiency is the aim of lean production. | Reduce the inefficiency caused by wasted time/resources. |

### Tools to help businesses implement total quality management (TQM)

The core concept behind Kaizen is that the best people to know the most efficient way of carrying out a task are those employees who work on the task. Therefore, employees should be given some control over making changes, to their jobs, to improve efficiency and quality. The idea is that employees should be improving their work, slightly, all the time – continuous improvement. Kaizen must apply to all processes and all staff so that it is part of the business **culture**. The business needs to commit to Kaizen over the long term – it is not a 'quick fix'.

▼ **Table 9.4** Kaizen

| Kaizen will work if... | Kaizen won't work if... |
|---|---|
| employees are empowered to make changes | employees do not understand it or are unwilling to be involved |
| there is a culture of team working | the nature of the business is not suitable |
| there is management support | management do not provide the necessary resources |
| all staff are involved. | not everyone 'buys-in' to the ideas of Kaizen. |

**Worked example**

Explain the benefits of lean production to a business. [6]

**Answer**

Lean production means using resources as efficiently as possible to minimise waste ✓ and improve quality. ✓ Inefficient production processes increase costs ✓ so lean production can reduce unit costs, ✓ help businesses meet their operational objectives, ✓ and increase value added to product. ✓

★ **Exam tip**

When answering questions on lean production remember that it applies to the whole organisation and the ideas behind lean production methods can be linked to employee motivation.

Just-in-time (JIT) production can be applied as a tool of lean production to reduce the waste of materials by ensuring the business holds as little stock as possible and that as soon as products are completed they are immediately delivered to customers. JIT reduces costs, avoids the risk of outdated stock and reduces time checking as the emphasis is on getting it right first time.

🔗 **Link**

See Unit 4, topic 4.3, inventory management, for detail on just-in-time inventory control.

## Methods and importance of quality assurance

Businesses should know the quality levels customers expect and to help them do this they can use a combination of three approaches:

➤ quality control

➤ quality assurance

➤ total quality management (TQM).

💡 **Remember**

It is easy to confuse quality assurance and quality control or even to think that they are the same. Quality assurance **(A)** focuses on the process **(P)**, quality control **(C)** on the result **(R)** of the process. One way to remember is that A comes before C and P before R.

**Key terms**

**Quality control**: a system for improving quality based on inspection, normally using sampling.

**Quality assurance**: a system for making sure that agreed standards are met at each stage of a process to ensure customer satisfaction.

▼ **Table 9.5** Quality control and quality assurance

| Approach | Explanation | Key features |
|---|---|---|
| Quality control | Focuses on the end result and is based on inspection of the product before it reaches the customer. Assumes that errors are unavoidable so detects errors and puts them right. Quality control inspectors are responsible for quality and are used to check work. | <ul><li>prevention</li><li>inspection</li><li>testing</li><li>random sampling</li><li>correction and improvement</li><li>involving the workforce.</li></ul> |
| Quality assurance | Works on the principle of 'right first time' and focuses on the processes so that the end result meets an agreed standard. Assumes errors can be avoided and aims to prevent errors. Employees are responsible for quality and check their own work so that good quality work passes to the next part of the process. | Improved processes and procedures in:<ul><li>product design</li><li>quality of inputs</li><li>production procedures</li><li>customer relations.</li></ul> |
| Total quality management (TQM) | Continuous improvement with employees responsible for the quality of their own part in the process (see kaizen above). | <ul><li>**quality chains**</li><li>**quality circles**</li><li>**internal customer**.</li></ul> |

**Key terms**

**Quality chains**: setting up a procedure so that parts of the procedure can be identified as 'internal customers'.

**Quality circles**: groups of employees who meet regularly, to discuss work-related issues and problems and to identify potential improvements.

**Internal customer**: part of a process where the output of one part of the process is dependent on another part for quality i.e. they are the 'customer' of the preceding process.

**Benchmarking**: comparing a procedure with other similar procedures, particularly the best available, in order to identify ways to improve the procedure.

## The importance of benchmarking

Benchmarking is often part of a quality assurance programme. This means comparing to 'best practice' in the industry. This involves researching and collecting data which can be difficult and expensive and the techniques may not always work in another business. However, it can help focus on those areas which need improvement, may be cheaper and quicker than other methods of quality improvement.

All methods of quality improvement require the workforce to receive high level training so that they can undertake task effectively and that the whole organisation adopts a culture which allows the business to change and adapt. Without this training quality improvement methods are unlikely to be successful.

 **Link**

See Unit 2, topic 2.3 human resource management.

**Worked example**

Explain the difference between quality control and quality assurance. [6]

**Answer**

Quality control has specialised staff responsible for quality, ✓ assumes defects/mistakes are unavoidable ✓ and focuses on the end result. ✓ Quality assurance assumes that defects/mistakes are avoidable, ✓ makes all employees responsible for their own quality ✓ and focuses on the process to ensure a quality product. ✓

## 9.4 Project management

This topic is concerned with:

➤ the need for project management

➤ network diagrams and critical path analysis (CPA).

### The need for project management

**Project management** means the efficient planning, organising and managing of resources to achieve specific targets. A **project** involves a variety of **activities** and has a beginning and an end point. The focus here is on the time management of projects. Projects are usually a way of businesses responding to the need for change. Projects that are managed inefficiently so that delays, and even failures happen, can result in higher than planned costs and even result in products that cannot make a profit or for which there is very little demand. Projects can fail for a number of reasons such as costs higher than estimated; failure of communication to all involved; poor management; inefficient planning etc.

### Network diagrams and critical path analysis (CPA)

**Network analysis** is a tool to help the efficient time management of projects. You should make sure that you are familiar with **network diagrams** and **critical path analysis (CPA)**. Consider planning a project such as an essay.

▼ **Table 9.6** Planning a project

| Task | Activity | Dependent on | Time |
|------|----------|--------------|------|
| A | Analyse the question | Starting activity | 1 hr |
| B | Draft plan of work | A | 3 hrs |
| C | Find information | B | 6 hrs |
| D | Reading | C | 5 hrs |
| E | Take notes | C can be at same time as D | 6 hrs |
| F | Plan essay structure | E | 4 hrs |
| G | Draft essay | F | 3 hrs |
| H | Edit draft | G | 2 hrs |
| I | Rewrite essay | H | 3 hrs |
| J | Proofread | I | 1 hr |

> **Key terms**
>
> **Project management**: planning, organising, securing and managing resources to achieve specific targets in relation to a project.
>
> **Project**: a sequence of activities that has a clearly defined beginning and end designed to achieve a desirable business outcome.
>
> **Activities**: clearly identifiable stages, or tasks, in the completion of a project.

> **Key terms**
>
> **Network analysis**: a planning tool that identifies all the activities in a project and allows analysis of the project in terms of completion times and other key features.
>
> **Network diagram**: a diagram that shows, in a logical progression, the activities involved in a project together with their time sequence.
>
> **Critical path analysis (CPA)**: another name for network analysis.

A simple CPA for the essay project would look like:

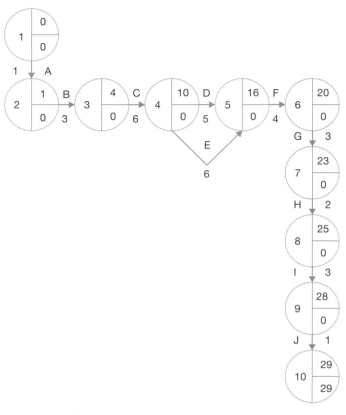

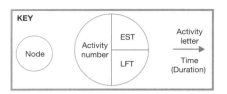

▲ **Figure 9.1** Critical path analysis for essay project

You should make sure that you are familiar with all the following elements of a CPA (network) diagram.

▼ **Table 9.7** Elements of a CPA diagram

| Element | Explanation |
|---|---|
| Circle | Node showing the beginning/end of an activity. |
| Earliest start time (EST) | The earliest possible time an activity can start relative to the beginning of the project. |
| Latest finish time (LFT) | The latest possible time an activity can finish relative to the beginning of the project. |
| Critical path | The sequence of activities that are critical to completing the project on time. |
| Critical activity | An activity within a project that cannot be delayed without delaying the overall project. |
| Non-critical activity | An activity within a project that can be delayed without delaying the overall project. |
| Dummy activity | An artificial activity used to ensure the logical representation of a project is not ambiguous. It takes no time and does not require any resources. |
| Total float | The maximum time an activity can be delayed without delaying the overall project. This is 0 for critical activities. |
| Free float | The maximum time an activity can be delayed without delaying the next activity in the sequence. This is 0 for critical activities. |

CPA can help to answer 'what if' questions by allowing a range of tasks/ activities and timings to be simulated. The technique can be linked to lean production so that all processes can be planned, co-ordinated and monitored. Knowing the critical activities can help prioritise tasks so that projects are completed on time.

## Revision checklist

**I can:**

➤ explain, calculate and interpret capacity utilisation calculations ☐

➤ discuss the problems of over- and under-capacity and explain methods for improving capacity utilisation including outsourcing ☐

➤ explain, analyse and evaluate methods of lean production including Kaizen and just-in-time ☐

➤ explain quality as related to customer demands ☐

➤ distinguish between quality control and quality assurance and evaluate each in managing quality ☐

➤ assess the role of TQM, benchmarking and training in quality control ☐

➤ explain the need for project management ☐

➤ discuss, with examples, the reasons for project failure ☐

➤ construct, analyse and interpret a network/CPA diagram ☐

➤ evaluate the usefulness of CPA as a management tool ☐

➤ apply all of the above to a range of businesses in different situations. ☐

## ⬆ Raise your grade

### Short answer questions

**1 (a)** Briefly explain the term 'capacity'. [4]

The maximum output ✓ that could be provided ✓ in a given time period ✓ using current resources. ✓

**[4 marks]** 4 marks means that you should give 4 elements to the explanation.

**(b)** Briefly explain the term 'Kaizen'. [3]

A lean production process ✓ meaning continuous improvement. ✓

**[2 marks]** It is important to consider the marks available. This question has 3 marks but the answer only includes 2 points. There needs to be a further explanation or an example. The answer could link Kaizen to TQM for the extra mark.

**2** Explain one method of improving capacity utilisation. [5]

If the problem is over-capacity ✓ then more resources could be employed. ✓ This would be a long-term solution ✓ but can be expensive ✓ and may take a long time to implement. ✓

**[5 marks]** A five-mark question does not need to have lots of writing but does need to focus on the question. This question only requires 'one method of …' but does ask you to explain. The command word 'explain' (and the 5 marks available) implies that some analysis is required, not just knowledge or definitions. The explanation above shows an understanding of 'capacity utilisation' and that the problem could be over-capacity. You could also answer in terms of under-capacity as long as you state which one you are referring to in your answer.

**3** Define the term 'benchmarking'. [2]

Comparing a product, service or process ✓ with best practice in the industry. ✓ This can be used to set new procedures. ✗

> **[2 marks]** While this is a full answer and well explained, there are only **two** marks available. The last sentence is not necessary for full marks here. If three marks were available, then the last sentence would be relevant. Don't waste your resources for no reward!

## Long answer questions

**4** Powers Ltd manufactures batteries for mobile phones. They have no system of quality control with the result that 10% of the batteries are defective and have to be thrown away. The production manager is aware that this has increased average costs, reduced productivity and increased waste which has to be disposed of safely – another cost to the firm. Ali, the production manager, has researched methods for improving quality and is considering implementing one of the following methods:

➤ quality control

➤ quality assurance

➤ total quality management (TQM).

**(a)** Explain to Ali the meaning of 'quality'. [4]

The fitness for purpose of a product or service, ✓ with 'fitness' defined by the customer. ✓ It may relate to durability, ✓ lack of defects, reliability. ✓

> **[4 marks]** Remember that, in a business context, quality is linked to customer expectations. In the case of batteries durability, lack of defects and reliability are important factors. The answer could have referred to appearance but that is not as relevant as the other factors mentioned.

**(b)** Explain the difference between 'quality control' and 'quality assurance'. [6]

Quality control focuses on the end result. ✓ Quality assurance focuses on the processes ✓ to ensure that the end result meets an agreed standard. ✓ Quality control requires the use of specialist staff, quality inspectors, ✓ whereas quality assurance involves all employees in checking the quality of their own tasks/output ✓ so saves the cost of employing specialist quality staff. ✓

> **[6 marks]** A concise answer which highlights the distinction between the two methods and includes some analysis of both methods.

**(c)** Analyse how Powers Ltd might benefit from implementing a method of quality improvement. [8]

It is important that businesses produce high quality products as poor quality leads to customer dissatisfaction and a bad business reputation. ✓ [1 knowledge mark] Powers Ltd supplies to mobile phone manufacturers so the orders for batteries are likely to be quite large. ✓ [1 contextualised knowledge mark] Throwing away 10% of the output ✓ [1 contextualised knowledge mark] would mean materials are wasted, ✓ [1 analysis mark] workers' time has not been used efficiently so employees are less productive ✓ [1 analysis mark] which leads to increased unit costs and lower profits. ✓✓ [2 contextual analysis marks] If mobile phone manufacturers think the batteries are unreliable they may look for other suppliers. ✓ [1 contextual analysis mark]

**[8 marks]** Some good analysis, in context, means that this answer quickly achieves full marks. Notice that there is a nice chain of reasoning, in context, starting at 'Throwing 10%...', which achieves 5 marks. A chain of reasoning requires you to keep answering 'so what'. For example, in the answer above, it states that workers' time is wasted (so what?) – workers are less productive (so what?) unit costs rise (so what?) and the business makes lower profits.

**(d)** Evaluate the usefulness, to Powers Ltd, of implementing total quality management. [18]

Total quality management (TQM) is an approach to quality that changes the culture of all aspects of a business and all employees with the aim of ensuring the best possible processes ✓ [1 knowledge mark] and involves the continuous improvement of products and processes. ✓ [1 knowledge mark] Powers Ltd currently have no methods of quality control ✓ [1 contextual knowledge mark] so implementing TQM would require a change in the company culture. ✓ [1 contextual knowledge mark] If TQM is implemented then all parts of the production process, management, workers, suppliers and customers are required to work together ✓ [1 analysis mark] to achieve the quality that customers expect. ✓ [1 analysis mark] As there is no method of quality improvement this would require extensive training for all employees ✓ [1 contextual analysis mark] which could be very expensive. ✓ [1 contextual analysis mark] Powers Ltd might use quality chains where one part of the process is a supplier for the next part of the process, ✓ [1 contextual analysis mark] a supplier/customer relationship. ✓ [1 contextual analysis mark] This would mean that employees in each part of the process are put into teams. ✓ [1 contextual analysis mark] Another method that could be used is quality circles ✓ [1 knowledge mark] where employees meet together, on a regular basis, to discuss ways of improving quality, in this case, reducing the number of defective batteries. ✓ [1 contextual knowledge mark] TQM might take time to introduce as it requires strategic change. ✓ [1 evaluation mark] It is not a solution but a way of doing things which requires the whole organisation to 'buy-in' to the changes required. ✓ [1 evaluation mark] If employees are not happy with the changes and do not want the responsibility of improving quality, the system may fail to achieve an increase in the quality of batteries produced. ✓ [1 evaluation mark] Powers Ltd could achieve TQM through the ideas of Kaizen but this would require a change in culture so that management trust the workers to 'know best'. This might be resented by managers and employees and, therefore, not achieve the improvements in quality they desire but if it was successful then quality would improve. ✓✓ [2 marks for an evaluative statement]

**[18 marks]** Evaluation questions are always higher mark questions. Evaluative questions will either require a judgement, based on the preceding analysis, or a statement which weighs up the preceding analysis. In this question the evaluation considers why TQM may not work and also the outcome if it is successful.

This section will allow you to practise writing answers for exam-style questions. Remember, it is useful to be aware of the mark schemes for the questions which can be found on relevant websites or from your teacher.

**Paper 3**

**Short answer questions**

1  (a) Briefly explain the term 'quality circles'.  [2]

   (b) Briefly explain the meaning of 'the internal customer'.  [3]

2  (a) What does lean production mean?  [2]

   (b) What are the three stages of quality control?  [3]

3  Explain two reasons why high quality reduces costs.  [6]

**Long answer questions**

4  Analyse the Kaizen method for improving quality.  [8]

5  Evaluate the usefulness of critical path analysis as a project management tool.  [12]

6  Discuss the benefits of outsourcing.  [20]

# 10 Finance and accounting

## Key topics

- ➤ costs
- ➤ budgets
- ➤ content of accounts
- ➤ analysis of published accounts
- ➤ investment appraisal.

## 10.1 Costs

This topic is concerned with:

- ➤ full and contribution costing.

### Full and contribution costing

There are two methods of costing used by businesses: **full costing** and **contribution costing**.

Full costing requires all of the costs, direct and indirect, of a business to be included into the costs of the products made by the business.

Full costing is used when businesses produce a range of products and need to calculate the price of each specific product. It is easy to identify the variable or direct cost of each product but difficult to share out the indirect or fixed costs of the business. Businesses have to make a judgement on how allocate fixed costs between products which means that the allocation of such costs is open to debate as some departments in a business may see the allocation of these costs as unfair. It might also prevent the use of **penetration pricing**.

Contribution costing is also known as marginal costing. Any revenue gained above the marginal cost of a product will be a contribution to the fixed/indirect costs of production; if these costs have been covered by other products then then it is the contribution to profits.

> **Key terms**
>
> **Full costing**: when all of the costs of a business are 'absorbed' into the costs of the products made. The cost will include a portion of the fixed (indirect) costs of the business.
>
> **Contribution costing**: the cost of a specific product is based on the variable or direct costs of production.
>
> **Penetration pricing**: setting the price for a new product very low allowing a business to quickly gain high market share and customer loyalty.

> ✓ **What you need to know**
>
> All businesses need accounting information and you should be able to apply this information to strategic decision making, the performance of a business and investment projects.

> 🔗 **Link**
>
> See Unit 5, topic 5.3 for more detail on costs and an explanation of contribution linked to break-even output.

> 📐 **Maths skills**
>
> It is useful to calculate contribution and to understand the different ways this can be done:
>
> Contribution per unit = price per unit – variable cost per unit
>
> Total contribution = total revenue – total variable cost
>
> OR
>
> Total contribution = contribution per unit × quantity sold

**A Level**

You should only refer to contribution costing in the following situations:

➤ 'One-off' special orders – a firm may be willing to supply a batch of products at a lower price if it has the spare capacity and regular customers do not find out and when using full costing would mean that they would reject the order. It is likely that the fixed costs have been covered by the 'normal' products so any price above marginal cost would contribute profits.

➤ 'Make or buy' decisions – a business can often choose to manufacture all its products or to buy some of them from other manufacturers. Marginal costing is useful here as the business can see if making the product covers the variable cost and contributes to fixed costs. If so they would choose to manufacture it.

➤ Deciding whether to stop production of a product – using full costing might mean that the product appears to make a loss but if the product covers the variable cost and contributes to fixed costs (contribution costing) it might be worthwhile continuing production. This might also apply when the business does not have the capacity to keep producing all products so calculates the contribution made by each product.

➤ When entering a new market – in order to compete in a new market firms may have to use penetration pricing in order to establish a customer base. In the short term the business may be content to cover just the direct costs so that in the long-term prices can be raised to a level which covers all costs and provides a profit.

---

**Worked example**

Wooden Productions plc (WP) manufacture a range of kitchen cabinets. WP are considering stopping production of the kitchen cabinet range 'Meadows' and are considering the following financial information:

| Meadows range | $000 |
|---|---|
| Sales revenue | 200 |
| Fixed costs | 88 |
| Direct labour | 50 |
| Direct materials | 53 |
| Salaries | 33 |
| Office expenses | 6 |

Discuss whether WP should stop production of the Meadows range. [11 marks]

**Answer**

If WP use the full costing method then this product would appear to make a loss. ✓ [knowledge mark]

Sales revenue = $200 000

Variable costs = $50 000 + $53 000 = $103 000 ✓✓ [2 analysis marks for the identification and correct calculation of variable costs in context]

Fixed costs = $88 000 + $33 000 + $6000 = $127 000 ✓✓ [2 analysis marks for the identification and correct calculation of fixed costs in context]

Therefore, revenue – costs = $200 000 – ($103 000 + $127 000) = –$30 000 ✓ [1 analysis mark] and the Meadows range appears to make a loss. If contribution costing is used ✓ [1 knowledge mark] so that fixed costs are ignored, then the range makes a contribution to fixed costs/profit of $97 000; $200 000 − $103 000. ✓ [1 analysis mark] If WP stop production of the range, then the fixed costs would have to be covered by the other products ✓ [1 evaluation mark] so WP should compare the cost information, using contribution costing, on all its products before making a decision. ✓ [1 evaluation mark] I would advise WP to continue producing the range as it covers all its direct costs and makes a positive contribution which might be difficult for other products to cover. ✓ [1 mark for justified judgement based on preceding analysis]

## 10.2 Budgets

This topic is concerned with:

➤ the purpose of budgets

➤ variances.

### The purpose of budgets

Budgets are financial **plans** for the future. Unit 5, topic 5.5 dealt with cash flow **forecasts**, budgets have a much wider scope than simply considering cash flowing in and out of a business.

> **Key terms**
>
> **Plans**: what the business *wants* to happen in the future.
>
> **Forecasts**: what the business *thinks* will happen in the future.

▼ **Table 10.1** Businesses often have more than one budget

| Budgets can be for… | Explanation |
|---|---|
| Sales | Plans the volume and value of sales over a specified time period. |
| Production | Plans production levels and input costs over a specified time period. |
| Marketing | Plans the finance required for marketing strategies over a specified time period. |
| Financial | Plans the need for external sources of finance over a specified time period. |
| Project | Plans the tasks, timings and costs of a project over a specified time period. |
| Capital expenditure | Plans the level of capital expenditure over a specified time period. |
| Master | The total of all budgets aggregated into one main budget over a specified time period. |

Budgets are useful but can also cause problems.

▼ **Table 10.2** Benefits and problems with budgeting

| Benefits of budgeting | Problems with budgeting |
|---|---|
| Budgets can be useful for… | Budgets can present problems if… |
| <ul><li>allocating resources</li><li>monitoring and evaluating business performance</li><li>identifying problems before they happen</li><li>improving decision making</li><li>motivating employees</li><li>managing money effectively</li><li>planning for the future.</li></ul> | <ul><li>based on unrealistic assumptions</li><li>managers unskilled in budgeting</li><li>they are over-optimistic</li><li>there is no previous experience of a project</li><li>there is a lack of data available</li><li>unrealistic targets set</li><li>managers stick rigidly to budgets and cannot adapt to change.</li></ul> |

> ★ **Exam tip**
>
> Budgets are important in total quality management and you can link ideas about this as well as linking to management and motivational theories in answers. Always consider the assumptions made when producing a budget and make reference to these when answering questions.

**Remember**

The difference between a plan and a forecast. A plan shows what the business wants in the future whereas a forecast is what might happen in the future.

Objectives set → Strategies planned → Approval and authorisation → Plans executed → Progress monitored

▲ **Figure 10.1** How budgets are produced

There are several types of budgets such as **incremental**, **zero** and **flexible**.

**Key terms**

**Incremental**: budgets are prepared for a variety of situations to anticipate outcomes that are out of the control of budget holders.

**Zero**: creating new budgets for each time period. Managers have to justify the budget 'from scratch'.

**Flexible**: budgets are prepared for a variety of situations to anticipate outcomes that are out of the control of budget holders.

**Adverse variance**: the variance contributes to a lower-than-budgeted profit.

**Favourable variance**: the variance contributes to a greater-than-budgeted profit.

**Variance analysis**: the process of calculating and examining variances in order to improve business performance.

### Worked example

Explain **two** reasons as to why budgets can be useful to business. [6 marks]

**Answer**

Budgets are financial plans for the future. ✓ [1 knowledge mark] Businesses can use budgets to allocate resources, ✓ [1 knowledge mark] managers are forced to think about the resources they will need, ✓ [1 analysis mark] when they will need them and how much they will cost. ✓ [1 analysis mark] Budgets are also useful for controlling and monitoring a business ✓ [1 knowledge mark] as businesses can compare the planned budget with actual spending to ensure that managers remain on target. ✓ [1 analysis mark]

## Variances

Variances are the difference between budgeted and actual performance. For example, if the budgeted spend on a project is $1000 but actual spending is $1200 then there has been an overspend of $200 known as an **adverse variance**. If the actual spending had been $900 then there would have been an underspend known as a **favourable variance**. Businesses that use **variance analysis** can take action to minimise problems, assess the quality of the budgeting process and the performance of departments and managers. A better understanding of costs and revenues can also help to control future events.

### Worked example

Complete the final column of the budget below by commenting on the variance. [8 marks]

| | Budget ($000) | Actual ($000) | Variance ($000) | Comment (Answer) |
|---|---|---|---|---|
| Sales revenue | 250 | 300 | 50 | Favourable ✓ sales are more than expected which increases profit. ✓ |
| Variable costs | 80 | 105 | 25 | Adverse ✓ variable costs are more than expected which decreases profit. ✓ |
| Fixed costs | 50 | 80 | 30 | Adverse ✓ fixed costs are more than expected which decreases profit. ✓ |
| Profit | 120 | 115 | 5 | Adverse ✓ adverse variances > favourable variances so the net result is lower profits. ✓ |

## 10.3 Contents of accounts

This topic is concerned with:

➤ financial statements

➤ inventory valuation

➤ depreciation.

**🔗 Link**

Unit 5, topic 5.4
Accounting fundamentals.
Tables 5.4 and 5.5.

### Financial statements

In Unit 5 the income statement and the statement on financial position are outlined. This section considers amendments to those statements. If we consider the statement from section 5.4 again:

▼ **Table 10.3** Example of an income statement

| First Development Ltd | | | |
|---|---|---|---|
| **Income Statement** | 2017 | 2017 (amended) | 2016 |
| Year ended 31 December | $000 | $000 | $000 |
| | | | |
| Revenue | 3 880 | 4 268 | 2 945 |
| *Less* cost of sales | 1 455 | 1 455 | 1 170 |
| Gross profit | 2 425 | 2 813 | 1 775 |
| *Less* Expenses | 1 226 | 1 226 | 1 050 |
| Operating profit | 1 199 | 1 587 | 725 |
| *Less* Finance costs | 98 | 98 | 72 |
| Profit before tax | 1 101 | 1 489 | 653 |
| *Less* Tax | 275 | 372 | 163 |
| Profit (attributable to shareholders) | 826 | 1 117 | 490 |

If the sales revenue had been miscalculated so that instead of $3 880 000, it should be $4 268 000, but costs remained the same, which figures would have to be amended? As the revenue has increased but costs remain unchanged then the following figures are amended (as shown above): Gross profit; Operating profit; Profit before tax; Tax; Profit – all have risen.

Changes in the income statement have an impact on the statement of financial position. If we now consider the same firm's statement of financial position from AS section 5.4, we can see that because the profit attributable to shareholders has increased then the retained profit in the statement below needs amending. Current assets also change as the higher sales revenue will be either in cash or in the bank, this is true for both net current assets and net assets.

**⭐ Exam tip**

It is easy to see why profit changes as revenue has increased but don't forget that tax is a percentage of profits; as the firm has higher profits it will have to pay more tax.

▼ **Table 10.4** An example of statement of financial position

| First Development Ltd statement of financial position as at the 31 December 2017 | | | |
|---|---|---|---|
| | Amendments required | $000 | $000 |
| Non-current assets | None | | 2 580 |
| Current assets | 2 743 | 2 355 | |
| *Less* Current liabilities | None | 1 362 | |
| **Net current assets (working capital)** | 1 381 | | 993 |

| First Development Ltd statement of financial position as at the 31 December 2017 | | | |
|---|---|---|---|
| | Amendments required | $000 | $000 |
| *Less* non-current liabilities (long term) | None | 255 | |
| **Net assets** | **3 706** | | **3 318** |
| **Financed by** | | | |
| Reserves | None | 2 492 | |
| Retained profit | 1 214 | 826 | |
| **Equity** | **3 706** | | **3 318** |

## Inventory valuation

Inventories (non-current assets) have to be valued and businesses should not understate or overstate the value. Accounting principles require that inventory is valued at cost or net realisable value (whichever is lowest).

Businesses usually value inventory as the original cost of purchasing it. However, this does not always result in the lowest cost valuation as required. If a firm has 100 laptop computers (selling price $200) in stock, originally bought for $100 each, then the cost valuation would be $100 × 100 = $10 000. If the technology in the laptops becomes outdated before the firms sells them then the laptops might only be sold off for $80 each making the net realisable value of the inventory $8000. As $8000 is the lower valuation then this must be recorded on the statement of financial position.

Valuing inventory can be problematic for businesses for many reasons:

➤ Damage to inventory might need repairing, adding to the cost of the stock.

➤ Some inventory may never be sold, so will have no financial value to the business.

➤ Inventory has to be checked and counted for a valuation. The date it is checked might not represent other times of the year or it might be a different date to the statement of financial position.

**Worked example**

Malik's Antiques income statement for the year ending 31 December 2017:

| | $000 |
|---|---|
| Sales revenue | 25 |
| Cost of goods sold | 10 |
| Gross profit | 15 |
| Office expenses | 8 |
| Operating profit | 7 |

Malik forecasts that sales revenue will increase by 20% next year and cost of goods sold will increase by 10%. Prepare Malik's income statement for the year ending 31 December 2018. [6]

**Answer**

Malik's Antiques income statement for the year ending 31 December 2018:

Sales revenue = 25 + 20% = 30

Cost of goods sold = 10 + 10% = 11

|  | $000 |  |
|---|---|---|
| Sales revenue | 30 | ✓ ✓ |
| Cost of goods sold | 11 | ✓ ✓ |
| Gross profit | 19 | ✓ |
| Office expenses | 8 |  |
| Operating profit | 11 | ✓ |

## Depreciation

**Depreciation** measures the wearing out of capital over a period of time. There are many ways of calculating depreciation but the **straight-line method** is the simplest.

> **Maths skills**
>
> Straight line depreciation is calculated as:
>
> Depreciation = (Cost of equipment – Residual value) ÷ Estimated lifetime of the machinery.

> **Worked example**
>
> Kaisa has purchased a t-shirt printing machine for $28 000 which is expected to have a useful life of 5 years at which time it can be sold for $3000.
>
> Calculate the yearly depreciation rate for Kaisa's machine.     [4]
>
> **Answer**
>
> Depreciation = (Cost of equipment – Residual value) ÷ Estimated lifetime of the machinery ✓
>
> $28 000 – $3000 = $25 000 ✓
>
> $25 000 ÷ 5 years ✓ = $5000 per year ✓

In the worked example above the depreciation rate of $5000 would be entered on the income statement as an expense. On the statement of financial position three figures are entered: The original cost, the accumulated depreciation and the **carrying amount (net book value)**. After the first year this would be:

▼ **Table 10.5** Cost, accumulated depreciation and carrying amount (net book value)

|  | $ | $ | $ |
|---|---|---|---|
| Equipment | 28 000 | 5 000 | $23 000 (carrying amount) |

> **Key terms**
>
> **Depreciation:** spreading the cost of a non-current asset over its expected useful life.
>
> **Straight-line method of depreciation:** assumes that the cost of the asset is spread evenly over its expected lifetime. Three elements to this method; asset cost, expected lifetime and **residual value**.
>
> **Residual value:** the estimated resale value of an asset at the end of its useful life.
>
> **Carrying amount (net book value):** the value of a non-current asset calculated by: Purchase price – accumulated depreciation.

> **Exam tip**
>
> The straight-line method is the simplest method for calculating depreciation and the only method you need to know for the exam.

It is difficult to estimate the useful life of equipment but it is important that businesses take care when doing this as depreciation is recorded in the income statement and has the effect of reducing operating profit, gross profit and profit before tax. This means that the amount of tax paid is also reduced and tax authorities in many countries have rules on how businesses calculate depreciation.

## 10.4 Analysis of published accounts

This topic is concerned with:

➤ use of ratio analysis.

### Use of ratio analysis

In Unit 5, topic 5.4 profitability and liquidity ratios were discussed. In addition to these you also need to be able to calculate and interpret other ratios. The ratios required are shown below:

▼ **Table 10.6** Ratio calculation

| Ratio | Calculation | Explanation |
|---|---|---|
| Profitability | You will need to know the two profitability ratios from Unit 5, topic 5.4: Gross profit margin and profit margin. | Measures different types of profit generated by a business in relation to sales revenue or assets. |
| Return on capital employed (ROCE) | (Operating profit for the year ÷ Capital employed) × 100 | Measures the rate at which the assets of a business generate profit. Known as the 'primary' ratio and measures the rate at which the assets of a business generate profit. Potential shareholders would use it to calculate potential returns on money invested in the business. |
| Financial efficiency | You need to know the two liquidity ratios in Unit 5, topic 5.4: The acid test and current ratios. | Measures how well business manages current assets in a business. |
| Inventory turnover | Cost of products sold ÷ Average inventory held. | Measures the rate at which inventory enters and leaves the business. The result tells us in, on average, how many days or how many times inventory is sold (turned over). |
| Days' sales in receivables | (Trade receivables [debtors] × 365) ÷ Credit sales | Measures the average time that debtors take to pay their debts to the business. It is important as businesses have to keep money flowing into the business so that they can pay their debtors. It is important to put the figure in the context of the business and to consider the proportion of credit sales to cash sales. |
| Gearing | Debt ÷ Equity or<br><br>Debt ÷ (Equity + Debt) | The proportion of finance that is provided by debt relative to the finance provided by equity.<br><br>There are various methods of calculating gearing but be guided by the question. It is the interpretation of the calculation that is important when selecting a source of finance. |
| Gearing ratio | (Non-current liabilities ÷ Capital employed) × 100 | Measures the proportion of the business capital that is provided by debt, i.e. the proportion of assets invested in a business that are financed by long-term borrowing. A business with 50% or higher gearing is said to be 'highly geared'.<br><br>Generally, the higher the level of gearing the higher the risks to a business as, unlike dividends, debt has to be repaid and incurs interest. However, if the business has strong, predictable cash flows then gearing can be an important part of the business capital structure.<br><br>Gearing can be a financially sound part of a business's capital structure particularly if the business has strong, predictable cash flows. |

| Ratio | Calculation | Explanation |
|---|---|---|
| **Investor ratios** | You are only expected to know the three ratios below: | Shareholders/potential shareholders use these ratios to determine whether or not to retain/buy shares in that company. |
| Dividend yield | (Dividend per share ÷ Market price per share) × 100 | Measures the rate of return that a holder of ordinary shares receives for each share held. Shareholders/potential shareholders can compare the dividend yield to other returns achievable elsewhere such as other companies or in a savings account. Sometimes a high dividend yield is an indicator of a high-risk investment. |
| Dividend cover | Profit after tax and interest ÷ Dividend paid | Measures the number of times that the total dividend could be paid out of the company's profit after tax and interest. This can indicate how likely it is that the company can keep paying a dividend in future years. |
| Price/earnings ratio | Current market price per share ÷ Earnings per share | Measures the relationship between the earnings per share and the market price of the share. The higher the ratio the more confidence shareholders will have in the company. |

**Maths skills**

Earnings per share is calculated as profit after tax ÷ number of ordinary shares.

**Exam tip**

One or two ratios on their own are not that useful. Ratio analysis should be interpreted in the context of the business and alongside other financial information. It is important that you analyse and interpret the significance of your results to the business in the question.

**Link**

See Unit 5 for ratios.

## Worked example

Utopia plc has selected the following financial information from the accounts for 2017.

| Ordinary shares of $1 | $200m |
|---|---|
| Market price of the shares | $3 |
| Dividend per share | $0.18 |
| Profit before tax and interest | $35.7m |
| Non-current liabilities | $22m |

**a)** Calculate the dividend yield for 2017. [3]

**b)** Calculate the ROCE for 2017. [3]

**Answers**

**a)** (Dividend per share ÷ Market price per share) × 100 ✓ = ($0.18 ÷ $3) × 100 ✓ = 6% ✓

**b)** (Operating profit for the year ÷ Capital employed) × 100 ✓ = ($35.7m ÷ $222m) × 100 ✓ = 16.08% ✓

## 10.5 Investment appraisal

This topic is concerned with:

➤ the concept of investment appraisal

➤ methods of investment appraisal

➤ discounted cash flow methods

➤ qualitative factors in investment appraisal.

## The concept of investment appraisal

In business, **investment** usually refers to spending on capital such as machinery and vehicles but can include other types of non-current spending such as on a marketing campaign. The need for **investment appraisal** is to ensure that the business is spending money to get a sufficient return on the investment in the future.

Investment projects are often long-term, a new rail track might take 20 years or more to complete, so the return is many years in the future. Therefore, it is important that decision-makers need to be aware of the uncertainty and **risk** in an investment decision. Taking decisions where the project time is years means that decision-makers have to be aware of 'known' factors; 'known unknown' factors and that there will be 'unknown unknowns' that will affect the risk of the investment decision.

For example, businesses know that exchange rates might change (known unknown) and affect overseas returns but they don't know if the government of a country will change future taxes on company profits (unknown unknown).

Investment appraisal involves making a **net cash flow forecast** for the investment project that tries to predict future cash inflows and outflows.

> 💡 **Remember**
>
> Do not confuse the cash flow forecasts of a business with the cash flow forecasts of a project. If you refer to a 'net cash flow forecast' it will remind you that this relates to an investment project not the whole business.

▼ **Table 10.7** Forecast net cash flow of investing in a new machine $000

| Year | Forecast cash outflow | Forecast cash inflow | Net cash flow forecast |
|---|---|---|---|
| 0 (initial investment) | 80 | | −80 |
| 1 | 15 | 40 | 25 |
| 2 | 15 | 40 | 25 |
| 3 | 15 | 45 | 30 |
| 4 | 15 | 45 | 30 |

## Methods of investment appraisal

▼ **Table 10.8** Basic methods of investment appraisal

| Method | Explanation | Calculation | Benefits | Limitations |
|---|---|---|---|---|
| Payback | The length of time it will take, in terms of net cash flows, to pay back the capital cost of an investment. In the table above the initial investment is paid back at the end of year 3. | The number of years for cash outflow = cash inflow | • Simple.<br>• Easy to compare many projects.<br>• Can easily use a range of forecast figures for 'what if' analysis.<br>• Gives lenders an idea of how long it might take to repay if financed by a loan. | • Does not take account of overall profitability.<br>• Does not consider cash flows after the payback period.<br>• Should be used with other methods. |

| Method | Explanation | Calculation | Benefits | Limitations |
|---|---|---|---|---|
| Accounting rate of return (ARR) | Measures the average annual profit of an investment as a percentage of the initial investment. It can be compared with interest rates on saving accounts. | (Average annual net cash flow ÷ original investment) × 100 = ARR% | • Easy to compare ARR and interest rates.<br>• Includes cash flows over the life of the project.<br>• Easy to compare with an expected rate of return.<br>• Easy to compare projects. | • More uncertainty the further into the future.<br>• Does not consider the timing of net cash flows so should be used with payback.<br>• Assumes cash flows have the same value in the future as they do now (the time value of money) – major weakness. |

## Discounted cash flow methods

Money in the future has a lower value than money today because:

- we want things now rather than waiting (the time preference for money)

- the opportunity cost of interest foregone by waiting for future returns

- future price rises, inflation, reduces the amount that can be bought with a specific sum of money in the future

- risk means that the longer the time period of the project the more uncertain the outcomes.

To find the value of future cash flows as compared with money spent on an investment now, discounting is used. The discount rate chosen by a business is often based on current or expected interest rates. Often two or three discount rates are used in a 'best' and 'worst' case scenario. When future cash flows are discounted the result is that the present value of future cash flows.

Discounted payback is the payback method but discounting future cash flows. For example, if we consider the investment above, where payback happened at the end of year 3, and use a discount factor of 5%:

▼ **Table 10.9** Forecast net cash flow of investing in a new machine $000

| Year | Net cash flow forecast | Discount factor 5% | Net cash flow forecast discounted 5% |
|---|---|---|---|
| 0 (initial investment) | −80 | | −80 |
| 1 | 25 | 25 ÷ 1.05 | 24* |
| 2 | 25 | 25 ÷ (1.05)$^2$ | 23* |
| 3 | 30 | 30 ÷ (1.05)$^3$ | 26* |
| 4 | 30 | 30 ÷ (1.05)$^4$ | 25* |

\* Figures rounded.

**Key terms**

**Opportunity cost:** the value of the next best opportunity that is lost by taking a particular decision.

**Discounting:** the process of recognising that money in the future has less value than the same amount today.

**Discount rate:** the percentage rate at which each future year is discounted.

**Present value:** the value today of a given amount of money in the future.

**Discounted payback:** The discounted payback period is the amount of time that it takes to cover the cost of a project, by adding positive discounted cash flow coming from the profits of the project. This contrasts with payback which uses unadjusted net cash flows.

Net present value (NPV) goes further than discounted payback by taking account of all the cash flows over the life of the project and applying discount factors. In the example from above this would give:

| $000 |
|------|
| 24 |
| +23 |
| +26 |
| +25 |
| −80 |
| =18 |

The $80000 initial investment is not discounted as it is expenditure now. The NPV of the project is $18000, positive, which suggests that the project should go ahead as it gives a higher return than the next best alternative.

NPV is dependent on the discount rate chosen. To avoid having to choose some discount rate businesses can use a technique called **internal rate of return (IRR)**. IRR asks 'What discount rate would give a NPV = 0?' Decision makers can then decide if the rate of return is worth the investment, easier than trying to decide a discount rate.

We can see how this works with our previous example of NPV.

▼ **Table 10.10** Example of NPV

| Discount rate | 5% | 10% | 15% |
|---------------|-----|------|------|
| Net present value $000 | 18 | 8 | −2 |

So NPV = 0 will be somewhere between 10% and 15%. Discount rates between 10% and 15% could be tried or a graph drawn up so that a more accurate figure is calculated.

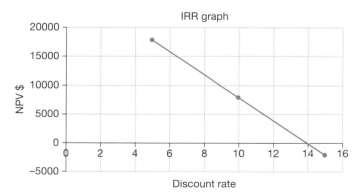

▲ **Figure 10.2** IRR Graph

You can see that NPV = 0 at a discount rate of 14%.

★ **Exam tip**

Discount factors will be given in questions. You are not expected to calculate the IRR but you may have to interpret the results.

### Worked example

Complete column 4 of the table below, rounding the results to the nearest whole number. [4]

Forecast net cash flow of a new product launch ($000):

| Year 1 | Net cash flow forecast 2 | Discount factor at 10% 3 | Net cash flow forecast discounted at 10% 4 |
|---|---|---|---|
| 0 (initial investment) | −25 | 1.00 | −25 |
| 1 | 6 | 0.91 | 7 × 0.91 = 5 ✓ |
| 2 | 7 | 0.82 | 7 × 0.82 = 6 ✓ |
| 3 | 12 | 0.75 | 12 × 0.75 = 9 ✓ |
| 4 | 12 | 0.68 | 12 × 0.68 = 8 ✓ |

### Qualitative factors in investment appraisal

So far we have considered **quantitative** tools for investment appraisal. However, there are also **qualitative** considerations in any business decision such as:

- attitude to risk – are the owners of a business 'risk averse' or 'risk takers'?

- impact on stakeholders

- changes in the internal and external environment in which businesses operate

- ease and availability of finance

- the fit with objectives and strategies.

It is important that decision makers consider all the available evidence before making a decision.

**Key terms**

**Quantitative:** based on numbers that can be calculated or estimated.

**Qualitative:** cannot be calculated or estimated in numerical terms.

### Revision checklist

**I can:**

➤ explain, analyse and produce different types of budgets ☐

➤ discuss the advantages and disadvantages of budgets ☐

➤ show how marketing and operations are linked to value added ☐

➤ analyse and evaluate the use of budgets ☐

➤ explain, calculate and interpret variances ☐

➤ make amendments to income statements and statements of financial position ☐

➤ understand the link between information on income statements and statements of financial position ☐

➤ discuss the net realisable value method of valuing inventory and the difficulties of inventory valuation ☐

➤ understand the role and impact of depreciation on income statements and statements of financial position ☐

➤ calculate depreciation using the straight-line method ☐

➤ discuss and calculate ROCE, inventory turnover, days' sale in receivables and the gearing ratio of a given business ☐

➤ calculate and assess dividend yield, dividend cover and price/earnings ratio ☐

➤ comment on the use, benefits and limitations of ratio analysis ☐

➤ define investment appraisal and discuss the need for it ☐

➤ assess the significance of risk in investment appraisal ☐

➤ explain, calculate and interpret payback, ARR, discounted payback and NPV ☐

➤ explain and interpret IRR ☐

➤ discuss qualitative factors that may influence investment decisions ☐

➤ evaluate investment appraisal methods and make recommendations based on them ☐

➤ and apply all of the above to a range of businesses in different situations. ☐

## ⬆ Raise your grade

### Short answer questions

**1 (a)** Briefly explain the term 'payback'. [3]

The length of time it will take, ✓ in terms of net cash flows, ✓ to pay back the capital cost of an investment. ✓

> **[3 marks]** It is important to explain all elements of the definition: time, net cash flows and related to investment projects.

**(b)** Briefly explain the term 'discounting'. [2]

The process of recognising that money in the future ✓ has less value than the same amount today. ✓

> **[2 marks]** It is important to consider the marks available. This question has two marks so the answer only includes two points.

**2** Give one advantage and one disadvantage of using ARR as a method of investment appraisal. [4]

ARR is the accounting rate of return ✓ and measures the average annual profit of an investment as a percentage of the initial investment ✓ advantages are it is easy to compare with an expected rate of return ✓ and to compare projects. ✗

> **[3 marks]** The question asks for one advantage and one disadvantage of ARR but the answer above gives two advantages so does not get the mark for a disadvantage.

**3**   Sounds Electronics plc (SE)

In recent years the shareholders of SE have been very unhappy with the company's performance, especially as the board of directors have announced a cut in the dividend payable to shareholders. The following extract is from the company's accounts:

|  | **2017** | **2016** |
|---|---|---|
| Ordinary shares of $1 | $1000m | $900m |
| Market price of the shares | $3 | $2 |
| Dividend per share | $0.36 | $0.40 |
| Profit before tax and interest | $155.7m | $140.8m |
| Non-current liabilities | $22m | $15m |

**(a)**   Calculate the dividend yield for 2016.                                                                 [3]

(Dividend per share ÷ Market price per share) × 100 ✓ = ($0.36 ÷ $3) ✗ × 100 = 12% ✓ [OFR]

> **[2 marks]** The 2017 figures have been used although the question clearly states 2016. However, this is one mistake so the formula can get a mark and the application of the calculation another mark. Showing each step means it is often possible to get some marks.

**(b)**   Discuss the possible effects, on shareholders, of the reduced dividend in 2017.                [8]

A key focus of shareholders is their return on investment. ✓ [1 knowledge mark] The returns from investing in shares of a company come in two main forms; the payment of dividends out of profits and the increase in the value of the shares (share price) compared with the price that the shareholder originally paid for the shares. ✓ [1 knowledge mark] The reduction in dividend reduces the dividend yield from 20% to 12% ✓ [1 contextualised knowledge mark] so shareholders have a reduced income from their shares. ✓ [1 analysis mark] However, the share price has risen by 50%. ✓✓ [1 contextualised knowledge mark and 1 contextualised analysis mark] This means that shareholders may want to sell their shares to take advantage of the increased share price and because the yield has fallen on their shares. ✓ [1 contextualised analysis mark] Whether they sell their shares depends on how much the shareholder paid for the shares – i.e. what the dividend means in terms of a return on investment and how much profit per share was earned which might have been distributed as a dividend. ✓ [1 contextualised analysis mark]

> **[8 marks]** A good, concise answer. Notice that half the marks are for context.

**Long answer question**

**(c)**   Evaluate two sources of finance available to SE for further expansion.                          [16]

SE could choose to raise the additional finance by long-term loans ✓ [1 knowledge mark] or by issuing more shares. ✓ [1 knowledge mark]

SE have a very low gearing ratio, ✓ [1 knowledge mark] 1.6% in 2016 ✓ [1 contextualised analysis mark] and 2.1% in 2017. ✓ [1 contextualised analysis mark] This means that further borrowing could be undertaken without putting the business at risk. ✓ [1 evaluation mark]

If they increase their long-term liabilities, they need to make sure that interest payments are be paid or assets might be at risk. ✓ [1 analysis mark] Interest payments reduce profitability and might therefore cause a decrease in dividends paid to shareholders ✓ [1 analysis mark] who are already unhappy with the performance of the company and the decreased dividend. ✓ [1 contextualised evaluation mark] Shareholders may even sell their shares resulting in a lower market price of shares ✓ [1 contextualised analysis mark] this could make it difficult to raise future finance by selling more shares. ✓ [1 contextualised evaluation mark] The advantage of issuing more shares is that it is permanent capital and if the company is unprofitable in the future, dividends need not be paid. ✓ [1 analysis mark] The raising of finance through a loan does not change the ownership of the company ✓ [1 knowledge mark] whereas the selling of more shares to the general public dilutes ownership. ✓ [1 knowledge mark] If there is a danger that a rival business might buy the shares and try to gain some control, then a loan might be better. ✓ [1 evaluation mark] Given the low gearing ratio and the risk of loss of control I would advise SE to take a loan. ✓ [1 evaluation (judgement) mark]

**[16 marks]** Good analysis, chains of reasoning and evaluation. Notice that evaluation can be rewarded at any point – the first evaluation mark comes in line 5 of the above answer. In longer mark questions about a third of the marks are for evaluation.

## ? Exam-style questions

This section will allow you to practise writing answers for exam-style questions. Remember, it is useful to be aware of the mark schemes for the questions which can be found on relevant websites or from your teacher.

**Paper 3**

**Short answer questions**

1   (a) Briefly explain variance. [2]

   (b) Calculate the gearing ratio of a firm with $2 m long term liabilities and capital employed of $6.8 m. [3]

2   (a) Define the term 'capital employed'. [3]

   (b) Briefly explain the term 'dividend'. [2]

3   Explain why investors might be interested in the price/earnings ratio. [5]

**Long answer questions**

4   Analyse **two** methods of measuring the financial efficiency of a firm. [8]

5   Discuss the practical uses of budgets. [12]

6   Evaluate the usefulness of investor ratio analysis to potential investors. [20]

# 11 Strategic management

A 6.1–6.4, SB pages 501–557

## Key topics

- ➤ what is strategic management?
- ➤ strategic analysis
- ➤ strategic choice
- ➤ strategic implementation.



## 11.1 What is strategic management?

This topic is concerned with:

- ➤ the meaning of corporate strategy, tactics and strategic management
- ➤ the need for strategic management
- ➤ how business strategy determines competitive advantage in an increasingly competitive world.

### The meaning of corporate strategy, tactics and strategic management

To successfully complete the 20-mark questions on Paper 3, candidates will need to be able to understand, apply and use **strategic management**. There are three main questions that need to be considered for successful strategic management:

**Key term**

**Strategic management**: the analysis, decisions and actions an organisation undertakes to create and sustain competitive advantages.

**Remember**

Strategic management simply means looking at the bigger picture – all of the different aspects of the business must be utilised for a plan to be successful.

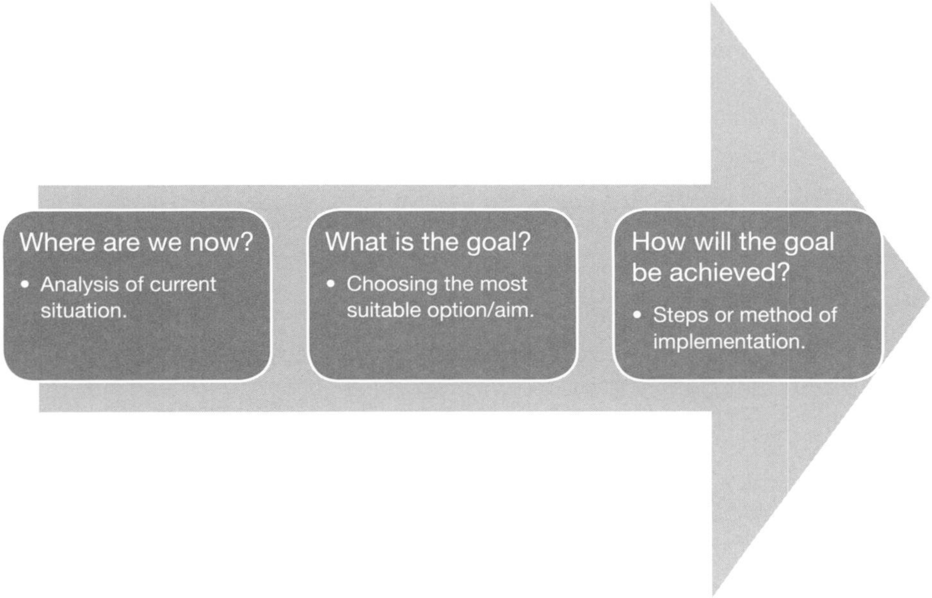
Where are we now?
• Analysis of current situation.
What is the goal?
• Choosing the most suitable option/aim.
How will the goal be achieved?
• Steps or method of implementation.

▲ **Figure 11.1** Three main questions for successful strategic management

Strategic management occurs at three different levels:

The pyramid illustrates how corporate strategy creates the base for all further strategies.

**Functional strategy**
- specific strategy for a functional area such as marketing
- decisions on the specific methods of achieving a particular objective.

**Business strategy**
- general strategy for a division or area of the business
- decisions made to complement the corporate strategy.

**Corporate strategy**
- overall purpose and general direction
- is the base for all further strategies and decisions.

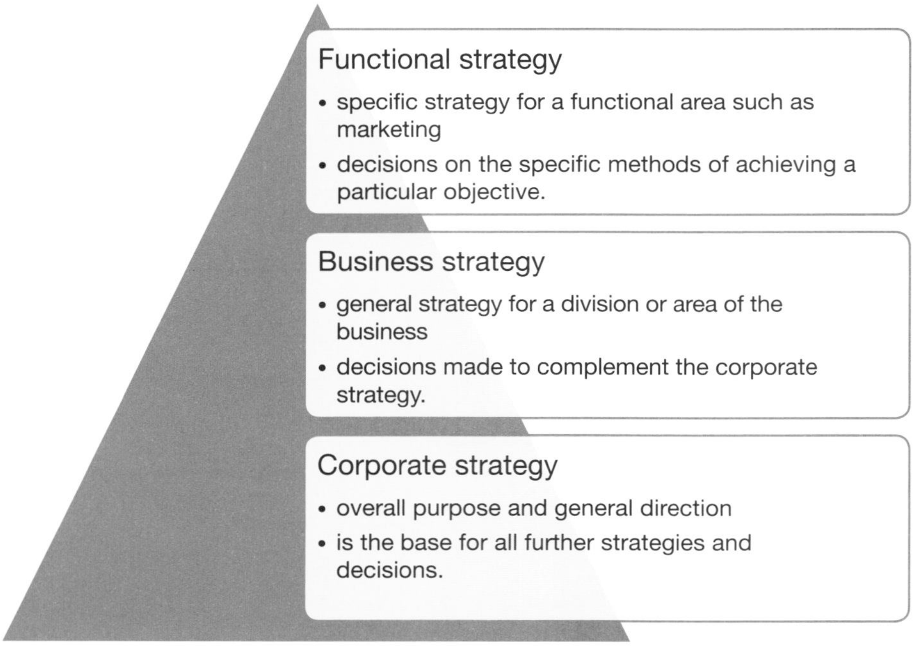

▲ **Figure 11.2** Three levels of strategic management pyramid

Strategic management integrates the key objectives and plans from the corporate strategy throughout the organisation.

Businesses use both strategies and tactics to reach specific objectives. Tactics are created by breaking down the strategy into specific and manageable tasks.

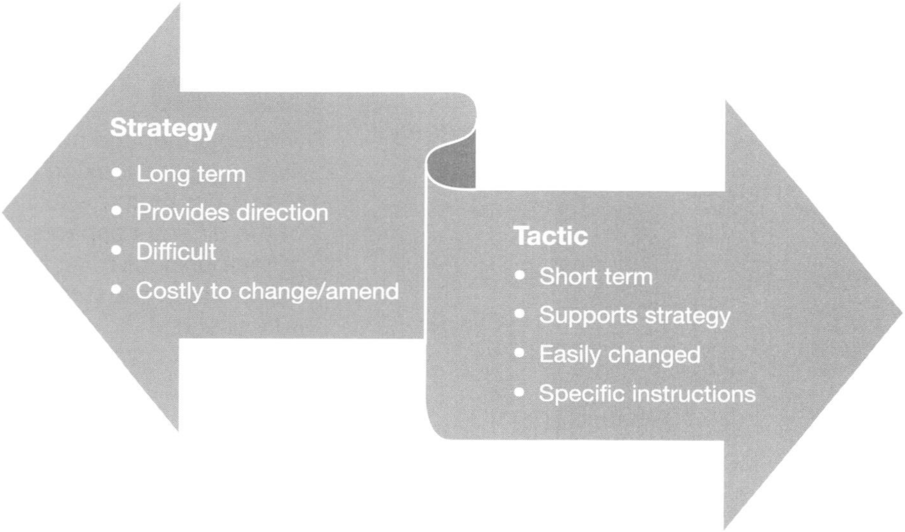

**Strategy**
- Long term
- Provides direction
- Difficult
- Costly to change/amend

**Tactic**
- Short term
- Supports strategy
- Easily changed
- Specific instructions

▲ **Figure 11.3** Strategies and tactics used to reach specific objectives

## The need for strategic management

Businesses that have poor strategic management tend to fail due to missing opportunities, not having a unified brand or ineffective planning techniques. There are many reasons why strategic management is important – the key reasons are shown in Figure 11.4.

▲ **Figure 11.4** The need for strategic management

## Chandler's assertion that strategy should determine organisational structure

(Alfred) Chandler's assertion is that strategic management decisions lead to the structure of the business. As strategic decisions made at the centre or the top of the organisation are communicated to individual managers lower down the hierarchy and in individual business units, the business structures adapt to meet the needs of the new decisions.

Chandler's observations are shown in Figure 11.5.

Management strategy decided at the head of the business.

Communication to junior managers and decision makers.

Individual business units free to decide own tactics within strategy.

▲ **Figure 11.5** Strategic management decisions lead to the structure of business

## How business strategy determines competitive advantage in an increasingly competitive world

To become successful, businesses must have a competitive advantage. This will allow businesses to maintain their market positions and remain in business. There is no specific business strategy that will bring success as each business is unique, however a well thought out strategy will help focus the business and maximise chances of business success.

▲ **Figure 11.6** Effects of poor business strategy

## Worked example

Evaluate the importance to SG of undertaking strategic analysis before the decision to merge with PPL Garages. [20 marks]

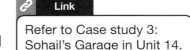

**Link**

Refer to Case study 3: Sohail's Garage in Unit 14.

### Answer

If SG does not undertake strategic analysis before they merge with PPL Garages, there will be a high chance of business failure as tools such as a SWOT analysis or Ansoff's Matrix will assist in identifying the used car environment and help to form future strategies that could utilise current market knowledge and provide a corporate strategy that would be the framework for the new organisation, especially if the business centralises its headquarters and merges the different divisions. ✓✓✓✓

If SG undertakes a SWOT analysis, which is a key tool, they will be able to identify the internal strengths and weaknesses of the merger; strengths include the increased market share that will make them twice as large as their nearest competitor and reduced operating costs that will allow for a more dominant market position. However, the weakness would be the increased risk of having a less diverse product family, something that Sohail wants to move away from as he does not want to be reliant on one market segment especially with increased threat of internet sales channels becoming a more popular method of purchasing products over time. This ties in with Ansoff's Matrix, which shows that Sohail would be moving backwards into market penetration with the same product and market, which although would provide cost opportunities of scale due to the merged organisations, would place him further at risk if the used car market was to change in its approach to the customer.

However, the opportunity to reduce the number of direct competitors is very important. As the owner of PPL wants to sell his business and allow another person to take control, if Sohail did not merge then he may have an even stronger competitor who would want to invest in the current operation and become the market leader, which would force Sohail to invest into his own business in order to compete with a stronger and more dedicated competitor. ✓✓✓✓

It is extremely important to undertake strategic evaluation before the decision to merge with PPL Garages as Sohail is considering two options and although there may be a gut reaction to stick with the area he is comfortable in, i.e. the used car sales, minimise competition and increase the cost efficiencies, this course of action is directly opposite to the direction that Sohail mentioned he wants to take the business. ✓✓

The joint venture option would allow Sohail to diversify his product range and target a new market with a supplier who also would like to make inroads into a new market, which means that NRG Autos may offer favourable terms and increased levels of support in the new venture that would not only help to increase the brand value and therefore attractiveness of the new product, but could also allow for a spreading of the increased financial risk of expansion. ✓✓✓

Strategic analysis could also identify potential pitfalls to Sohail. Although he has mentioned the desire to diversify, Sohail's organisation currently needs to consolidate its administrative functions which is a huge weakness and could put the entire organisation under threat from a better organised competitor. This analysis could therefore help to temper Sohail's ambition of diversification with the reality of his existing position; merging with a similar, existing business would therefore allow Sohail to also have access to a competing administrative system which may be better organised than the current method, which would make the merger a much more attractive option than face value. ✓✓✓✓✓

## 11.2 Strategic analysis

This topic is concerned with:

➤ SWOT analysis

➤ PEST or external environment analysis

➤ business vision/mission statement and objectives

➤ Boston Matrix

➤ Porter's Five Forces

➤ core competencies.

 **Exam tip**

All strategy questions are worth 20 marks. Candidates have a choice of two questions and must choose one only.

## SWOT analysis

The second stage of the management strategy, strategic analysis can also be used to clarify and refine business objectives. Strategic analysis is used to identify the business environment at the time and situation, considering the following aspects:

The internal environment
• Available resources.

The external environment
• Influence of competition and PEST(LE) factors.

Forces and factors
• Derived from internal and external situations.

▲ **Figure 11.7** Identifying the business environment

### Undertake and interpret SWOT analysis in a given situation

One of the most common and easily understood models, the SWOT analysis is a template that helps to explore internal and external factors that may affect or influence a business of its products.

**Key term**

**SWOT analysis**: investigation into the controllable strengths, and weaknesses that may influence a business and its products and external opportunities and threats that need to be harnessed and controlled that may affect a business and its products.

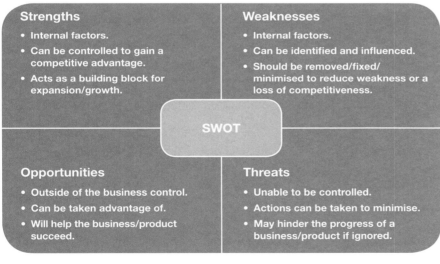

**Strengths**
• Internal factors.
• Can be controlled to gain a competitive advantage.
• Acts as a building block for expansion/growth.

**Weaknesses**
• Internal factors.
• Can be identified and influenced.
• Should be removed/fixed/minimised to reduce weakness or a loss of competitiveness.

**SWOT**

**Opportunities**
• Outside of the business control.
• Can be taken advantage of.
• Will help the business/product succeed.

**Threats**
• Unable to be controlled.
• Actions can be taken to minimise.
• May hinder the progress of a business/product if ignored.

▲ **Figure 11.8** Example SWOT analysis

A SWOT analysis is the first step of a process that will be used to create objectives both tactical and strategic.

**Remember**

A SWOT analysis is only as good as the data entered and the ability of the user. The matrix does not tell a business what to do but can be used to inform strategic decisions.

**Remember**

The analysis will be subject to the views of the analyst – two different people may read or rank the information differently and create different objectives – this is immaterial as the justification is what is important.

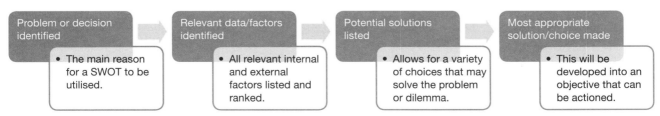

Problem or decision identified
• The main reason for a SWOT to be utilised.

Relevant data/factors identified
• All relevant internal and external factors listed and ranked.

Potential solutions listed
• Allows for a variety of choices that may solve the problem or dilemma.

Most appropriate solution/choice made
• This will be developed into an objective that can be actioned.

▲ **Figure 11.9** Development of the outcome of a SWOT analysis into strategic objectives

## PEST or external environment analysis

While businesses can easily identify internal strengths and weaknesses from a simple audit, there needs to be a framework to identify and classify external factors and their potential influence on the business. The **PEST analysis** is commonly used for this function.

| Political (and legal) | Economic | Social (and environmental) | Technological |
|---|---|---|---|
| • Policies and regulation; frameworks businesses have to work in.<br>• Have to be closely followed. | • Taxation and monetary policy.<br>• Affect profitability and accounting ratios. | • Demographics and attitudes that affect demand.<br>• Can be changeable and unpredictable. | • The differing methods of communication and production.<br>• Change processes and procedures. |

▲ **Figure 11.10** PEST (political, economic, social, technological) analysis in a given situation

While PEST can be a useful tool, there are a number of issues that need to be taken into consideration.

| Advantages | Disadvantages |
|---|---|
| • Relies heavily on secondary data.<br>• Relatively quick and easy to use.<br>• Easy to present and understand.<br>• Can explain a SWOT and give detail to a SWOT analysis. | • Can become outdated easily.<br>• Does not respond easily to market changes.<br>• Simplicity can be misleading.<br>• Relies on assumptions about future changes.<br>• May be subjective due to the views of the author. |

▲ **Figure 11.11** Advantages and disadvantages of PEST

## Business vision/mission statement and objectives

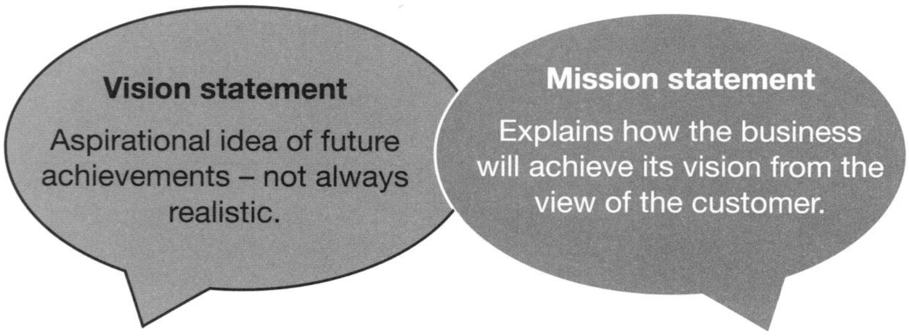

**Vision statement**
Aspirational idea of future achievements – not always realistic.

**Mission statement**
Explains how the business will achieve its vision from the view of the customer.

▲ **Figure 11.12** Difference between vision and mission statements

Although they may only consist of one or two lines, mission and vision statements are very important to most businesses:

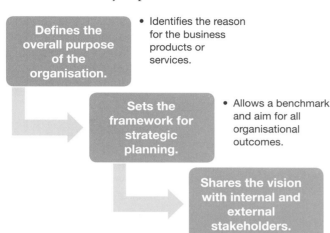

▲ **Figure 11.13** Evaluation of the role of business vision/mission statements and objectives in strategic analysis

## Boston Matrix

A framework for identifying the relative success of a product or stage in its life cycle. Useful for businesses with many products in its range. This allows businesses to assess the viability of products.

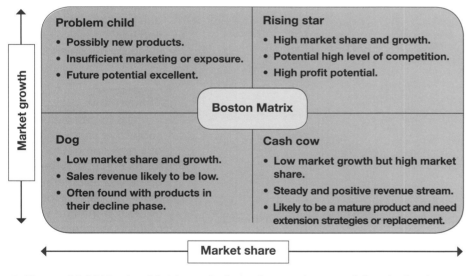

▲ **Figure 11.14** Boston Matrix analysis on the product portfolio of a business

The Boston Matrix allows the analyst to identify at what stage of the product lifecycle a product is and create strategies to maximise the potential sales if appropriate by matching promotional activities and spend to the product. Useful for managing a large product portfolio.

Businesses will need to have products in all four areas to ensure business longevity. Just having all cash cows, for example, means that there are no replacement products available for the decline stage.

## Porter's Five Forces

While the Boston Matrix analyses the products as internal factors, Porter's Five Forces analysis deals with five external influences to determine the level of competition.

### Porter's Five Forces analysis as a framework for business strategy

Reasons for using Porter's Five Forces analysis:

- assess existing position or potential for entry into a market
- assess the chances of survival or growth
- highlights internal strengths and weaknesses.

Problems with Porter's Five Forces analysis:

- best for simple markets
- difficult to reduce all influences to five forces
- competition and customers are not simple
- markets change quickly leading to redundant analysis.

▲ **Figure 11.15** Porter's Five Forces

## Core competencies

Core competencies are the capabilities that are essential for a business to gain a competitive advantage in the market are represented by the common skills, techniques or relationships that a business can apply successfully to a range of products or sectors. This management theory was introduced by Prahalad and Hamel.

### Prahalad and Hamel's core competencies analysis as a framework for business strategy

Core competencies of a business can be identified by the significant contribution levels of several factors, as illustrated in Figure 11.16.

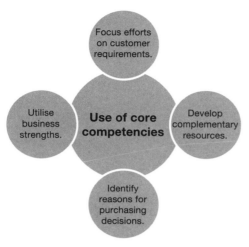

▲ **Figure 11.16** Use of core competencies

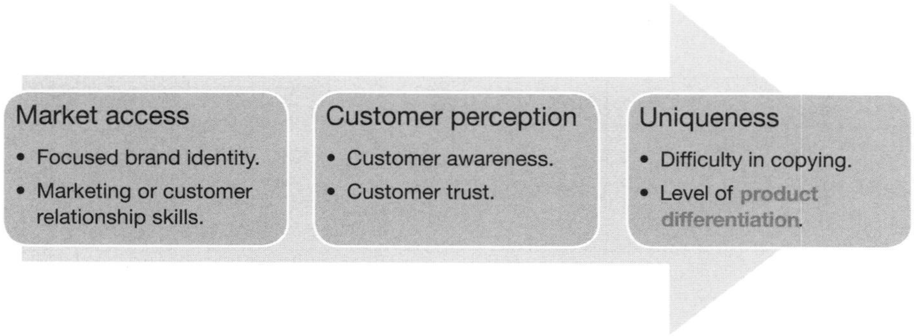

| Market access | Customer perception | Uniqueness |
|---|---|---|
| • Focused brand identity.<br>• Marketing or customer relationship skills. | • Customer awareness.<br>• Customer trust. | • Difficulty in copying.<br>• Level of product differentiation. |

▲ **Figure 11.17** The three factors used to decide on core competencies

**Exam tips**

There are unlikely to be any questions that specifically require models of strategic analysis to be used. Candidates can identify appropriate places for a suitable framework to be used and use the following methods to maximise their potential in their answers:

**Step 1**: Identify the relevant frameworks that may bring value to your answer; there may be a use for all, however you must choose the most suitable and limit yourself to these.

**Step 2**: Rather than wasting time and effort defining the frameworks, an exercise that is unlikely to earn any additional marks, consider utilising the information within the case study to complete each of your frameworks; limit yourself to a maximum of 2–3 points for each component of a framework due to time constraints.

**Step 3**: Instead of using each framework in isolation consider any crossover between frameworks; does the outcome of a PEST analysis support the findings of a SWOT analysis. Linking two frameworks is a simple way to gain analysis marks.

**Step 4**: Identify any limits on the analysis deduced; is there any further information that may be critical and may change the outcome? When will the information be used: if it is not to be used in the near future it may become outdated and provide erroneous data.

**Step 5**: Arrange the analysis into paragraphs that complement the question asked and use the findings after all limitations in the evaluation to help support the strategy chosen, supported or discussed.

**Key terms**

**Product differentiation:** the minor variation of a product that engages and attracts a customer when buying a product or service.

**USP**: unique selling point – a factor that differentiates a product from its competitors.

## 11.3 Strategic choice

This topic is concerned with:

➤ Ansoff's Matrix

➤ force field analysis

➤ decision trees.

### Ansoff's Matrix

While the previous chapter focused on how strategic analysis can help a business identify its current position and any threats and opportunities, this chapter focuses on how a business can use the information from SWOT and PEST analyses to make strategic choices to develop markets.

#### The structure of Ansoff's Matrix and how it analyses the link between business strategy and risk

Ansoff's Matrix assesses the relative risk of expansion by investigating the current and future markets and products to help a business decide on a strategy that suits its propensity to risk.

> **Key term**
>
> **Ansoff's Matrix**: a decision tool for assessing the risk of strategies that can be used for future growth.

> **✗ Common error**
>
> Some candidates confuse Ansoff's 'Market penetration' with 'penetration pricing' which is a strategy used when launching a product.

> **💡 Remember**
>
> Ansoff's Matrix is a starting point to assess the likely level of risk in a new strategy. The tool is largely ineffective when used without further analysis as the information is limited and does not factor in many influences such as profitability.

▼ **Table 11.1** Use of Ansoff's Matrix to analyse and evaluate different business strategies in a given situation

|  | Products | | |
|---|---|---|---|
|  | **Present** |  | **New** |
| **Present** | **Market Penetration**<br><br>*Existing products and markets*<br><br>Low risk<br><br>Advantages:<br>• Already know and understand the market.<br>• May increase efficiencies.<br><br>Disadvantages:<br>• Lead to increased competition.<br>• Reliance on limited market. |  | **Product Development**<br><br>*Existing markets, new products*<br><br>Medium risk<br><br>Advantages:<br>• Customer knowledge but untested product.<br>• Expands the product range utilising existing customers.<br><br>Disadvantages:<br>• Extensive research and development costs for new products.<br>• Market research also required. |
| **New** | **Market Development**<br><br>*Existing products, new markets*<br><br>Medium risk<br><br>Advantages:<br>• Product knowledge but unknown customer base.<br>• Expands the customer base meaning less reliance.<br><br>Disadvantages:<br>• Large market research costs.<br>• Increased spending on advertising an unknown brand. |  | **Diversification**<br><br>*New products and markets*<br><br>High risk<br><br>Advantages:<br>• Potential new markets and revenue streams.<br>• Expanded product and customer portfolio spread risk.<br><br>Disadvantages:<br>• No experience of customers or markets.<br>• Huge investment into product development and market research. |

(Markets labels the left vertical axis with *Present* and *New*.)

## Force field analysis

Another valuable tool for making strategic choices, force field analysis is used when deciding whether to change, amend or implement a plan.

**Force field analysis** identifies a potential plan of action, separates forces for and against change with a score out of 5, which is then added up. The highest total signifies whether the decision to proceed should be taken.

▼ **Table 11.2** The use of simple force field analysis as a means of making strategic choices in a given situation

| | Forces for change | | Forces against change | |
|---|---|---|---|---|
| 5 | Improved quality of products | Move to new, high tech premises | Loss of employee satisfaction | 3 |
| 4 | Reduced cost of labour | | Employees fear of redundancy and IT | 2 |
| 3 | Financial support via grants | | Disruption | 4 |
| 12 | | | | 9 |

The higher total for forces against change suggests that the project should be undertaken.

## Decision trees

**Decision trees** are different from previous frameworks as they are used to choose between multiple options rather than deciding on whether a choice should be made.

They are particularly useful when:

➤ all choices are suitable

➤ there are estimates of costs and benefits available.

Results from decision trees will allow:

➤ probabilities of success or failure to be factored

➤ calculations of the potential highest yield

➤ **'what if?' analysis** of outcomes if different assumptions are made.

### Construction of simple decision trees from information given

Decision trees are constructed from lines connecting decision points (squares) to outcomes (circles). Each outcome will either be a definite result or an uncertain outcome that has further outcomes.

Decision trees always start from the left-hand side.

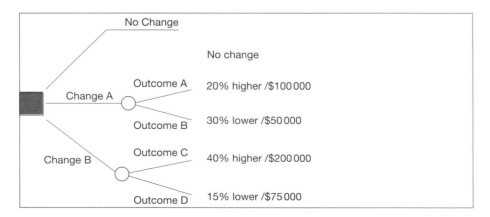

▲ **Figure 11.18** Example decision tree

## Calculation of the expected monetary values from decision trees and use of the results to assist in selecting the most appropriate strategy

The decision tree in Figure 11.18 shows a simplistic view of the options available. To calculate monetary values, **probability values** will have to be utilised for the outcomes of each change.

Therefore, to calculate the probability of change A being higher, the calculation would be:

➤ Step 1

- Outcome A:

  ○ $100\,000 \times x\%$ = **expected monetary value**

- Outcome B

  ○ $50\,000 \times x\%$ = expected monetary value

➤ Step 2

  ○ Expected monetary value (A) + expected monetary value (B) = Y

➤ Step 3

  ○ Expected monetary value (Y) − cost of change = Final expected monetary value

The results of each change are calculated as above, compared against no change and the most suitable option is recommended.

### The usefulness of decision trees

Decision trees are only as useful as:

➤ the analyst

➤ the available data

➤ the options available.

They provide:

➤ options, associated costs and benefits

➤ a quantitative analysis taking into account the level of risk

➤ an opportunity to investigate the impact of decisions and assumptions based on 'what if' analysis.

## 11.4 Strategic implementation

This topic is concerned with:

➤ business plans

➤ corporate culture and strategic implementation

➤ developing a change culture

➤ managing and controlling strategic change

➤ contingency planning and crisis management.

---

**Key terms**

**Probability values (decision trees):** the chance of each option being realised expressed as a percentage.

**Expected monetary value:** the value of, in financial terms, taking into account forecast returns and expected probability.

**X Common error**

Candidates sometimes forget that all of these are predictions, which means they are not guaranteed and will be subject to both internal and external changes in the business environment.

**Remember**

You are unlikely to have to draw a decision tree; you may be asked to either complete sections or make calculations based on assumptions provided.

**Remember**

All of the strategic choice tools are unsuitable where market conditions are changing rapidly as they are all predictions based on historical data.

## Business plans

All businesses have business plans, whether they are detailed or not. Without business plans, all businesses will struggle to implement strategy as an effective plan will contain the strategic analysis, market conditions and future forecasts that will give the whole organisation an aim that objectives can be derived from.

## Key elements of business plans

There is no set format for a business plan; every financial institution will have a template and every business will have a business plan that is specific to their needs, however the following elements should be present in most.

| | |
|---|---|
| **Executive summary** | • Business name, history, legal structure and basic introduction to product or services.<br>• A brief statement of objectives and aims. |
| **Product or service** | • Detailed outline of the main or core products or services.<br>• Focus on how the product/service meets a market need and any differentiation. |
| **Market analysis** | • Size of market, competition, target customer and trends.<br>• Indication or outcome of market research. |
| **Marketing plan** | • The marketing mix.<br>• Explanation of how the customer needs will be met. |
| **Production plan** | • Patents or licenses held.<br>• Costs and outline of premises, equipment, employees and suppliers required. |
| **Organisational plan** | • The people in the business and their roles.<br>• Organisational structure. |
| **Financial plan** | • Cash flow and profit and loss forecasts.<br>• Outlines current and future borrowing needs and return. |
| **Summary and long-term ambitions** | • Reason for investment.<br>• Future objectives and plans for growth and expansion. |

▲ Figure 11.19 Key elements of business plans

**Remember**

A good business plan will answer four key questions:

- reason for the business
- where the business wants to go
- how it will get there
- how much it will cost.

There are also costs to business plans:

- time and resources required to develop the plans
- forecasts may be inaccurate or based on erroneous data
- difficulty to be precise about future developments
- plans may be too rigid and inflexible and discourage change.

## The value of business plans for large and small, established and start-up businesses

Whatever the size of the business, there is value for a business plan:

- often required for loan and finance applications and presentations
- gives examination of current and future business ideas and prospects
- shows commercial viability of the product and the business
- provides a sense of direction for the organisation
- good review of resources, requirements and chances of success.

## Corporate culture and strategic implementation

Corporate culture is the way in which businesses organise themselves and how they approach business. Corporate culture varies from business to business and there is no 'best culture'.

Key term

**Corporate culture:** the values, beliefs and behaviours that determine how a business and its employees interact to complete business activities.

Common error

Culture is not the same as leadership styles, although there is a crossover in the theories.

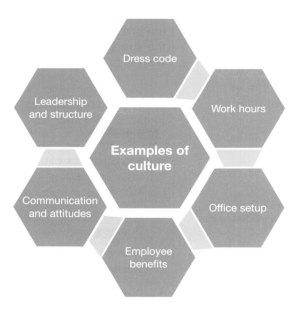

▲ **Figure 11.20** Different types of corporate culture such as power, entrepreneurial and task

Different types of culture exist due to the historical origins of the business and the philosophy of the managers or the type of industry the business operates in.

Although there are many cultures, three common corporate cultures are described below. Each has its own strengths and weaknesses and are useful in specific situations.

| Power culture | Task culture | Entrepreneurial culture |
|---|---|---|
| • Decision making concentrated in the centre with few people with responsibility.<br>• Autocratic leadership styles.<br>• Narrow, tall organisations. | • Team approach with groups of skilled employees completing tasks.<br>• Power is from expertise not position.<br>• Democratic leadership.<br>• Flat or matrix structures. | • Embraces change and takes risks.<br>• Employees listened to and respected.<br>• Democratic or laissez-faire leadership style.<br>• Creativity is valued.<br>• Flat organisational structures. |

▲ **Figure 11.21** Corporate culture styles

### Importance of corporate culture in strategic implementation

The strategic implementation of strategy is influenced by social, economic and market situations. Having the correct corporate structure will give a business a competitive advantage over another that is not able to meet the market requirements.

| High tech products | • Task and entrepreneurial cultures most suitable.<br>• Ability to develop new products and ideas.<br>• Responsive to market change. |
|---|---|
| Growing market | • Entrepreneurial culture is most suitable, due to responsiveness to new ideas.<br>• Power culture, however, has the advantage of quick and decisive decision making. |
| International expansion | • Clear direction associated with the power culture.<br>• Task culture allows specialists to work on projects with room for debate and argument. |

▲ **Figure 11.22** The suitability of different corporate cultures

## Developing a change culture

Change culture is important for businesses to be able to respond to new market conditions and changing methods of production.

### Importance of developing a change culture to allow effective implementations of new strategies

Any new strategy requires change; without the change culture there will be:

➤ resistance from employees due to insecurity and a fear of the impact on them

➤ a slow uptake of new products, techniques and markets that may cost a business market position

➤ increased costs associated with a slow and difficult change period.

## Managing and controlling strategic change
### The importance of leading and managing change

All businesses rely on management to lead a business. Every business needs an effective leader to motivate and encourage employees and provide direction:

➤ Without effective management, leadership and communication, the employee base will be unlikely to accept change.

➤ Without acceptance and management, strategic change is unlikely to achieve organisational objectives.

➤ This will overcome resistance which is natural in any change situation by engaging in effective communication.

➤ Effective leaders and management are able to communicate the reasons and need for change involving all employees.

### Techniques to implement and manage change successfully

Project champions are effective in implementing change. Champions must have real status with the workforce, a commitment to change and people skills to allow interaction with different types of employees.

---

**Remember**

It is important to refer to the role that the corporate culture plays in the implementation of business strategy.

**Key terms**

**Change culture**: the ability of an organisation to accept and embrace change in order to advance the aims and objectives of the organisation.

**Project champions**: an influential employee assigned to support and drive a project to a team.

**Remember**

Any new strategy requires change; if a business and its employees are able to change rapidly, the business will be ideally placed to exploit new markets and achieve organisational aims and objectives.

**✗ Common error**

Candidates may refer to businesses forcing change onto employees especially in power cultures. It is important to realise that forcing change will be met with resistance and is often the worst way to effectively change the direction of a business.

**Remember**

There are many techniques available; not all are suitable for all situations, and often there may not be the time or the resources available to manage and lead change effectively, which means a need for an engaged and motivated workforce that embrace new ideas.

**Kotter's eight steps** strategy is also a useful model for promoting change and can be utilised effectively.

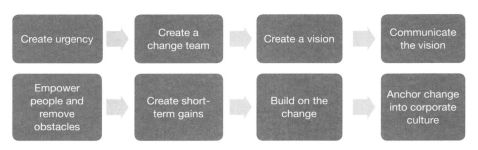

▲ **Figure 11.23** Kotter's eight steps strategy

▲ **Figure 11.24** Techniques for sucessful change management

## Contingency planning and crisis management

However, detailed the strategic plan may be, there are influences both internal and external that may cause the plan to stray from its original aims. For this reason, businesses must have a **contingency plan** and be able to **manage crises** effectively.

### Development of a strategy to manage change

There are a number of steps that must be followed in order to effectively manage unexpected change:

➤ Recognise the need for an alternative plan.

➤ Identify potential events that could negatively affect the business.

  ○ Assign probability ratings and rank according to the most likely or the most damaging.

  ○ Assign potential costs and benefits of minimising negative events.

  ○ Determine which are critical and which are disruptive.

  ○ Critical events must be planned for even if unlikely to occur.

➤ Develop specific plans.

➤ Increase staff training to ensure staff are able to effectively react to and manage crises.

➤ Test plans and revise where needed.

## Importance of contingency planning and crisis management

**Importance**

Quick response times.

Reassures customers and other related stakeholders.

Maintains confidence.

Effective public relations and marketing.

**Drawbacks**

Costly and time consuming.

May detract from and divert finance from other essential business activities.

Likely to be wasted resources as unlikely to be used.

**Remember**

The propensity of the owner for risk can affect a business ability to make effective contingency plans, however may allow for a responsive leader when managing crises.

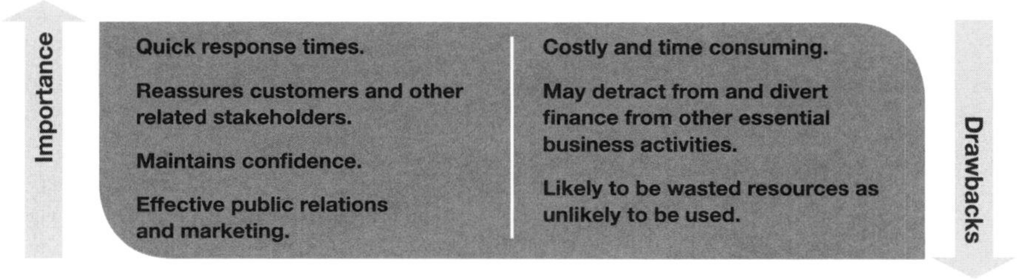

▲ **Figure 11.25** Importance and drawbacks of contingency planning and crisis management

---

### Worked example

Evaluate whether the information in the tables for Sohail's Garage is sufficient to allow SG's directors to choose between the two strategic growth options. [20]

🔗 **Link**

Refer to Case study 3: Sohail's Garage in Unit 14.

Plan of answer.

**Introduction to the answer (knowledge and application)**

Summarise the two options highlighted and identify the most important factors that might influence the decision; these could include:

- director's future aims

- the most important current and future internal and external factors.

Briefly summarise the main types of information given without going into detail and how the business may use the data.

**Content (to achieve mainly analysis marks)**

Select the main piece of information from each table, manipulating the data so that you use figures you have created rather than using what is already there in its raw state:

- Table 1: Total GP increase from 2015–2016.

- Table 2: The total NPV and payback.

- Table 3: The difference between changes in annual salary and inflation.

Write one piece of good analysis for each of these; focus on how the data may be beneficial for:

- assessing both options including why it is useful and if there are any concerns from the data

- assessing the link between director's future aims and objectives.

Make sure that you use specific numerical or case data to back up your analysis. Ensure that each piece is fully and competently analysed. You may want to add what further details from the case study or your own learning may be useful.

**Summary (to achieve mainly evaluation marks)**

Within this section you give your answer to the question. Do you think the information is sufficient? Your answer can either agree or disagree as long as you fully justify your opinion.

'No, the information is not enough as there are too many variable factors.'

Remember there are 10 marks available for evaluation. Evaluation must have the following factors to score well:

- good, supported judgement

- effective use of the case study to ensure the answer is specific to this business and its options.

✗ **Common error**

Candidates often start their answers with their opinion or judgement. Judgement must be based on evidence and analysis; therefore, your interim judgement must be at the end of each piece of analysis, followed by a final judgement based on all of your findings.

**I can:**

➤ analyse the benefits of and need for strategic management ☐

➤ undertake and interpret a SWOT and PEST analysis and integrate the results into strategic objectives ☐

➤ evaluate the role of mission and vision statements for a business ☐

➤ undertake and interpret various business models such as the Boston Matrix, Porter's Five Forces, Ansoff's Matrix and decision trees in relation to business objectives ☐

➤ explain the use and benefits of business plans and their effects on corporate culture ☐

➤ explain the need for managing and controlling strategic change and the uses of contingency planning and crisis management. ☐

---

 **Raise your grade**

 **Link**

These questions refer to Case study 3: Sohail's Garage in Unit 14.

The strategy questions in section B of Paper 3 require the candidate to combine all of the knowledge learned within the AS and A Level units. Candidates must prove they are able to bring together knowledge of different and competing functional areas when composing an answer.

1 Recommend which one of the two strategic options SG should choose for their future growth option. Justify your recommendation. [20 marks]

> The question requires the candidate to utilise the appendices and make a decision. It is therefore useful to outline the choices and the information that will be necessary in an introduction.

SG has the option of either extending their dominance in an existing market by taking over their biggest competitor, PPL Garages or, diversifying into a new market with an untested product that is new to the country. While Sohail's preference within the case study is to diversify, there are risks and benefits for both strategic options.

> While this introduction may not be worth any marks, it is vital to show the examiner that the candidate is aware of the choices and knowledge of business frameworks such as Ansoff's Matrix, even though it is not explicitly mentioned.

If SG chooses option A, which is diversification as their future strategy, a number of key benefits and disadvantages must be considered.

Diversification will allow SG to spread their risk by targeting a new market; the predicted payback time is 1 year and 5 months, which is a full 10 months shorter than the payback time for option B. This means that the financial risk is minimised, as even though inflation is relatively low at 1.5%, this could change very quickly in response to unforeseen global factors such as a global economic crash or recession. The investment of $100m dollars is also 6 times less than option B, which means the risk of entering a new market is substantially lower.

In addition to this, there is a growth in GDP and a positive increase in actual annual salaries, which means that customers have more disposable income in a country that is enjoying a sustained economic boom. This is an indication that customers may want premium cars that they could afford on credit, which would therefore make the investment into the premium market attractive.

However, the predicted NPV is only 2/3 of the NPV of option B, which means that in the long term, diversifying may be less profitable than expansion, which would negatively affect the shareholders returns. Shareholders may therefore be more interested in future gains than the short-term safety in what is a positive external market environment.

> The paragraph above has critical analysis of option A, which is clearly linked to the case study and uses the information from the appendices. The candidate will now need to repeat the above for option B.

If SG chooses option B, then as mentioned above, there is a much higher short-term risk of financial failure as the investment of $600m will need to be financed from either increased investment from shareholders, which would either increase the personal investment risk or dilute the shareholding of the limited company. Neither of which are seen as positive steps as future returns, especially if the shareholding is diluted will decrease.

However, the payback is still relatively short at 2 years and 3 months, which means that the market is obviously considered to be strong and is a solid future investment as mentioned with the NPV being half as much again as in option A. A further consideration is that even if the economy does suffer, this would be a positive influence for second-hand car sales, as customers with less disposable income would go for the value option, which is the second-hand car market, and the luxury end of the business would undoubtedly suffer from a lack of sales, especially as the brand would be relatively new in the country.

> The critical analysis does not have to consider many variables: while the exam is 3 hours long, the amount of time for this question is only 20% (40 minutes) which must include reading the case, identifying all the relevant issues and selecting the most appropriate. At this point, it is suitable to start the recommendation.

Based on the information above, I would recommend that SG choose option B. SG could prove to lenders that both the existing business and the proposed merger would be successful and is built on solid foundations.

Sohail has already begun the implementation of merging the three divisions into one head office, and there may be additional savings from merging a similar business into the mix, as PPL might have more advanced administrative functions that could be utilised. While the investment is large, the external economic climate is positive and the stable interest rate would allow SG to plan confidently for the future.

While Sohail does want to diversify, this may not be the correct time. The business is currently remodelling its administrative functions which will cause some unforeseen issues, and if Sohail and the senior managers are distracted with a new business venture, the entire operation may be put at long term risk.

The shareholders would also be more inclined to risk additional borrowing in the stable environment as the potential return is much higher, and may not need to dilute their own shareholding. Even though a separate premium brand does have some advantages, Sohail could slowly turn some of the redundant forecourts into 'premium' sales floors and sell new or nearly new vehicles from established manufacturers, which would reduce the risk and investment and increase the long term prosperity of Sohail's Garage.

> The evaluation is as long as the analysis, which is needed due to the amount of marks awarded – it is impossible to gain 10 marks for evaluation with a brief, one sided statement of fact.

**2** Discuss the importance of strategic management to the future success of SG. [20 marks]

> The plan below is a method for candidates to ensure they have all the necessary information structured in a suitable manner before writing an answer. Planning allows for corrections and a final review before the answer is written.

## Introduction

What is strategic management?

Definition.

How does it apply to SG?

Investment choice of option A or B or consolidating.

What tools, techniques or frameworks can be used within strategic management?

PEST, SWOT, Force Field analysis or investment appraisal (only analyse a limited number).

## Application

How would SWOT/PEST help with the two options available?

Importance of making the right choice – future success.

Strategic implementations of the new sector or the merger – e.g. organisational cultures.

## Analysis

Both options are expensive, difficult to undo and involve many different departments – without the use of the tools above, may jeopardise the long-term stability of the whole organisation.

A corporate plan with clear objectives may give a sense of direction and motivate employees, which will result in better outcomes.

Contingency planning is required to protect reputation and financial stability.

## Evaluation

Strategic management is essential for future success as it operates in a competitive, cost conscious market.

Effective strategic management does not guarantee success – external influences could have major impacts.

Managing change is essential, as is the ability of managers to effectively communicate changes to the workforce.

A plan similar to this will allow for a candidate to start identifying key areas that must be discussed. A basic plan such as this may also allow for additional data to be added when reviewed without losing any of the cohesiveness that may happen when paragraphs are added into written essay style questions.

 ## Exam-style questions

This section will allow you to practise writing answers for exam-style questions. Remember, it is useful to be aware of the mark schemes for the questions which can be found on relevant websites or from your teacher.

 **Link**

These questions refer to Case study 3: Sohail's Garage in Unit 14.

**Paper 3**

1 Evaluate the most important factors SG's directors should consider when making the strategic choice between options A and B. [20 marks]

2 Evaluate the importance of developing a culture of change within SG when introducing new growth strategies. [20 marks]

3 Discuss the importance of contingency management if SG is to continue being successful. [20 marks]

# 12 Raising your achievement

## During your course of study

### Sharing some ideas about how to achieve the best possible result in your Business examinations

Study time is important – it is even more important to make good use of your study time.

Recent research shows that there are some important things you can do from the very start to make sure you achieve your best.

The first thing is to set yourself some definite goals. Here are some important questions which may help you to plan your approach to study:

### Question 1

What grade do you want or need to achieve in your Business exam? What grade will be worth all the effort over the last two years of study and will allow you to progress to the next stage in your education or employment? Setting yourself a specific target may motivate you to study, not only your revision notes but also the grade descriptors.

> ★ **Exam tip**
>
> Set a specific goal to motivate you and give you something to focus on.

### Question 2

How much extra-curricular time do you spend developing your knowledge and skills in Business? You may already spend many hours a week in private study, but if this is not the case, it is a good idea to increase your study time. This can be done gradually, for example you could plan to add an extra hour to your normal study time for the next two weeks, then add an extra hour to this increased time, and so on.

> ★ **Exam tip**
>
> Make a definite plan to increase your study time.

### Question 3

What is your reaction when a piece of work from your Business course is returned by the teacher and you have not done quite as well as you had hoped, despite having made a real effort to get a good mark? You may feel a bit deflated and focus on the negative comments. However, you could think a little differently. Students who focus on the learning points and say "Okay, this did not go so well; let me reflect on my performance and learn from my mistakes", are able to turn a negative experience into something far more positive – which then leads to real progress.

> ★ **Exam tip**
>
> Don't focus on disappointment, but try to learn from your mistakes.

### Question 4

What do you do with all the work completed during your course of study? Some student's answers may be: "I have it all here somewhere, it just needs sorting out". Students usually find it helpful to keep a carefully-organised collection of the work they do. Have a separate section for each topic with your notes and all the answers you have prepared together with the questions. When preparing for the examination, having a well-organised file will mean you can get on with revision without wasting time trying to find the relevant materials.

> ★ **Exam tip**
>
> Organise your work to make it easier to revise.

At this stage you could be working towards the following position:

➤ you have a definite goal (the final grade you would like to achieve)

➤ you have a plan to increase the time spent on private study

➤ you view each result you achieve as an opportunity to learn from your mistakes

➤ you are building up a well-organised file of work which will be invaluable for revision.

## Practical ideas to help you learn more effectively

**Self-assessment**: this means that you mark your own work making use of model answers or mark schemes provided with past examination papers.

Research has shown that there are many benefits to doing this if you carry out the process on a regular and frequent basis, for example:

➤ you find out for yourself how well you have done after completing a task

➤ you can get immediate information about any errors or omissions in your answer, so you can start to learn from your mistakes right away

➤ if you use mark schemes (for example exam paper mark schemes) you can learn exactly how marks are allocated to answers so that you are better-prepared to produce the answers expected in exam situations.

**Peer-assessment**: by marking a friend's practice exam answer, peer assessing can help by not only identifying errors and omissions your friends have made but also challenging you to write down all the necessary answers and explanations needed for the questions.

**'Repairing' your answers**: the more substantial benefits of checking your own work appear when you go on to analyse any aspect of your answer which was not correct or where an aspect was missing. It is a good idea to spend time trying to understand why the model answer is showing a different outcome to the answer you have provided. Try and work out for yourself how the right answer was achieved, or maybe ask your teacher or a friend to explain the right answer to you if you really cannot see how it was done. Make a point of adding some notes about the correct answer to your work; these notes will be useful when you look back at the question and the answer and may also help you to remember the points in your exam.

Below you will find some examples illustrating how to repair answers:

## ▼ Example 1: repairing an answer where a calculation is incorrect

Calculate the percentage increase in revenue for product X between 2016 and 2017 using the information provided:

| Product X | $ |
|---|---|
| Total revenue 2016 | 500 |
| Total revenue 2017 | 750 |

★ **Exam tip**

Always check your answer to make sure the figure calculated is correct.

In this example, Revenue 2016 × 133% is $500 × 133% = $665, which is the wrong figure – Revenue 2017 should be $750.

| Student answer | Model answer |
|---|---|
| For a percentage increase you must work out the difference between the numbers you are comparing and then divide the increase by the original number and multiply by 100.<br><br>This is:<br><br>750 − 500 = 250<br><br>250/750 = 0.33 × 100 = 33% | $$\frac{\text{Revenue 2017} - \text{Revenue 2016}}{\text{Revenue 2016}} \times 100$$<br><br>$$\frac{\$750 - \$500}{\$500} \times 100$$<br><br>$$= 50\%$$ |

### Repaired answer

For a percentage increase you must work out the difference between the numbers you are comparing and then divide the increase by the original number and multiply by 100.

This is:

750 − 500 = 250

*This should have been written as a formula.*

250/750 = 0.33 × 100 = 33%

*This then turns to 50%*

*This is the data from 2017, the wrong year. The figure used should be 500, from 2016.*

## ▼ Example 2: repairing an answer with an incorrectly written response

Discuss appropriate methods of selection for a shop manager.

| Student answer | Model answer |
|---|---|
| One appropriate method could be a work trial where the manager is given a basic task to complete.<br><br>Another is an interview where questions are asked about the role the manager will complete. | An appropriate method of selection is a work trial.<br><br>This allows the recruiter to see if the recruit is able to complete the manager's daily tasks, however a recruit may be nervous and not complete the tasks to the best of their ability. |

| Student answer | Repaired answer |
|---|---|
| One appropriate method could be a work trial where the manager is given a basic task to complete.<br><br>Another is an interview where questions are asked about the role the manager will complete. | Instead of listing the methods of selection I know, I should have focused on some I know well and given analysis for each one.<br><br>This then shows my ability to analyse, which allows me to reach the top grades in a long mark answer. |

## So why is assessing my own work and then 'repairing' answers such a good idea?

Extensive international research has shown that this 'repairing' approach, carried out systematically, will make a big difference to what a student can gain from all the practical work which is carried out – and over a course of study can boost an individual's performance by as much as two examination grades!

In the first illustration, the student has focused on the incorrect year as the original number when calculating the percentage increase. If this process is repeated whenever this type of error is made, then it is likely the student will learn the correct formula for calculating a percentage increase.

In the second illustration, the student has focused attention on delivering knowledge instead of focusing on the analysis which is the important element of the question. As a result of this, the student would have scored poorly, but the student now has their own personal record of what is needed to avoid repeating the error. If the student repeats this process for similar questions, it is much more likely they will remember this distinction between a lower mark knowledge question and a higher mark analysis question.

Remember that each correction you make represents a step – maybe just a small step – towards improving your examination performance.

## Making progress with written answers

In order to boost your ability to demonstrate knowledge, understanding and analysis of key Business ideas and concepts, you could try the following process when you are reading through a passage in a textbook or case study about a particular topic. The process helps you organise information and consists of several steps:

**Step 1**: highlight key points in the text.

**Step 2**: prepare a table in which you make some notes that summarise key points about a particular aspect of the topic.

**Step 3**: prepare a second table, this time making some notes that summarise key points about a different aspect of the topic, and so on. More tables can be added if necessary.

▼ **Example 3: using tables to analyse knowledge and ideas in an AS Level topic: leadership styles**

Having highlighted key points in a textbook about the different types of leadership style, you could produce tables along the following lines:

| Table 1: the definitions and reasons for using leadership styles | | |
|---|---|---|
| Autocratic | A leadership style in which leaders dictate without consultation of subordinates. | Used for unskilled and untrusted employees. |
| Democratic | A leadership style involving consulting with subordinates and evaluating their opinions before making a decision. | Used for skilled and experienced employees. |
| Laissez-faire | A hands-off approach to management where employees manage themselves. | Used for motivated and trusted employees who want responsibility. |

| Table 2: advantages and disadvantages of the leadership styles | | |
| --- | --- | --- |
| Autocratic | Allows complete control of processes where speed and accuracy are important, *which minimises* chances of error. | Limits creativity and ideas from employees that *could improve* productivity are ignored. |
| Democratic | Greater employee involvement encourages teamwork, loyalty and positive atmosphere, *which can improve* productivity. | Greater discussion leads to a slower decision-making process, *which can mean* time critical deadlines or opportunities are missed. |
| Laissez-faire | Employees have freedom to do what they think is the best option, *which can lead to* more motivated and efficient working practices. | Little overall management control and overview, *which might result in* a fragmented and uncoordinated approach in the workplace. |

The next table may look at specific situations in which the management style would be most or least effective, with reasons.

This process of building layers of knowledge and analysis in tables with a clear focus can be a powerful learning and study tool. It makes information easily accessible and can be separated into subject specific elements.

### Avoiding the most common errors in exam answers

When using the 'Raise your grade' feature in the units within this book, you will soon become aware of a number of key errors made by students. It is important that you know how to avoid some of the most common errors in examination answers.

### Common error 1: misreading the question

Although you may have read the question once, have you understood what it is asking you to do? It may be useful to highlight key pieces of text before you start your answer to make sure that you have fully understood the question.

**Exam tip**

Make sure you answer what the question asks.

When the question asks about 'recruitment':

➤ Is it asking for methods of recruitment or recruitment strategies?

➤ Is it asking to analyse one method/strategy or is it only asking to analyse the advantages?

### Common error 2: not looking at the amount of marks allocated

Students who run out of time have often not looked at the amount of marks allocated to a question. This is obvious when a three mark 'briefly explain' question may have an answer that is written over one or two whole pages.

**Exam tip**

Make sure you understand what is required from each question.

This not only wastes valuable time in an exam, but may also make it harder for an examiner to correctly allocate the marks, as the key points can be hidden in a long essay type answer. Then, for the last questions, the student is forced to use bullet points which means it is very difficult to gain analysis marks.

**Common error 3: not identifying the 'command' word**

This is closely linked to the point above. Candidates often focus on the content element in the question, such as business objectives or the size of the business. While this important, it is also vital to look carefully at the command word being used, as this indicates what the examiner is actually asking you to do.

For example:

➤ 'State' or 'define' only requires basic knowledge which can easily be answered in a few short sentences.

➤ 'Analyse' will require the candidate to look at the advantages or disadvantages, strengths or weaknesses. (Depending on the question.)

➤ 'Discuss' requires the candidate to make a judgement based on the preceding analysis. The student must usually make a decision about what is the *most suitable*. This must be based on two-sided analysis and a strong answer will compare the strongest with the second and third options. (If available.)

**Common error 4: incorrect or poor answer structure**

Although it is understandable that students may rush answers within an exam setting, it is important to remember that there is always enough time to answer all the questions set.

However, it is also important to realise that the exam is not the best place to start learning how to structure an answer. It may be useful to have revision tables as in the section above, which are linked to the type of question set:

Two-mark questions will use command phrases such as: *define/state/identify* and will need basic knowledge with one form of expanded answer.

| Question: | Define the term 'sole trader'. [2 marks] | |
|-----------|------------------------------------------|--|
| Mark 1 | A business owned by one person. | This is a simple definition, but it is the most important aspect. |
| Mark 2 | Who has unlimited liability. | This expands the answer with a simple point. |

Whereas three-mark questions will usually begin with: *describe/briefly explain* and will usually need **two pieces** of expansion.

| Question: | Describe the business structure of a sole trader. [3 marks] | |
|-----------|------------------------------------------------------------|--|
| Mark 1 | A business owned by one person. | This is a simple definition, but it is the most important aspect. |
| Mark 2 | Who has unlimited liability. | This expands the answer with a simple point. |
| Mark 3 | Which means all of his personal possessions are at risk if made bankrupt. | This shows the candidate fully understands the term. |

★ Exam tip

Make sure you identify the command word.

Five-mark questions, usually found on Paper 1, usually start with: *explain two ways* and need **two fully expanded** examples.

| Question: | Explain two types of business ownership. | [5 marks] |
|---|---|---|
| Mark 1 | A sole trader. | This is a simple definition, but it is the most important aspect. |
| Mark 2 | Who has unlimited liability. | This expands the answer with a simple point. |
| Mark 3 | Which means all of his personal possessions are at risk if made bankrupt. | This shows the candidate fully understands the term. |
| Mark 4 | A partnership. | This is a simple definition, but it is the most important aspect. |
| Mark 5 | Which means 2–20 people can share ownership *and* share ideas and strengths. | This answer has to have **two** pieces of expansion to score full marks. |

Eight-mark questions depend on whether the question is for Paper 1, which is general knowledge, or Paper 2 which is data response.

For Paper 1, which is general knowledge, a suitable structure might be:

| Question: | Analyse the benefits of a large business using a limited structure. | [8 marks] |
|---|---|---|
| Level 1 [1 mark] | A limited structure, such as an LTD or a plc. | This is a simple definition, which shows basic understanding of limited structures. |
| Level 1 [2 marks] | Means that the investors only stand to lose the capital invested. | This is a simple expansion, which shows understanding of limited structures. |
| Level 2 [3 marks] | This means that investors are more likely to invest their capital as they know this is the maximum they can lose. | This shows the candidate is able to apply the idea to a business. |
| Level 2 [4 marks] | Banks are willing to lend capital as limited businesses are seen to be more secure. | This shows the second benefit asked for and the idea is applied to a business. |
| Level 3 [5–6 marks] | *Which means* businesses have more opportunity to raise capital easier than in an unlimited structure, as investors and banks are more confident. | This answer has some analysis of the benefits of the limited structure which relates to both the banks and investors. |
| Level 4 [7–8 marks] | *Which can lead to* the capital needed for a business to reach its organisational goals, such as expansion or brand awareness through marketing, which requires large amounts of capital. | There is good analysis shown as there is a continued, logical progression of the benefits of a limited structure, with an example to show full understanding. |

★ Exam tip

It is important to use and understand the significance of connecting phrases such as: 'which means' and 'this leads to', as this is what will allow the student to reach the Level 4 'Good analysis' marks.

For Paper 2, which is data response, the following excerpt from a case study shows the type of information presented to students in an exam paper:

> ABC Ltd is a successful shoe retailer based in country X, which now wants to expand from one shop in the capital to other major cities…
>
> ABC Ltd wants to grow quickly, so needs to raise $10 000. They have asked their bank, who have asked for a business plan to be produced…

A suitable structure might be:

| Question: | Analyse the benefits to ABC Ltd of using a limited structure. [8 marks] | | Similarities and differences |
|---|---|---|---|
| **Knowledge [1 mark]** | A limited structure, such as an LTD or a plc. | This is an expanded definition, which shows basic understanding of limited structures. | These stay the same as the first two marks are always awarded for knowledge. |
| **Knowledge [2 marks]** | Means that the investors only stand to lose the capital invested. | | |
| **Application [3 marks]** | As ABC Ltd want to *expand from one to two shops.* | These are two pieces of specific data from the case study (it is important to be as specific as possible). | These however change, as specific examples from the case study are needed. |
| **Application [4 marks]** | And they require a *bank loan of $10 000.* | | |
| **Analysis (without using the case study) [5–6 marks]** | *Which means businesses* have more opportunity to raise capital easier than in an unlimited structure, *as investors and banks are more confident.* | This answer has unrelated analysis of the benefits of the limited structure which relates to both the banks and investors. | This is similar as two marks are awarded for analysis without any reference to the case study. |
| **Good analysis [7–8 marks]** | *Which means ABC Ltd is* trusted more by its bank *when it takes in its business plan, which will* give more of a chance to raise the $10 000 needed for their plans for expansion. | This is now good analysis as it is expanded and in context. | This is different as there is specific reference made to the case study when expanding the answer. |

In summary:

➤ read the questions carefully and correctly

➤ make a note of the number of marks awarded

➤ identify the command word

➤ structure your answer appropriately to the question and the exam paper.

**Understanding what is expected by different types of question**

Each question in an examination will start with a particular command word which asks you to do something (as explained above). It is important to understand why particular words are used and what they mean, otherwise

> ★ **Exam tip**
>
> It is important to use and understand the significance of connecting phrases such as: 'which means' and 'this leads to', as this is what will allow the student to reach the Level 4 'Good analysis' marks.

it is possible you will waste time by misunderstanding what is required and lose marks for not doing what is expected of you.

Examination papers will be designed:

| To test | By asking you to |
|---|---|
| Knowledge | Identify<br><br>State<br><br>Define |
| Understanding | Describe<br><br>Briefly explain |
| Application of knowledge or the case study material. | Explain<br><br>Calculate |
| Ability to analyse elements of the course. | Analyse |
| Ability to look at a situation or a problem from different points of view, consider a range of factors, make a judgement and provide a conclusion. | Discuss<br><br>Justify<br><br>Assess<br><br>Evaluate<br><br>Recommend |

| Words used | What is expected | Examples of questions | |
|---|---|---|---|
| **Identify**<br>**State**<br>**Define** | A brief response that shows you can remember basic facts and ideas. | AS Level | **Identify** two management styles. **State** two business objectives.<br><br>**Define** opportunity cost. |
| | | A Level | **Identify** one aspect of a multinational business.<br><br>**State** two types of merger and takeover.<br><br>**Define** demographic change. |
| **Describe**<br>**Briefly explain** | A fuller written statement giving facts and (especially where 'explain' is used) requiring some development; that is a further statement designed to show understanding. Sometimes the development can take the form of examples. | AS Level | **Describe** the aims of a social enterprise.<br><br>**Briefly explain** a method of measuring the size of a business. |
| | | A Level | **Describe** the difference between hard and soft HRM.<br><br>**Briefly explain** management by objectives. |
| **Explain**<br>**Calculate** | Answers are required about a particular situation, using extended knowledge or data. | AS Level | **Explain** the difference between a fixed and variable cost.<br><br>**Calculate** the gross profit margin. |
| | | A Level | **Explain** the need for labour legislation.<br><br>**Calculate** the contribution cost of X. |

| Words used | What is expected | Examples of questions | | |
|---|---|---|---|---|
| **Analyse** | Where you study some information in some depth, separating out different aspects of the information. | AS Level | **Analyse** the benefits of price skimming. | |
| | | A Level | **Analyse** the benefits of an income statement. | |
| **Discuss** **Justify** **Assess** **Evaluate** **Recommend** | Where you look at both sides of a particular proposal or idea, pointing out the benefits but also the drawbacks. You may be asked to make a judgement and give reasons to support it. | AS Level | **Discuss** the most appropriate methods of selection. **Justify** the most appropriate marketing strategy for a new business. | |
| | | A Level | **Discuss** the suitability of profitability ratios when applying for long term loans. **Justify** the most suitable corporate culture for an entrepreneurial business. | |

## Preparing for the exam

### Exam preparation top tips

When preparing for an exam, it is always important to remember that exam preparation begins long before the day of the exam. Organisation is key to exam success, and below are some tops tips to success:

➤ Make sure your notes are well organised and that you can easily find your notes.

➤ Make sure you have practiced past papers. Look not at the final mark, but at what you didn't do so well on, and how you lost marks.

➤ When doing exam practice scripts, always time yourself! There is no point in doing a practice exam in two hours when the real one only lasts for 90 minutes.

➤ Make sure you have one good, up-to-date course book which will give you hints, tips, and the basic knowledge needed to succeed in your Business exam.

➤ Keep up to date with news and new developments. This is especially important for Paper 1, where you need to show application to relevant examples.

➤ Download a copy of the syllabus and make a checklist; use a highlighter to check off what you are confident in and especially where you have a lack of knowledge.

➤ Get a study buddy. It is much easier to study when you know there is somebody else with you.

➤ Revise sensibly and practise all your skills. If you focus only on knowledge, you may end up losing marks in the long answer questions.

➤ Create model answers and structures that you can use in your exams. Remember, examiners are not trying to trick you, so if you can focus on the subject, that will help you to relax and give good answers.

➤ Understand what the examiner will be looking for and try to focus your attention on meeting those requirements. The key concepts below will help.

## The key concepts

Studying business should not just mean being able to remember lots of facts and being able to analyse effectively, it should help you, the learner to make links between topics and develop a deep and meaningful relationship with the topic. The table below is designed to help focus your mind on what are the most important elements.

| Key concepts | Description |
|---|---|
| Change | Often described as the only constant, students of business must realise that business can only develop and grow with change. Change is good! |
| Management | Good leadership should mean a highly motivated workforce, effective systems and an efficient method of communication. |
| Customer focus | Without customers, businesses would not exist, therefore, customers should be understood and their needs and wants met. |
| Innovation | Reinvention is the only way that a business can stay ahead of its competitors. As times change, so must the business. |
| Creating value | Businesses exist to meet the needs of their stakeholders. These could be either the shareholders or the recipients of social enterprise. Businesses must both create and measure value. |
| Strategy | If you know where you are and where you want to get to, you should then be able to create a plan to achieve your long-term goals. |

# The exam

You have studied, you know the key concepts, your notes are excellent … now it's the exam.

➤ **Don't panic** You have spent a full year studying, revising and living the subject – you know what you need to do and there are no tricks. Show the examiners how good you are.

➤ **Read the instructions and the questions carefully.** Don't overlook the details, don't rush to be the first one to finish and make sure you have time to review your answers.

➤ **Manage your time.** You know how much time you have, you know how long each question should take and there is a clock in the exam hall. Do not run out of time and do not rush questions.

➤ **Remember this is a business exam.** You have spent the last year learning business terminology, rules and methods. Use this vocabulary to show your deeper understanding of the subject.

➤ **Follow the order of the questions.** Students who mix up the order of the questions often miss out entire questions. This therefore means they cannot score maximum marks. Questions are also laid out to make sense and information in question 1 may help in following questions.

## Time management

### AS Level exam papers

Papers 1 and 2 are AS Level exam papers.

In **Paper 1**, you have one hour and 15 minutes to complete two sections. Each section is based on your own knowledge and you are provided with no materials or case study.

**Section A** consists of four short answer, five-mark questions, three of the questions are split into parts (a) and (b). You should spend no longer than 35 minutes on Section A.

**Section B** consists of one essay style question worth 20 marks. This may also be split into parts (a) and (b). There are three questions available for you to choose from: **you must only choose one**. The time allocation for Section B is therefore 40 minutes.

In **Paper 2**, you have one hour and 30 minutes to complete two questions. Each question has its own short case study, which must be used to provide evidence for your answers.

Both questions are split into multiple sections and each question has a mark allocation ranging from a minimum of two marks to a maximum of 11 marks.

It is recommended that you do not spend more than 45 minutes on each question.

### A Level exam paper

Paper 3 is an A Level exam paper.

In **Paper 3**, you have three hours to complete two sections. There is an extended case study which must be used as evidence for all of your answers. If you answer the questions using only your own knowledge, and do not refer to the case study, you will not score well. As the case study is in depth, it is recommended that you read the case study carefully and allow at least 20 minutes to fully read the background material provided.

**Section A** consists of five questions, each of which may be split into a number of parts. You are recommended to spend no more than two hours to answer this section.

**Section B** consists of one 20-mark question. You have a choice of two questions and **you must choose only one.** You are recommended to spend no longer than 40 minutes on this question.

These timings are a guide only. You may need to spend more time on one question and less on another. As long as you are aware of the time available and the questions left, then you should be able to allocate your time appropriately.

# 13 Exam-style questions

## Assessment for A Level Business

The assessment structure for A Level Business is as shown below:

| Component | Type of paper | Marks | Time | Weighting AS Level | Weighting A Level |
|---|---|---|---|---|---|
| Paper 1 | Short answer and long answer (essay) questions Based on the AS Level syllabus content. Section A: Four short answer questions. Section B: One essay from a choice of three long answer questions. | 20  20 | 1 hr 15 minutes | 20%  20% | 10%  10% |
| Paper 2 | Data response Two data response questions based on AS Level syllabus content. | 60 | 1 hr 30 minutes | 60% | 30% |
| Paper 3 | Case study Section A: Five questions based on an extended case study. Section B: One essay from a choice of two questions, based on the case study. Based on the additional A Level syllabus content and also assumes knowledge and understanding of the AS Level syllabus content. | 100 | 3 hrs | N/A | 50% |

**Note:** Although Paper 3 tests new content, it is in addition to the knowledge and understanding of the AS Level syllabus content.

## Paper 1

### Section A (short answer questions)

Section A consists of four questions, three of which will be separated into two parts. You must answer all of the questions.

1   (a)  Define the term penetration pricing. [2]

   (b)  Briefly explain why penetration pricing may be used. [3]

2   (a)  Define the term 'leadership'. [2]

   (b)  Briefly explain one style of leadership. [3]

3   Explain the costs and benefits to a business of holding high levels of inventory. [5]

4   (a)  Distinguish between 'leadership' and 'management'. [2]

   (b)  Briefly explain why a business may use different leadership styles. [3]

### Section B (long answer questions)

Section B consists of three questions, of which you should answer only **one**.

5   (a)  Analyse why a business needs to consider the viewpoints of its stakeholders. [8]

   (b)  Discuss how there could be conflicts between the stakeholders of a clothing retailer. [12]

6   Discuss how Goleman's 'four competencies of emotional intelligence' could be used by managers of a retail business to motivate its employees. [20]

7   (a)  Analyse why effectives job descriptions and person specifications are important to a manufacturing business. [8]

   (b)  Discuss the advantages and disadvantages for a manufacturing business of using staff training as a method of boosting staff motivation. [12]

**Paper 2**

In Paper 2 you are required to answer the two data response questions presented. Each question is split into many parts and must be answered using the case study when asked to provide evidence. Four sample questions, based on case studies, are provided here for practice.

**1 Case study: José's Builders (JB)**

José is a sole trader who employs three people and has specialised in renovating houses and building extensions for over ten years. He has built a good reputation in his local area for quality work at competitive prices. He is able to trust his staff and there is large demand for his skills. His main business objective is to expand over the next five years.

To achieve this objective, José is thinking of expanding into another area. He is considering two possible neighbouring towns and has collected the data below.

▼ **Table 1:** Location information

| Town A (High income area) | Town B (Middle income area) |
|---|---|
| • A small town with a large percentage of houses which are large but have not been extended. <br> • The population is generally wealthy. <br> • There is already an established builder in the area. <br> • José can travel to this location easily. | • A large town with smaller houses, many of which have not been extended. <br> • The area is a working-class area. <br> • A national company has recently started advertising in the area. <br> • The location adds 30 minutes each day in relation to town A. |

José is now ready to expand, however, he is concerned that he may not have all the skills his business needs, as he does not have a qualified electrician working for him.

▼ **Table 2:** Key financial information

| | ($) |
|---|---|
| Stock | 7500 |
| Cash in bank | 3000 |
| Trade payables | 5000 |
| Trade receivables | 25000 |

(a) Explain the following terms:

   (i) sole trader [3]

   (ii) business objective. [3]

(b) (i) Referring to Table 2, calculate the acid test ratio. [3]

   (ii) Using your answer to the above, comment on the liquidity of JB. [3]

(c) Analyse one advantage and one disadvantage of JB expanding into a new market. [8]

(d) Recommend whether José should enter into the new business venture. Justify your choice. [11]

## 2 Case study: Jill and John's Jackets (JJ)

Jill and John's Jackets (JJ) is a small partnership that sources and sells coats for farmers and other outdoor people who need tough and useful jackets for their outdoor businesses. Jill and John started their business ten years ago as they realised that many jackets weren't waterproof or tough enough, and were also expensive. After asking colleagues in other local businesses, they found this was a common problem.

After doing some more market research, JJ designed a limited range of jackets that suit the needs of farmers and outdoor workers. JJ found an overseas manufacturer who was able to batch produce the jackets for a reasonable price.

The business has grown rapidly and has started selling its jackets online and to specialist clothing stores who require trade credit. JJ now needs to increase the size of its storage facility. JJ has cash flow problems as its suppliers want to be paid for the jackets on delivery, but JJ's trade customers want to have credit facilities and have up to 60 days' trade credit.

Jill and John think that JJ may now have to change its legal structure to protect their personal assets and also arrange suitable cash flow for their business.

| Per jacket | $ | Quantity |
|---|---|---|
| Average cost of jackets | 20 | |
| Average trade selling price | 40 | |
| Average trade sales per year | | 800 |
| | | |
| Average online selling price | 60 | |
| Average online sales per year | | 1200 |
| | | |
| Cash in bank | 5000 | |
| Debtors (money owed) | 7500 | |

(a) Explain the following terms:

   (i) market research [3]

   (ii) trade credit. [3]

(b) (i) Referring to Table 2, calculate JJ's online breakeven level. [3]

   (ii) Explain the results of the breakeven level. [3]

(c) Analyse two ways in which JJ could improve their cash flow. [8]

(d) Recommend whether JJ should change its legal structure. Justify your choice. [11]

## 3 Case study: Paul's Paper Supplies

(a) (i) Define sales turnover. [2]

   (ii) Briefly explain the term 'small business'. [3]

(b) (i) Referring to Table 1, the total value of sales of paper in country A in 2018 was $10m.

     Calculate Paul's market share. [3]

   (ii) Explain one method that Paul would NOT use to measure his business. [3]

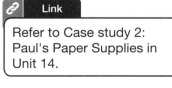

**Link**

Refer to Case study 2: Paul's Paper Supplies in Unit 14.

**(c)** Analyse two factors that Paul should consider when deciding to increase the size of his business. [8]

**(d)** Evaluate whether Paul should increase the size of his business. [11]

### 4 Case study: Paul's Paper Supplies

**(a) (i)** Define the term 'business objective'. [2]

**(ii)** Briefly explain the term 'business stakeholder'. [3]

**(b) (i)** Referring to Table 1 calculate the profit margin for 2018. [3]

**(ii)** Explain one possible reason for the change in profit margin between 2018 and 2019. [3]

**(c)** Analyse two factors that might influence Paul's future objectives. [8]

**(d)** 'Paul's suppliers are his most important stakeholder.' To what extent do you agree with this statement? [11]

Link

Refer to Case study 2: Paul's Paper Supplies in Unit 14.

## Paper 3

### Section A

Section A consists of five questions, which will be split into separate parts. You must answer all the questions.

**1** Analyse the benefits for SG of having a diverse product range. [10]

**2 (a)** Refer to the data in the case study.

**(i)** Calculate the net present (value) for the investment in each option. [4]

**(ii)** Refer to the data in the case study. Calculate the payback period for the investment into each option. [4]

**(b)** Discuss the usefulness of investment appraisal to SG when making investment decisions. Refer to your results in 2(a). [14]

**3** To what extent could a detailed marketing plan lead to a successful launch of SG's proposed new joint venture? [16]

**4** Refer to the case study.

**(a)** Calculate the accounting rate of return over the five-year projection of both options. [4]

**(b)** Refer to your answer to 2(a) and other relevant information. Recommend whether SG should invest into either of the proposed options. Justify your answer. [16]

**5** Evaluate the use of financial motivators for SG's future success in its sales departments. [14]

Link

Refer to Case study 3: Sohail's Garage in Unit 14.

### Section B

Within this section you will have a choice of two questions of which you will have to answer **one**. These questions rely on the candidate having a broad depth of knowledge and the ability to bring together multiple elements of the Business syllabus.

**6** Discuss the importance of contingency planning if SG is to continue to be successful. [20]

**7** Discuss the importance of strategic management to the future success of SG. [20]

Link

Refer to Case study 3: Sohail's Garage in Unit 14.

A Level

## 14 Case studies

### Case study 1: Dingle's Dairy (DD)

Fred Dingle is a farmer who has 100 goats and sells the milk they produce to local, independent shops who sell his product as a healthy alternative to cow's milk. He is a sole trader who set up his business five years ago and has recently broke even on his original investment. He now has some capital available that he is thinking of reinvesting into his business to help him grow and be more profitable. He has one farm assistant who helps with the milking every day and any other jobs around the farm.

The business made a healthy profit last year as he has less expenses due to his original loan being repaid (see Table 1).

▼ **Table 1** Accounts for Dingle's Dairy 2015 and 2016

|  | 2015 ($) | 2016 ($) |
|---|---|---|
| Revenue | 50 000 | 60 000 |
| Cost of sales | 30 000 | 35 000 |
| Gross profit | 20 000 | 25 000 |
| Expenses (including interest payments) | 25 000 | 10 000 |
| Profit for the year | (5 000) | 15 000 |

Fred would now like to expand the business further. He has identified that there is a potential market for other products based on goat's milk, such as ice cream and cream. There isn't enough retained profit to finance the new equipment he will need for his new venture, which will cost $40 000, so he has decided to explore other sources of finance.

## Case study 2: Paul's Paper Supplies

Paul's Paper Supplies is a small sole trader who sources and sells specialist papers for industrial printers and other companies who need specialised paper for their business. He started the business one year ago as he saw that the printing company he worked for found it hard to find specific types of paper. After asking colleagues in other local businesses, he found this was a common problem.

After researching the market, he found some good international contacts from paper suppliers who were willing to let him act as an agent and sell their papers wholesale in the UK, so he left his job and started his business.

It has grown rapidly as he has started supplying businesses nationally with different types of specialist paper, and he is struggling to manage the business by himself. He also has cash flow problems as his suppliers want him to pay for their paper on delivery, as he buys small quantities of paper and is a sole trader, but his customers, who are asking for larger orders, want to have credit facilities, so they have 30 days to pay their bill after delivery. His bank only gives him a small overdraft.

Paul thinks that changing his legal structure and increasing his size will help his business develop and give him some personal security.

▼ **Table 1** Accounts for Paul's Paper Supplies

|  | 2018 | 2019 (predicted) |
|---|---|---|
| Turnover $ | 100 000 | 500 000 |
| Number of customers | 12 | 30 |
| Average size of order ($) | $500 | $1500 |
| Gross profit ($) | 30 000 | 200 000 |
| Types of paper sold | 5 | 20 |
| Size of market ($) | 1 500 00 | 2 000 000 |

## Case study 3: Sohail's Garage (SG)

Sohail Khan has grown a small one-man business into country A's leading used car sales company. He started with a $2500 government grant and bought a single car at auction that he repaired and sold for a profit. Since then his business has expanded rapidly and it recorded sales revenue of $320m last year. He is now one of the country's best known used vehicle sales companies, praised for its excellent customer service.

SG is a private limited company with Sohail owning 55% of the shares. It is split into three divisions, each one operated as a separate profit centre. The three divisions are as follows.

➤ Private vehicle sales. This is the largest of the three divisions. Sohail's business buys cars at auction, ensures they are mechanically sound and sells them on, usually with a small mark up. Sohail relies on the quantity of cars sold to ensure high profit levels.

➤ Fleet vehicle sales and service. This division deals exclusively with larger businesses who lease 10+ vehicles over a number of years. The total revenue of fleet vehicles is around 20% of SG. Each fleet vehicle is leased for a maximum of three years which covers around 80% of the total purchase price and is then sold on, which is where Sohail makes his profit on each car.

➤ Commercial vehicle sales and service. This is the smallest division in terms of sales turnover. Sohail spotted an opportunity through his fleet vehicle sales operation to open a new business venture, based on his brand name, however, sales have been slow. Many larger operators deal directly with manufacturers and commercial customers have been reluctant to leave their existing companies, especially where they already have built up a good reputation.

Accounting data for the three divisions is shown in Table 1.

### New offices and infrastructure needed

While Sohail has a number of forecourts and garages where he services and sells his cars, the infrastructure of his business is unreliable and each division uses its own computing systems and contacts, causing management and communication problems. Sohail and the other company directors want to relocate to a new head office that will centralise all the back office systems in one new, purpose built and future proof location.

### Style of leadership in the three divisions

Sohail has often described himself as being a well organised person who believes there are certain set methods and rules that should be used when leading a business. He has appointed three managers to lead the three business divisions. Interestingly, each manager takes a different view of the best business leadership style.

➤ The private vehicle sales division is led by Umar. He considers that office workers should be given clear instructions, non-financial incentives and temporary employment contracts to – in his words – 'make them focused on keeping their jobs'.

➤ The fleet vehicle sales division is led by Steven. He is a charismatic leader who is liked and respected by most of his workers. Steven encourages workers to be involved in making all major decisions and he keeps them well informed.

➤ The commercial vehicle sales division is led by Sara. Commercial vehicle sales started out as a minor extension of fleet vehicle sales and built up just enough custom to become an independent division. Sara is a mechanical engineering graduate who encourages her teams of sales and customer service managers to solve problems themselves and arrive at solutions with little central direction.

Having different leadership styles does not worry Sohail as long as the divisions deliver the profits and business growth that are his main objectives. However, he has recently been asking himself whether the leadership styles used are contributing to the different levels of profitability in the three divisions.

## Financial efficiency

Sohail is able to compare the financial efficiency of all three divisions because they are separate profit centres. He does this by calculating accounting ratios. Recent results for Sohail's Garage are shown in Table 1. He is worried about the financial efficiency of the commercial vehicle division. He is thinking about how to improve this without damaging staff morale or reducing levels of customer service.

## Marketing in the mass market

Sohail's Garage is currently profitable but operates in an increasingly competitive mass market. SG has a strategy of keeping average costs as low as possible, with a low profit margin on each unit sold to increase turnover and gain a reputation as the best value car sales garage. The price elasticity of demand is high. Sohail has asked the board of directors to discuss strategies for making demand less sensitive to price increases. He said at the last board meeting: 'We need to look at all parts of Sohail's Garage's marketing strategy if we are going to increase sales of cars profitably.'

## Strategic choices

Despite his business success, Sohail wants to expand SG into new markets and products. He recognises the potential danger of relying on a limited number of market segments. He knows diversification will be risky and that there will need to be a huge financial investment due to the nature of holding stock. However, to stay within one segment is also taking a chance because new rivals and selling channels such as the internet could make SG uncompetitive.

At a recent board meeting, two ideas were identified as possible options; both will need substantial external financial investment.

### Option A

The owner of NRG Autos plc, a foreign manufacturer of premium cars hoping to enter a new market, offered Sohail a joint venture opportunity where Sohail would use his existing back office network and experience to be the sales agent for imported NRG Autos cars within country A. The cars would be sold at 'independent' NRG forecourts using SG's skills and experience.

### Option B

The CEO of PPL Garages, SG's biggest competitor, has suggested PPL and SG merge, and that SG could effectively take control of the larger business. This increase in size would mean a much larger share of the market and a company at least twice the size of the nearest competitor. This could increase brand awareness and marketing opportunities as well as reducing costs by closing forecourts that are close to each other without minimising the customer experience.

Choosing between the two options will not be easy. Both options will require significant financial investment. Sohail has prepared the data in the tables below to help him make his choice.

▼ **Table 1** Accounting data for the three divisions of SG

| | | Private vehicles | Fleet vehicles | Commercial vehicles |
|---|---|---|---|---|
| Revenue 2016 | $m | 120 | 92 | 15 |
| Revenue 2015 | $m | 110 | 67 | 14 |
| Gross profit 2016 | $m | 45 | 32 | 3 |
| Gross profit 2015 | $m | 39 | 21 | (5) |
| Inventory level at end of 2016 | $m | 20 | 3 | 2 |
| Inventory turnover ratio | 2016 | 17.2 | 9.2 | |
| Debtor days 2016 | | 13.5 | 42.1 | |

▼ **Table 2** Required investment – forecast net cash flows for the two financing options

| Year | Option A ($m) | Option B ($m) |
|---|---|---|
| 0 | (100) | (600) |
| 1 | 75 | 300 |
| 2 | 100 | 300 |
| 3 | 150 | 350 |
| 4 | 200 | 350 |
| 5 | 200 | 350 |

10% discount factors: Year 1: 0.92, Year 2: 0.87, Year 3: 0.76, Year 4: 0.71, Year 5: 0.65

▼ **Table 3** Forecast data

| | 2018 |
|---|---|
| Annual real GDP growth rate 2016–2020 | 3.0% |
| Inflation 2016–2020 | 1.5% |
| Exchange rate index 2018 (2017 = 100) | 102 |
| Change in annual salary 2016–2020 | 2.5% |
| Change in interest rate 2016–2020 | 0% |

# Index